Praise for
The Complete Guide to College Transfer

"Jaime Smith turns what feels like a maze into a map. A clear, compassionate, and practical guide for transfer students navigating a system that too often overlooks them."
— **Jeffrey Selingo**, New York Times bestselling author of
Who Gets In and Why: A Year Inside College Admissions

"The number of students transferring between colleges continues to increase significantly and so do the challenges. In this book, you'll find practical advice, timely insight, and solace in what can too often be an unclear and daunting experience."
— **Rick Clark**, executive director of Strategic Student Access
at Georgia Tech and coauthor of
*The Truth About College Admission:
A Family Guide to Getting In and Staying Together*

"*The Complete Guide to College Transfer* is a smart, student-centered resource that demystifies the transfer process and empowers learners to take control of their academic journey. With thoughtful nods to Phi Theta Kappa and the unique strengths of community college students, this guide recognizes the potential in every transfer story — and offers practical tools to help students make the most of it."
— **Lynn Tincher-Ladner, PhD**, president and CEO of the
Phi Theta Kappa Honor Society

"By illuminating behind-the-scenes institutional processes — credit articulation, partnership programs, admissions, and financial aid — Jaime Smith guides learners to claim ownership of their academic histories and make informed decisions about their futures. This book is grounded in real student experiences and written in accessible language. You simply will not find a more approachable or comprehensive resource for successfully undertaki
— **Janet L. Marling,**
National Institute for the Study

"Finally, a book that demystifies the college transfer process! Certified educational planner Jaime Smith brings years of practical experience to her exceptional new book. Case studies and helpful advice make this a must-have text for any student contemplating a transfer. *The Complete Guide to College Transfer* counsels students to assess their credits, weigh financial options, and ultimately make their right-fit college decision. Whether their reason for transferring is academic, financial, social, or personal, students will benefit from Smith's thoughtful and astute guidance."

— **Andrea Malkin Brenner, PhD**, creator of Talking College™ card decks and coauthor of *How to College: What to Know Before You Go (and When You're There)*

"Jaime Smith's *The Complete Guide to College Transfer* is a long-overdue resource for the millions of students who begin but don't finish their college journey. With clarity, empathy, and deep expertise, Smith offers practical strategies and advice for navigating the often overlooked complexities of transferring schools. This book is a road map for students seeking a second chance at finding their right college fit. Its real-world examples allow students to see themselves throughout the entire book."

— **Sydney Matthes**, chief programs officer of Service to School

"This outstanding book offers invaluable guidance to the millions of students who transfer colleges during their academic journey. Through compelling case studies, it not only highlights the diverse reasons students choose to transfer but also normalizes an often overlooked yet common part of the college experience. Jaime Smith, already recognized as a national expert on college transfers, shares her deep knowledge and remarkable storytelling to great effect. As the parent of a student whose personal growth led her to seek a new college — and who blossomed into a true scholar at her new school — I understand both personally and professionally the profound impact of finding the right fit, even if it doesn't happen straight out of high school. I only wish we'd had this book when we were navigating the complexities and emotional weight of the transfer process."

— **Mark Sklarow**, CEO emeritus of the Independent Educational Consultants Association (IECA)

"*The Complete Guide to College Transfer* is a lifeline for transfer students striving for success. Jaime Smith provides a clear, comprehensive road map that helps students navigate the complexities of changing colleges. This well-researched guide offers practical advice on everything from comparing credit transfers to understanding financial aid options. With expert tips, insightful case studies, and a detailed timetable for the transfer process, Smith empowers students to avoid common pitfalls and make informed, confident decisions."

— **Steven R. Antonoff, PhD**, author of *College Match* and *A Student of Colleges*, coauthor of *The College Finder*, independent educational consultant, trainer, and certified educational planner

"Jaime Smith brings needed clarity and authenticity to a complex and growing student population: college transfers. Her use of case studies and emphasis on financial literacy make this book an essential part of a student's transfer journey."

— **April Gamble, MEd**, associate director of admissions at The College of Wooster

"Jaime Smith provides a timely and important guidebook on the many nuances of becoming a successful transfer student. There's never one right way to do higher education, and this book gives many wonderful examples and case studies for how to make college work for a variety of students. I'm sure this resource will be a huge asset to many students."

— **Mia Nosanow, MA, LP**, author of *The College Student's Guide to Mental Health*

"This book is a gift to anyone navigating the complex and often overwhelming world of transfer admissions. At once a compassionate, step-by-step guide and an indispensable reference, it meets students exactly where they are — whether transferring from a community college, starting over after a false start, or seeking a better fit — and empowers them with clarity, strategy, and encouragement."

— **Sheila Akbar, PhD**, president and CEO of Signet Education

THE COMPLETE GUIDE TO COLLEGE TRANSFER

Find Your Ideal School, Maximize Your Credits, and Earn Your Degree

JAIME SMITH
MA, MSEd, CEP

New World Library
Novato, California

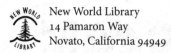

New World Library
14 Pamaron Way
Novato, California 94949

Copyright © 2025 by Jaime Smith

All rights reserved. This book may not be reproduced in whole or in part, stored in a retrieval system, or transmitted in any form or by any means — electronic, mechanical, or other — without written permission from the publisher, except by a reviewer, who may quote brief passages in a review.

Some names and identifying characteristics have been changed to protect privacy.

The material in this book is intended for educational purposes only. No expressed or implied guarantee of the effects of the use of the recommendations can be given nor liability taken.

Text design by Tona Pearce Myers

Library of Congress Cataloging-in-Publication data is available.

First printing, August 2025
ISBN 978-1-955831-00-0
Ebook ISBN 978-1-955831-01-7
Printed in Canada

10 9 8 7 6 5 4 3 2 1

New World Library is committed to protecting our natural environment. This book is made of material from well-managed FSC®-certified forests and other controlled sources.

Contents

Introduction..ix

Part I: Transfer Basics   1

Chapter 1: All Kinds of Transfers..3
Chapter 2: Why Transfer?..11

Part II: Assessing Earned Credit   25

Chapter 3: Collecting Transcripts...27
Chapter 4: Transcript Self-Evaluation...31
Chapter 5: Alternative Credit Sources...43

Part III: Searching for Colleges   55

Chapter 6: The Five P's for College Research...58
Chapter 7: Qualities of a Transfer-Friendly College...............................77
Chapter 8: Partnerships..97

Part IV: Planning   109

Chapter 9: Minimum Eligibility Requirements.....................................111
Chapter 10: General Education...120
Chapter 11: Majors and Prerequisites...128
Chapter 12: Transfer Timeline...136

Part V: Application   149

Chapter 13: Data Entry..151
Chapter 14: Writing..172
Chapter 15: Follow-Up Documentation......................................189

Part VI: Decisions   203

Chapter 16: Admissions Results..205
Chapter 17: Transfer Credit Evaluation Report..........................211
Chapter 18: Housing Options...222
Chapter 19: Financial Aid Awards and Cost Comparisons..............231

Part VII: Post-Acceptance   249

Chapter 20: The Fine Print...251
Chapter 21: Academic Planning...259
Chapter 22: Tips for Success...266

Final Thoughts...272
Acknowledgments..273
Notes...275
Index...282
About the Author...293

Introduction

There is no single "right" way to do college. Your journey through higher education is uniquely yours — take the path that suits your life and helps you meet your goals. Whether you're considering a community college, switching between four-year universities, or returning to complete your degree after time away, you're part of a growing community of transfer students who are redefining the college experience.

As Jim Rohn, a successful entrepreneur and college dropout, wisely noted, "If you don't like how it is for you, change it.... You are not a tree."[1] Ultimately, your degree won't come with a footnote about the circuitous route you took to earn it. If something isn't working for you, take action! Your education is what you make of it, so make it a journey that is meaningful to you.

In this practical guide, you'll find everything you need to navigate the transfer process successfully. From researching schools and understanding credit transfers to managing applications and securing financial aid, this book provides step-by-step guidance for every type of transfer student. To get the most benefit, I recommend reading the book from beginning to end and taking the actions described in each chapter as needed. However, depending on your unique circumstances, some sections may be less relevant to your situation, and you should feel free to skim or skip ahead. Be sure to check the companion website at TransferSavvy.com for helpful resources and downloadable worksheets, which are mentioned throughout the book.

You'll encounter case studies based on real transfer experiences shared by my students. While names and identifying details have been changed to protect privacy, these stories offer authentic insights into the challenges and triumphs of the transfer process. You will also find excerpts from actual college transfer applications and university policies, but keep in mind that these quotes are just examples to help guide you through this process. When you begin researching colleges and working on your own transfer applications, please read the instructions and policies currently listed on live college websites and application forms — details of the college transfer process change frequently.

A note on language: I've made a conscious effort to use inclusive language throughout this guide. You'll notice terms like "first-year students" instead of "freshmen," and "test-free" policies rather than "test-blind." However, I've retained some widely used traditional terminology, such as "bachelor's degree" or "need-blind" admissions, to avoid unnecessary confusion.

As we embark on this journey together, keep in mind that your path may not be linear, and that's OK. This guide will equip you with the knowledge and strategies to make informed decisions, overcome obstacles, and successfully transfer to the college that best fits your needs and aspirations.

Higher education has a place for you. This book will help you find it.

PART I

TRANSFER BASICS

Understanding the college admissions process can be overwhelming for anyone. If you are thinking about pursuing transfer admissions, it might feel like wandering through the wilderness without a map. Just when you think you have cracked the code on transfer rules at one college, you discover another college with entirely different requirements and processes.

In order to make sense of it all, you first need to understand a few essential terms. Knowing the vocabulary of transfer will help you understand and articulate your transfer wishes and needs, become more efficient in your research, and learn to ask the right questions of college admissions officers.

CHAPTER 1

All Kinds of Transfers

Academic progress is not linear. It's full of zigzags and circles, mountains and valleys. Although we frequently refer to "four-year colleges" and "four-year degrees," in reality fewer than half of all college students graduate with a bachelor's degree in four years.[1] More than a third of all college students transfer between schools at least once, and almost half of those students transfer more than once.[2]

Although every transfer student is unique, there are a few common characteristics of transfers that can help us classify students into categories and subgroups. Transfers may be planned or spontaneous and can take the student through multiple types of postsecondary institutions. Let's explore the main categories and find the general terms that best describe your journey.

Vertical Transfer

Vertical, or upward, transfer is the most common pathway for students planning to transfer from the outset. These students begin at a two-year community college with the goal of building strong transcripts and becoming desirable transfer applicants at four-year universities. In an ideal scenario, a well-prepared student can study for two years at the community college, then transfer and spend another two years at a four-year university to earn a bachelor's degree in a total of four years. This can be a challenging timeline, but it is possible with careful planning and strategic scheduling.

Students may choose this pathway to a bachelor's degree for a number of reasons:

- Community colleges don't have a lengthy application process — you just sign up — making them accessible to late-blooming students who weren't ready for the first-year college search and application process during high school.
- Cost-conscious families may wish to utilize free and low-cost community college programs in their state.
- Students with diverse interests and talents, known as multi-potentialites, might enjoy inexpensively exploring numerous fields of study before settling into a particular major.
- Working students can take advantage of flexible scheduling, evening and online classes, and part-time attendance.
- Close-knit families can remain close when students live at home and commute to school.

Case Study: Jerry, Vertical Transfer

Jerry never planned to attend college. He didn't particularly enjoy high school, and his peer group was more interested in partying than planning for the future. His mother, who never had the opportunity to attend college herself, begged him to try just a class or two at a nearby community college. He took just one class to appease his mother and got a D. Originally, he planned to quit college the next semester, but that D nagged at Jerry. He didn't like the feeling of failure.

So he enrolled in three more classes and earned B's. Then, he took five classes and received A's and B's. Jerry realized that he loved math and economics, then discovered that these classes could prepare him for a lucrative career in finance. He researched the transfer pathways and articulation agreements between his community college and several well-respected undergraduate business programs and, ultimately, set his sights on the Haas School of Business at the University of California, Berkeley. He studied the transfer agreements carefully, met regularly with advisers at his community college and at Haas, and landed a prestigious internship that would set his application apart.

Jerry earned a bachelor of science in business administration and became the first in his family to graduate from college. He now mentors new community college students who are considering careers in business and finance.

Lateral Transfer

Lateral transfer, also called horizontal transfer, describes the process of a student moving from one four-year university to another. These students are not usually planning to transfer when they first enroll in college. However, something changes that necessitates a move to a different university. There may be an unforeseen mismatch between the student and the original university, or an on-campus event or change in personal circumstances might compel the student to seek admission elsewhere. In some cases, it may be in the student's best interest to first transfer to a community college and then plan for future vertical transfer.

Case Study: Amelia, Lateral Transfer

Amelia didn't give much thought to college fit. She was content to attend whatever college her twin sister selected. The two had been inseparable since birth and were excited to continue this next phase of life as a pair, staying in the dorm as first-year roommates. The two moved across the country, switching from the four distinct seasons of New England to the everlasting summer of the Southwest.

The first semester of college passed smoothly, and Amelia began to get serious about her studies. She had entered the university with an undeclared major and planned to

> work through general education (GE) requirements while exploring major and career options. One of her first GE courses was an introduction to biology, which rekindled Amelia's love of science. She remembered that she had once hoped to become a marine biologist, but this landlocked state university was not a practical place to explore that interest.
>
> Amelia also realized that she could thrive in college with or without her twin sister. Perhaps it was time to spread her wings and seek a coastal college with marine science majors. Amelia ultimately transferred to the University of Miami, where she could explore majors of interest while continuing to enjoy year-round sunshine.

Reverse Transfer

It is somewhat rare to see a student pursue reverse transfer, wherein they use credits from a bachelor's degree program to obtain an associate degree at a community college. Sometimes a student will withdraw entirely from the four-year institution to follow a more vocational trajectory or graduate with a credential sooner. However, in many cases, it is not necessary to withdraw completely. A student can continue working toward a bachelor's degree at the original institution while simultaneously attempting to transfer credits to an associate degree program. Ultimately, such a student may graduate with both associate and bachelor's degrees.

Case Study: Moe, Reverse Transfer

> Moe went directly from high school to a four-year liberal arts college. It seemed like the perfect fit, but as soon as Moe arrived on campus, he felt out of place. He had a strong case of impostor syndrome and worried that he wasn't really "smart enough" to attend such a college.

Although he had an ADHD diagnosis and an Individualized Education Plan (IEP) in high school, he did not seek accommodations at his new college. Somehow, that felt like cheating. Moe would only feel successful if he could complete college unassisted. He struggled through the first semester but didn't return for a second, deciding that he did not belong at this college, or maybe *any* college.

After several years of working successfully in the service industry, Moe found himself jobless during the Covid-19 pandemic. His skills didn't easily translate to a remote work environment. Moe began to think about a career change.

Moe's career aspirations didn't necessarily require a bachelor's degree. He would most likely be able to achieve his goals by completing an associate degree at his local community college. So Moe completed a reverse transfer, taking his earned credits from a four-year college and transferring them to his local two-year community college. Those transferred course credits fulfilled some of Moe's general education requirements so that he could focus primarily on his associate degree (AA) specialization. With appropriate support for his ADHD and a new goal in mind, Moe successfully completed his AA degree in under two years.

"Swirling" Transfers

Some transfer students don't fit neatly into any of the prior categories. They may already have experienced several types of transfer in their quest for an undergraduate degree. These transfer students are affectionately called "swirlers" because they "swirl" between two-year community colleges and four-year universities, collecting credits from various postsecondary sources. Such students typically have multiple college transcripts spanning several years and are looking for a way to bring their piecemeal credits together and complete a degree. With the rise of online learning, students now have even more opportunities to earn an eclectic collage of college credits, further complicating the transfer process.

Case Study: Hollie, "Swirling" Transfer

Hollie has been working on her bachelor's degree for over thirty years. A multipotentialite with a wide range of academic interests, Hollie had difficulty pinning down a single major on which to focus.

Community college was an obvious choice for her after high school; it allowed her the freedom to dabble in several academic subjects inexpensively. Frequent relocations led to multiple transfers between community colleges and local universities. Degree progress was slow but consistent. Then the births of her children and the onset of a chronic health condition interrupted Hollie's college trajectory.

By age forty-eight, Hollie had collected nearly ninety semester credits spread over eight separate transcripts from colleges and universities throughout the Pacific Northwest. Now an empty nester, Hollie was ready to complete her undergraduate education, but she needed more flexibility than a traditional brick-and-mortar university could provide. She also needed a program that would accept a high-unit transfer student with credits going back almost thirty years.

Enter Southern New Hampshire University. SNHU offered the flexibility and support she needed to finally complete her undergraduate degree. After submitting her transcripts, Hollie received a credit evaluation report showing that the vast majority of her credits would be applied to a bachelor's degree. She would need to complete a minimum of thirty credits at SNHU, including at least twelve within her declared major. By taking just one or two classes during each eight-week online session, Hollie quickly advanced through the final requirements to earn her long-awaited bachelor's degree eighteen months after enrolling.

Common Challenges and Questions

What if I have dual enrollment credits from high school?

College courses taken before graduating from high school may provide transferable college credit. These credits, often referred to as dual enrollment, concurrent enrollment, or dual credit, may receive different treatment during the transfer credit evaluation process. Each university establishes a policy specifically to address the transferability of these unique credits. In nearly all situations, students whose only college credits were earned through dual enrollment — that is, those who did not enroll in college classes after high school graduation — will apply for first-year admission rather than transfer admission. Such students should still share their college transcripts with prospective universities, as credits are often transferable even when students are not officially transfer students.

Will my swirling credit collection put me at a disadvantage?

It depends. If you have collected enough college credits to be a high-unit transfer, some universities will not consider your application. Others will review your application for admission but limit the number of transfer credits that can be applied to your degree. Even if you are not considered a high-unit transfer, the presence of numerous transcripts may be a red flag for admissions officers. Be sure to explain your educational journey in your essay or the "additional information" section. Put your transcripts in context for the reader.

I'm embarrassed to attend community college. Why do my friends from high school think it's for losers?

Your concerns are not unfounded. Community colleges (or junior colleges, as they were originally named) have a dark history rooted in discrimination and elitism, which led to the stigma that persists today.[3] Understanding the origins of the community college system may help you mentally separate historical inequities from the vital work that today's community colleges do.

The first American universities were designed to serve the elite. Women, people of color, and those without money or status were typically denied admission to these institutions. However, legislation in the late 1800s required public land-grant universities to prove they did not practice racial discrimination in admissions or else create separate institutions to serve minorities. Thus, the junior college was invented to be the "separate but equal" form of higher education for women, minorities, and low-status individuals so that four-year universities could preserve their elite reputations.

But times have changed! Community colleges have become respected providers of education and training for anyone who wishes to learn. In fact, students who have attended both community colleges and four-year universities often find that the quality of teaching is superior at community colleges. Tenured university professors may be more focused on research, while community college instructors generally consider teaching their primary job.

Many famous and successful people attended community colleges and now speak highly of their experience! Tom Hanks, Amy Tan, Jim Belushi, Aaron Rodgers, Dax Shepard, and Beverly Cleary are just a few of the big names who started out at public two-year colleges and went on to achieve great things, whether they ultimately earned a bachelor's degree or not. Despite all this, the stigma of community college persists in some social circles. Fight back! Represent your community college with pride, and join the #EndCCStigma campaign on social media to shine a light on your community college journey.[4]

CHAPTER 2

Why Transfer?

It is difficult to summarize the reasons for college transfer. Each transfer student is a unique individual who has followed a singular educational path that cannot be easily compared to others. Thus, their motivations for changing course are also unique and not easily compared.

In this way, transfer admission is entirely different from first-year admission. When high school students apply for first-year college admission, the vast majority have similar academic backgrounds: four years of English, US and world history, both life and physical sciences, math in a predictable sequence, and so on.

Not so with transfer students. Course requirements and offerings at colleges can differ wildly, and students can apply for transfer at multiple points in the undergraduate journey. Some students come from two-year community colleges, while others transfer from four-year universities. Transfer may be a choice made in response to experiences at a prior university or a requirement when a student is suspended or expelled from the prior college.

This chapter will explore some of the most common reasons students transfer between colleges.

Academic Reasons

Since higher education is an academic endeavor, let's begin with academic reasons for transferring between colleges. Educational needs are some of the best reasons to begin the transfer application process.

Degree Goals

Different kinds of colleges offer different kinds of degrees. When you think of getting an undergraduate education, a typical four-year bachelor's degree probably comes to mind. The shorthand for these degrees uses initials, such as BA for bachelor of arts or BS for bachelor of science. Some specialized bachelor's degrees also exist, such as BFA for a bachelor of fine arts. These degrees are typically only available at four-year institutions, whether small liberal arts colleges or large research universities, and can prepare students for careers or graduate school.

Community colleges, sometimes called junior colleges, usually offer a different type of degree — an associate degree. Here, AA stands for associate of arts, and AS means associate of science. These degrees are designed to be completed in approximately two years and often include some amount of vocational training so that graduates are prepared to enter the workforce immediately.

If a community college student wants to earn a bachelor's degree, they usually have no choice but to transfer vertically; the community college simply does not offer the type of degree they desire. Approximately half of all transfer students are transitioning from community college for the purpose of earning a bachelor's degree.[1] Because this is such a common transfer pathway, many community colleges have introduced specialized associate degrees for transfer, often abbreviated as ADT, or more specifically AAT or AST to represent the arts and sciences.

In recent years, the difference between two-year and four-year institutions has begun to blur. Some community colleges are now authorized to offer bachelor's degrees in certain high-demand majors.[2]

Students may enter both associate and bachelor's degree programs directly from high school. However, students who plan to attend graduate school in pursuit of a master's or doctoral degree must typically earn a bachelor's degree first. So, if a student's educational goals include the possibility of a graduate degree, that student must transfer from the community college to a bachelor's degree–granting institution first.

Desired Major

Most colleges require their students to declare a major, or specialized area of study, prior to graduation. In other words, a student might not just earn a bachelor of arts, but specifically a bachelor of arts in sociology, for example.

Some students know exactly what they want to learn, stating their intended major right on their first-year application! Other students may have no idea what to study and might pick a general subject area or select an "undecided" or "exploratory" major at first. Either way, first-year students are regularly exposed to fascinating new ideas and academic research, which can lead to a newfound love of a topic they never imagined studying before. If that topic is not available as a major at their current institution, they may wish to consider transferring to a school that offers the desired major and has respected professors doing research in that field.

Conversely, some students who enter college intending to pursue an area of passion may feel repelled by studying that subject after arriving on campus and experiencing college life related to that field. A transfer may then be necessary. For example, an artistic student might first enroll in a BFA program at an arts college but then discover that they appreciate art as a hobby rather than as a major or a career path. To pursue studies outside of the arts, that student will likely need to transfer, even if they aren't yet attracted to a new field. Once they have ruled out art as a major, transferring to a college with a greater variety of options will provide the needed exposure to alternative areas of study.

Academic Notice, Probation, or Suspension

Sometimes the decision to transfer is not entirely up to the student. If a student consistently underperforms in classes, the college may place the student on academic notice or probation. At first, this is usually just a warning to the student that they must improve their grades to continue studying at the college. If grades do not improve, the next step may be academic suspension or dismissal, where the student is asked to leave the school entirely.

Since most four-year universities have minimum GPA requirements for transfer, a student in this situation is unlikely to be eligible for lateral transfer to another four-year institution. A reverse transfer to a community college may be the only option for continued undergraduate study. After a period of remediation and GPA improvement,

14   Transfer Basics

the student may apply for reentry to the original university or for transfer to a different four-year school.

School Closure or Discontinued Majors

The Covid-19 pandemic led to a loss of revenue for many colleges and universities as students unexpectedly deferred admission and canceled housing contracts. This financial setback, combined with declining birth rates and increased skepticism about the value of college degrees, created an untenable situation for numerous institutions of higher education. To remain financially viable, some colleges have been forced to make difficult decisions to cut less popular majors, close small academic departments, cancel athletic programs, and, in some cases, cease operations completely.

Ideally, a college facing cuts and closures will coordinate with other institutions to provide smooth transfer pathways for affected students. Nevertheless, fewer than half of all displaced students successfully transfer to other institutions. Of those who do, very few persist in completing their degrees.[3]

Former Incarceration

Partnerships between colleges and correctional facilities enable incarcerated students to pursue higher education while serving their sentences. Higher education programs in prisons vary by region and can change frequently due to budget fluctuations and instructor availability. Some colleges offer only a limited number of courses through their prison partnerships, while others make full associate and/or bachelor's degrees accessible through a mix of in-person and remote learning options. Many programs establish transfer pathways for incarcerated students, allowing them to continue their studies at a partner institution upon release. They may also include reentry support services to facilitate the transition to post-prison life. Even without organized transition support programs, formerly incarcerated students who have earned college credits can apply for transfer admission to any college or university and continue pursuing their degrees.

Military Separation (for Veteran Students)

Although online colleges have made it possible to earn an entire bachelor's degree while serving in the military, many service members prefer to dive into traditional full-time undergraduate study after completing their contracted years of service. Transferring to brick-and-mortar institutions enables these student veterans to fully immerse themselves in campus culture as they transition from military to civilian life. Access to veteran-specific support services on campus can also help veterans navigate this significant life change as they simultaneously pursue their academic goals.

Case Study: Antonio

Antonio was an engineering student at a top public university. Covid restrictions led to his first semester of college being held online, a mode of learning that was not an ideal match for Antonio's personality. Living at home and taking classes online was a struggle, and unsurprisingly, his first-semester grades were lower than desired. As he moved into a dormitory on campus for the second semester, Antonio hoped that taking a mix of in-person and online classes while living in a student-focused environment would bring him greater success. Instead, his GPA fell further, and he sank into a deep depression.

Eventually, Antonio was placed on academic suspension and instructed to take classes at a local community college to rebuild his transcript and improve his GPA. His transfer to community college was also rocky, and he failed several more courses before finding a healthy and productive student routine with the help of a therapist. Antonio didn't want to continue repeating the same mistakes, so he dutifully attended classes, asked questions during weekly office hours, and began to replace his failing grades with A's and B's through academic renewal.

Despite this academic improvement and personal growth, Antonio's first application for reentry to his original university was denied. He began to wonder if that school was the right fit for him after all and decided to apply for transfer to engineering programs at other four-year universities. Engineering programs are notoriously difficult to enter as either a first-year student or transfer, but he was accepted to a handful of smaller colleges in the Midwest. Before making a final transfer decision, Antonio applied for reentry to his original university program one last time. He was readmitted and decided to return. Because he had taken classes at the local community college, which had a detailed transfer contract with his university, his newly earned credits were guaranteed to transfer and fulfill general education and major requirements. Although he took a detour through community college, Antonio's careful planning allowed him to continue making progress on his degree, which minimized the effect on his overall graduation timeline.

Financial Reasons

College can be expensive! But not all colleges are equally expensive. If the current tuition bills and associated costs far exceed a student's budget, it may be time to consider transferring. That said, the transfer process comes with its own costs, so students should not be too hasty with this decision.

Change in Circumstances

Family income may rise or fall a bit each year, but a drastic change in family circumstances could affect your ability to pay for college. If you have filed the Free Application for Federal Student Aid (FAFSA) or the College Scholarship Service (CSS) Profile, you know that need-based financial aid is calculated according to your family's income from the prior-prior year. (FAFSA and CSS Profiles are covered in detail in chapters 6 and 15.) For example, a student attending college during the 2025–26 academic year would complete these forms with income tax details from 2023. A lot can change in two years, though! If there has been an unexpected drop in your family's income due to a lost job or the death of a primary earner, for example, start by contacting your current university's financial aid office. College financial aid officers can make several adjustments to a student's financial aid profile, which could lead to additional grants and scholarships that lower the cost of attendance at the current college.

Lost Scholarship

Merit scholarships usually come with specific renewal requirements, such as maintaining a minimum GPA or continuing to enroll in college full-time. When such requirements aren't met, a scholarship can be revoked. Before jumping to transfer, talk with the organization that administers the scholarship and ask about the possibility of reinstatement. A term or two without a scholarship might still be cheaper than switching schools entirely. Remember that most scholarships are not transferable between schools, so enrolling at a new college means starting over with financial aid.

Facing Reality

You got into your dream school, and your parents said they would "find" the money to pay the high tuition. As the tuition bills roll in and/or student loan debt piles up, that dream school might seem more like a nightmare. Before you jump ship, do a detailed cost comparison between your current school and the college that appears less expensive. If you don't qualify for need-based aid, an in-state public school may very well be more affordable than a private school. If you have been receiving need-based aid, though, you might be surprised at how similar your net costs are at each school.

For example, if your FAFSA calculations show a Student Aid Index (SAI) of \$30,000, a private college that covers 100 percent of financial need will keep your yearly bill under \$30,000 even if the total cost of attendance is $80,000 per year. A public college that costs $40,000 per year but only covers 50 percent of financial need might end up charging you $35,000! The net price calculator available on each university's website can help you estimate your costs. However, read carefully to be sure that the calculator provides accurate information for transfer students — many colleges only guarantee accuracy for first-year students. (See chapter 6 for more information on financial aid and net price calculators.)

Personal Reasons

Life happens. As much as you might want to prioritize college, sometimes other life events get in the way. If a personal or family situation has derailed your original college plans, it might be wise to consider another path to achieving your higher education goals.

Health

Attending college can be physically challenging for anyone. Most students haven't trained for the athletic demands of college life. Who has the stamina to bike across campus and climb multiple flights of stairs after a fitful night's sleep, followed by a breakfast of coffee and sugar? Add in a new diagnosis or flare-up of a chronic condition, and maintaining high levels of academic achievement becomes near impossible.

When illness or injury disrupts a traditional full-time college education, students may need to withdraw and take a gap term to recover. If the health challenges are likely to be ongoing, transfer to a new institution may be necessary. Students might look for a flexible college that allows part-time attendance, is located closer to family or a medical facility, or offers a significant number of online classes.

Mental Health

To be clear, mental health *is* health. Dealing with depression or anxiety is every bit as challenging as navigating campus with a broken leg or taking a midterm with the flu. Simply because professors and classmates cannot see a mental health condition does not make it any less valid. Just as a student with a chronic illness may have changing college needs, a student facing mental health challenges may require a different atmosphere, both to succeed in academics and to attain mental well-being.

For example, a highly competitive atmosphere might be inappropriate for a student suffering from anxiety, but that student may thrive in a more collaborative environment. A student at a rural campus with limited access to therapists may find success at an urban school surrounded by private practitioners. If addiction and substance abuse are factors, a student may wish to consider a "dry" school or a campus with substance-free dorms. For a student who has suffered trauma at their first school, a transfer to any other college environment may allow that student to begin the healing process.

Family

In some cases, a reason for transfer comes not from the student directly but from a family member. For example, a parent's illness can easily disrupt a student's education because it may affect the student's ability to concentrate on academics or make them feel compelled to return home to support their parent. The loss of a parent's job may mean that the student must prioritize paid work to compensate for decreased family income. Some disruptions are temporary, allowing the student to return to the same college after a short break. Prolonged or more significant family challenges can interrupt college studies for years, necessitating a transfer to a different kind of college that can better accommodate the student's needs.

Social Reasons

Students often head into college believing the hype that these will be "the best four years of your life." They imagine hanging out in a dorm and talking with new friends at all hours, attending parties, cheering at football games, and studying in cafés with classmates. In reality, however, making friends is not always easy. After the welcome-week activities have ended, students sometimes struggle to connect with others and to settle into a comfortable social circle.

20 Transfer Basics

Homesickness or Transfer?

During the first semester of college, up to 94 percent of new students report regular feelings of homesickness.[4] Unsurprisingly, consistent feelings of homesickness correlate with difficulty adjusting to the college environment, lower grades, higher dropout rates, and strained friendships. When students go home for Thanksgiving or winter break, some may get a boost of confidence from being with loved ones and return to college with renewed enthusiasm. Others may find that the idea of returning to the discomfort of college fills them with dread.

When students feel lonely or out of place at college, they may begin considering transfer during that very first term. It's easy to believe that everyone else is happily living their best college lives when old high school classmates post smiling pictures on social media. Unhappy students think the grass must be greener at some other college.

Unfortunately, transfer is rarely the answer to social challenges. If anything, transfer students have a more difficult time adjusting to life and finding friends at a new college. The orientation and welcome-week activities for transfer students are usually much more limited, if they exist at all. Furthermore, transfer students may be unable to move into campus housing, where many friendships are made. If they can live in the dorms, they might be thrown into preexisting social circles that are difficult to crack open.

Try This First

Before jumping to the conclusion that transfer is required to find happiness at college, students should try making the following adjustments:

- Request a room swap if the current roommate is not a good match.
- Join a student club both to meet new people and to show campus engagement on a potential transfer application.
- Take a noncredit class to learn a craft or sport with others who share that interest.
- Look into honors programs or specialized majors that may host more like-minded students.
- Investigate Greek life. Even if the stereotypical sorority or fraternity doesn't appeal to you, an academic or service-oriented group might be a good fit.

- Set up regular calls with family and friends from home for support, but not so many that these calls interfere with friend-making opportunities on campus.

After trying all these tips, transfer might still seem like the answer. Maybe it is then! However, trying to make the best of the current situation will be helpful in any case. Even if it doesn't result in their feeling comfortable enough to remain at the current college, practicing these skills will better prepare the student to integrate themselves into a new college community as a transfer student.

Case Study: Amit

Amit was a motivated student in high school, but his GPA didn't always reflect his abilities or his desire to achieve. When applying for first-year admission, he was determined to apply to elite name-brand schools and then attend the most selective college that admitted him. When acceptances were released, Amit had several options. However, the most prestigious school to accept him offered a first-semester study-abroad program, followed by a traditional on-campus spring semester. Amit didn't stop to think what a January entry would entail; he was too enamored with the school to say no.

After a fun semester abroad, Amit was ready to begin "real" college. He signed up for spring classes, moved into the first-year dormitory, and got to work. A gregarious fellow, Amit did not typically have trouble making friends. So he was surprised to find himself struggling to integrate into the college community.

Amit didn't realize that many tight social circles had already formed among the fall-entry students. There were no welcome-week activities or club fairs in January. Amit was on his own. To further complicate matters, he discovered that the intended business major he had selected over a year earlier was not enjoyable. He found the required courses tedious and difficult, and his grades began to drop.

Amit realized that he had selected a university and a major for all the wrong reasons. He had prioritized the details that would be printed on his diploma without considering how unpleasant the journey might be. It was time to reevaluate the options, assess his needs as a student, and seek a better fit.

Ultimately, Amit transferred to the flagship public university just miles from his family home and declared an anthropology major. He had initially dismissed this nearby school. It wasn't especially prestigious, and attending a local school didn't feel like "going away" to college. Sometimes the best-fit college is right in your own backyard, though. Amit received a warm welcome as a transfer student and found immediate success in both social and academic endeavors.

Is Transfer Right for Me?

As you have read, students transfer for a multitude of reasons. Perhaps you identify with some of the students profiled so far. Or you may have your own unique reasons for wanting to transfer. Before you take that leap into transfer applications, pause and think about the pros and cons of this decision.

Obviously, if your only path to a degree is via transfer, you should do it! For example, community college students and students displaced by school closures have no other option but to transfer if they want to continue working toward a bachelor's degree. Similarly, adults who left college years ago may have the option to return to a previous school, but life changes sometimes get in the way. Transferring to a new school might be the only way to get back on a degree track while accommodating jobs, family, and relocations. Choosing to transfer is not such a difficult decision when the alternative is abandoning the pursuit of a degree altogether.

Prospective transfer students who are currently enrolled at four-year universities and have the option to remain there face a much more difficult decision. A degree can be earned at the current college, so is transfer worth the hassle? In most cases, remaining at your current school will be the most efficient path to a degree. Are you willing to trade some of that efficiency for a better college environment? Do the benefits you expect to receive at the new school outweigh the possible delays that can accompany the transfer path? If the answer is a whole-hearted "YES," then transfer might be the right path for you. If you don't feel so confident, consider discussing your options with trusted friends, family members, or a professional academic adviser.

Common Challenges and Questions

What if I was suspended or expelled from college for something other than low grades?

Students can be asked to leave a college for any number of reasons. Academic suspension is one of the most common reasons for students to withdraw and also one of the most straightforward issues to resolve through repeated classes, academic renewal, and raising the overall GPA.

Other issues that may lead to dismissal from a college include academic dishonesty (e.g., plagiarism or cheating), breaching the student code of conduct, allegations of abuse, criminal activity, or any behavior that could be interpreted as a danger to campus safety. Recovering from circumstances such as these can be more challenging, but it is not impossible! According to lawyer and educational crisis management specialist Hanna Stotland, the key to success is honest and "ethical disclosure."[5] Stotland has found colleges to be more open-minded when transfer applicants are able to demonstrate honest transformation after a problematic experience.

How do I prove that I'm in "good standing" at my current college? What if I'm not?

Most colleges have one or more application questions about your status at the most recent college you attended. These questions may ask about academic standing, student conduct, and eligibility to return to that college. It's important to answer honestly and then use the additional information boxes to explain the circumstances of any disciplinary actions or academic suspensions.

After submitting the online application, you may be required to have an official at your most recent college complete some forms that verify your standing. If you are currently enrolled at a college, you may also need to ask your professors to sign a form with predicted grades in their classes and send this document to prospective universities.

You won't necessarily be disqualified for past transgressions. No one is perfect! If you have made mistakes in the past, writing honestly about them and showing remorse and personal growth can mitigate the impact on your transfer application.

I know I want to leave, but I don't know where to go.

Sometimes your current college feels like the wrong fit, but you don't know what kind of college might be the right fit. In this case, don't rush to transfer! Make sure you are not running away from challenges but are running toward new opportunities.

If remaining at your current institution while examining your educational wants and needs is unsustainable, consider shaking things up with a study-abroad program, internships, or a gap term. Adding a variety of new experiences to your life can help you gain clarity before you embark on a transfer journey.

PART II

ASSESSING EARNED CREDIT

Before you can plan your future, you must unpack the past. If you're lucky, the exercise of tallying and documenting your existing credits will be a fun trip down memory lane. However, for some students, this is the hardest part of the transfer journey.

You may have unpleasant memories associated with prior colleges you attended. Perhaps you failed some courses, dropped out to address mental health concerns, or gave up a dream to care for your loved ones. Maybe you are embarrassed to have chosen the "wrong" college, or you feel shame because your college experiences don't look like your friends' social media posts. These feelings are perfectly normal and familiar to many transfer students.

You are not alone.

Whatever your feelings about your previous college history, it's time to gather your transcripts and objectively review your previously earned credits. You might be surprised at how much progress you have already made!

CHAPTER 3

Collecting Transcripts

Your transfer journey begins with a sea of paperwork.
When you apply to your next college, you will send them *all* transcripts from every postsecondary institution you have attended. Truly, the transfer admission committee wants to see everything from your academic past. They might even ask for your high school transcript or standardized test scores. These seemingly mundane documents are vital because they tell a story about you and your academic history.

Before you send these transcripts into the world, let's see what story they tell. Decoding these documents will help you understand your current student status and imagine how admissions officers might interpret your educational background. Knowing where you stand will also help you make wise decisions about your next steps in transfer.

Colleges Attended

Begin by making a list of colleges you attended and the approximate years you were enrolled. Include every college, even if you didn't earn credits there. If you took college courses while enrolled in high school, make a note of those colleges and your date of high school graduation. You will need to acquire copies of your transcript from every postsecondary institution you attended, even if you simply took a dual enrollment college class on your high school campus. You can find a worksheet to help with this on my website at TransferSavvy.com /Book.

Unofficial Transcripts

If you are currently in college, or recently left, you may be able to download a free unofficial copy of your transcript from the college's student portal. During this early planning stage, an unofficial copy works just fine.

If you are no longer able to access your college's student portal, you will need to acquire a copy of your transcript in a different way. Many colleges and universities now use third-party websites to manage transcript requests, usually for a fee. Two of the most common transcript sites are Parchment and National Student Clearinghouse. Other schools may handle their transcript requests in-house. Visit the website of each college you attended, locate the search bar or icon, and search for "order transcript" to find the pages that explain the transcript ordering process. You will probably find the instructions in the registrar's section of the website.

Fees for multiple transcripts can add up quickly, so if you have the option to order an unofficial transcript for free, take it. Official transcripts will need to be sent to your future college either with your application or upon enrollment, but you don't need anything fancy as you prepare. Simply choose yourself as the recipient of the transcript and select electronic delivery, if available. Email delivery of an unofficial transcript can often be completed immediately, so check your email right away.

Common Challenges and Questions

What if I didn't pass any classes at a particular college?

Order a transcript anyway. You need to know how your official record will appear to your future college so you can explain it in your application.

If you didn't earn any credits at this college because you failed or withdrew from all your classes, you might wonder if you can simply pretend you never enrolled there.

No, you cannot ignore any past college records.

When applying to a new college, you are obligated to disclose all prior postsecondary enrollments. If you try to hide some of your records, you risk rejection or expulsion when your history is uncovered, and it will be! Most universities periodically run a list of enrolled students through the National Student Clearinghouse database to verify student enrollment records and check for any undisclosed history. It's not worth the risk.

What if the college won't give me my transcript?

Some colleges place a financial hold on academic records, such as transcripts, if students owe money to the institution. If it is a small fee and fits within your budget, the simplest solution is to pay the bill and move on. However, if your transcript is being held hostage for several thousand dollars, fight back! There are federal regulations to prevent colleges from withholding your transcript if you used federal funds to pay for tuition. In addition, many states have enacted laws prohibiting the withholding of student records entirely. Do your research and request the records you are legally entitled to receive.[1]

What if the college I attended has closed down?

If your college no longer exists, it may be challenging to track down your records. However, schools are required to provide a way for students to access records indefinitely. If you cannot find a way to access your records online, contact the Department of Education in your school's home state.[2]

I don't remember my student ID number!

That's OK! There are multiple ways to locate your records. If you don't have the necessary information to order your transcript online, contact the college directly by phone or email. They can search for your records with other personal details you provide.

My transcripts are really old. Do credits expire?

While your earned college credits don't technically expire, certain colleges may choose not to accept older courses as transferable credits. Most core classes remain relevant for an indefinite period — it is unlikely that your next college will require you to retake English Composition 101, for example. However, in fields that evolve quickly, such as science, engineering, and computer programming, older courses may lose their relevance after several years. Your new college may ask you to demonstrate that you have kept your knowledge current, or they might require you to retake some courses. Colleges evaluate these situations on a case-by-case basis. If you have credits that are more than five to ten years old, check carefully with each potential university to determine their policy of aging credits.

CHAPTER 4

Transcript Self-Evaluation

Now that you have access to all your course records, it's time to dig into the details.

At first glance, it may seem like your transcripts are written in another language. There are so many unique terms and acronyms! However, not every detail on your transcript is of equal importance. We want to focus primarily on your classes, credits, and grades.

The number of transferable course credits you have earned so far will determine your student level, that is, sophomore, junior, and so on. Once you know how colleges define you, you can match your experience to the universities seeking students with your academic background.

Reading a Transcript

Most college transcripts include several pieces of information for each class taken:

- Course number
- Course name
- Credits (also known as units or hours)
- Letter grade
- Grade or quality points

Some transcripts also distinguish between attempted, earned, and graded credits. Attempted credits show how many credits you enrolled in, while earned or graded credits reflect only the classes you completed successfully.

32 Assessing Earned Credit

Here's an example:

Course	Course Title	Attempted	Earned	Grade	Qty Pts
BIL 101	INTR BIOLOGICL SCI	3.000	3.000	A	12.000

This student took BIL 101: Introduction to Biological Science. This was a 3-credit class, and the student earned all 3 credits by passing the class with a grade of A. Assuming this college operates on a 4.0 grade scale, this A is worth 4 quality points per credit, giving this student 12 "quality," or grade, points.

The most critical data points for each class are earned credits and grades. First you will add up the earned credits from your transcripts. Then you will calculate your college grade point average, or GPA.

Quarter or Semester

Almost all US higher education institutions operate on either the quarter or the semester system. To accurately interpret your transcripts and count your earned credits to date, you must know which system your previous colleges used. Some transcripts clearly state whether they use semesters or quarters; others can be more difficult to decipher.

If your school was on the quarter system, you will probably see classes divided into three sessions per year: fall, winter, and spring quarters. If your school was on the semester system, your transcript will instead show two sessions: fall and spring semesters. In both systems, there may be an optional summer session as well.

A typical bachelor's degree from a school on the quarter system requires approximately 180 quarter credits, while the same degree from a semester-based school usually requires 120 semester credits. It may look like the semester-based school lets you graduate faster, but both degrees require the same amount of time in college. The table below summarizes the differences between the two systems.

Quarter System vs. Semester System		
	Quarter	Semester
Number of sessions per year (not including summer)	3	2

Typical session length in weeks	10–12	15–16
Common session names	Fall, Winter, Spring	Fall, Spring
Credits needed for bachelor's degree	180	120
Start month	September	August
End month	June	May

Now that you know the difference between quarters and semesters, look for clues on your transcript:

- During which month did you begin classes?
- How many sessions do you see each year?
- Does the spring session start in January or March/April?
- Does your transcript show progress toward a 120- or 180-credit degree?

It's also possible that your college uses a nonstandard credit system, where each class might be worth one credit or even a fraction of a credit, depending on the workload involved. If you still aren't sure what system your college uses, visit the college's website and see if the academic calendar shows two or three primary sessions. Of course, you can always call and ask, too! Knowing this crucial fact is essential before you move forward with your transcript evaluation.

If all the colleges you attended award credits on the same system, adding up your total credits earned will be easy. However, if you have credits from multiple schools on different systems, you must do some math before proceeding to the next step.

Credit Conversion

Think of quarter and semester credits as centimeters and inches. If you have taken some measurements in centimeters and noted others in inches, you won't be able to compare lengths accurately. You also won't be able to add up the measurements until you convert all the numbers to the same system. The same goes for quarter and semester credits.

34 Assessing Earned Credit

Here's the standard conversion formula:

<u>1 semester credit = 1.5 quarter credits</u>

So a typical 3-credit class from a semester-based school will convert into 4.5 credits at a quarter school. Conversely, a 5-credit quarter class will convert into 3.33 credits at a semester school. Please note that these conversions are approximate. When your new college evaluates your transcript, they may assign more or less credit to any given class, depending on how your class aligns with those offered on their campus.

Let's look at an example:

Unofficial Transcript

Term: 2015 Fall Foothill

Academic Standing:	Good Standing

Subject	Course	Level	Title	Grade	Credit Hours	Quality Points
ANTH	F005	FU	MAGIC, SCIENCE & RELIGION	A	4.000	16.00
COMM	F012	FU	INTERCULTURAL COMMUNICATION	A	5.000	20.00

Term Totals (Foothill Undergraduate)

	Attempt Hours	Passed Hours	Earned Hours	GPA Hours	Quality Points	GPA
Current Term:	9.000	9.000	9.000	9.000	36.00	4.00
Cumulative:	34.500	34.500	34.500	34.500	138.00	4.00

Unofficial Transcript

Term: 2016 Winter Foothill

Academic Standing:	Good Standing
Additional Standing:	Dean's List

Subject	Course	Level	Title	Grade	Credit Hours	Quality Points
ENGL	F001A	FU	COMPOSITION & READING	A	5.000	20.00
SOC	F014	FU	SOCIOLOGY OF CRIME	A-	4.000	14.80

Term Totals (Foothill Undergraduate)

	Attempt Hours	Passed Hours	Earned Hours	GPA Hours	Quality Points	GPA
Current Term:	9.000	9.000	9.000	9.000	34.80	3.86
Cumulative:	43.500	43.500	43.500	43.500	172.80	3.97

Here, you can see that classes are listed for fall and winter sessions, which indicates that this school is most likely operating on a quarter system. This student earned 9 quarter credits in each session. To find out how many equivalent semester credits they earned, just multiply by 0.66667 and truncate the product at three decimal places.

$$9 \times 0.66667 = 6.000$$

In this case, the student's 9 quarter credits convert to 6 semester credits for each session.

Here's another example:

2023 Fall Semester

Program:
College of Business and Economics
Bachelor of Business Administration
Major: Pre-Finance
Martin-Gatton College of Ag Food Envr
BS in Equine Science and Management
Major: Equine Science and Management

CRS NUM	COURSE TITLE	GRADE	HOURS	QPTS
KHP 112	VOLLEYBALL	A	1.0	4.00
CHE 185	FOUNDATIONS OF GENERAL CHEMISTRY I Pass Fail Grade Scale	P	2.0	0.00
STA 296	STATISTICAL METHODS AND MOTIVATIONS	B	3.0	9.00
EQM 101	INTRO TO THE HORSE & HORSE INDUSTRY	A	3.0	12.00
AFE 100	ISSUES IN AG, FOOD AND ENVIRONMENT	A	3.0	12.00

	AHRS	EHRS	QHRS	QPTS	GPA
Semester	12.0	12.0	10.0	37.00	3.700
Cumulative	25.0	25.0	10.0	37.00	3.700
Status	Good Standing				
Status	No Academic Honors				

This time, the transcript clearly states that these classes took place during the fall semester, so we don't have to guess which credit system the school uses. This student earned 12 semester credits during the fall session. We can convert those to quarter credits by multiplying the semester credits by 1.5.

$$12 \times 1.5 = 18$$

36   Assessing Earned Credit

So we converted 12 semester credits into 18 quarter credits earned during the fall session.

Have you taken more classes on the quarter system or semester system? Convert the rest of your classes to that system. If you have equal numbers of courses in both systems, convert everything to semester credits. Many more colleges operate on the semester system these days.

If you have nonstandard credits that conform to neither the quarter nor the semester system, your credit conversions will unfortunately be far less precise. For example, at a college where each class is worth a single unit per term, you might multiply your credits by three or four (the average number of credits for a class on the semester system) to get a ballpark estimate. You may need to talk to an adviser at your college to learn more about how your credits translate to different systems.

When you have finished your credit conversions, you are ready to move on to counting your credits.

Credits and Levels

Most colleges require students to earn grades of C or better to transfer those credits into the new college. If you're lucky, your new school might accept C- or D grades, but don't count on it. Pass or P grades are acceptable for transfer at some schools if the student can show that a P grade is equivalent to a C or higher.

Let's begin with a conservative estimate of your transferable credits and add up only the credits from classes where you earned a C or higher. Make sure you are adding quarter credits to quarter credits or semester credits to semester credits. If you are working with multiple transcripts from schools on different systems, carefully convert quarter credits into semester credits or vice versa before you begin. (See prior section.) Visit TransferSavvy.com/Book for a worksheet for calculating and converting your credits.

How many credits do you have? The chart below shows how you will likely be classified when you apply for transfer admission to a new university.

Credit Level Classifications		
	Total quarter credits	*Total semester credits*
Low-unit transfer	Fewer than 45	Fewer than 30
Sophomore transfer	45–90	30–60
Junior transfer	90–105	60–70
High-unit transfer	More than 105	More than 70
Typical total for degree	**180**	**120**

Transferring at the sophomore or junior level is most common. Many universities have a residency policy that requires students to take the last 30–60 semester units (45–90 quarter units) while enrolled at the new university. (Sometimes this is referred to as being "in residence," though it does not dictate where you physically live.) Thus, students who arrive with less than half of their degree completed will be able to fulfill this requirement while maintaining their expected graduation timeline.

Additionally, admissions officers can more easily assess the academic performance of transfer students who have completed at least a year's worth of college credits. Students with fewer credits may need to submit high school records to be evaluated alongside their college transcripts. In some cases, low-unit transfers simply aren't admissible at all. Admissions officers typically want more data before they agree to admit a transfer student with few completed college credits.

Keep your unit status in mind as you research potential colleges for transfer. Many colleges have minimum or maximum unit requirements for admission. If you are a low-unit transfer, you may need to take additional courses before applying. If you are a high-unit transfer, your college options might be limited to those with lower residency requirements for graduation.

We will learn more about how your current credit count influences your college search in part 3.

38 Assessing Earned Credit

Transfer GPA

Your transcript probably has a GPA, or grade point average, printed right on it. If you only have one prior transcript, you can use this GPA to assess your transfer odds at various schools. Ensure you look at the cumulative GPA for all terms, not the GPA for any individual term.

If you have attended multiple schools, you must estimate your overall GPA from all schools attended. Make sure you have converted your units to the same system (semester or quarter) before you begin!

First, we need to assign a point value to every letter grade. Although some schools may assign a plus or minus to your grade, let's keep it simple and focus on round numbers to estimate your GPA.

The table below shows the point value assigned to each letter grade. Notice that the last two grades on the list, P for Pass and W for Withdrawal, do not have associated point values. Classes taken on a Pass/Fail grade basis or dropped before the withdrawal deadline are not included in your GPA.

Letter Grade Point Values	
Letter	*Grade points*
A	4
B	3
C	2
D	1
F	0
P	n/a
W	n/a

For each class, multiply the point value of the grade by the number of credits attempted in the class. For example, if you earned an A in a 4-credit class, you would have 16 grade or quality points for that class. If you earned a C in a 3-credit class, you would have 6 points.

Calculate your quality points for each graded class on your transcript this way. Then add up your total quality points for all graded, for-credit classes. Also add up the attempted credit values of all those classes. To calculate your GPA, divide your total quality points by the total number of credits attempted in those classes. Remember to skip over any classes graded W or P!

Visit TransferSavvy.com/Book to access a worksheet for calculating your GPA.

Let's work through an example.

Course		College	Description	Units Attempted	Units Earned	Grade	Grade Points
ART	80	LAN	BEGINNING CERAMICS	2.0	0.0	F	0.0
ENGL	1B	LAN	Composition and Reading	4.0	4.0	A	16.0
MATH	1	LAN	PRE-CALCULUS	4.0	4.0	A	16.0
MATH	215	LAN	Support for Pre-Calculus	2.0	2.0	P	0.0

This student took four classes. Math 215 was a noncredit support class for Precalculus, and it was graded on a Pass/Fail basis, so we won't include that class in our calculations. The other three classes were taken for transferable credit and letter grades. First, we assign a number value to each grade, and then we multiply by the number of credits attempted.

Class	Letter grade	Grade points	Units attempted	Total points
Art 80	F	0	2	0
English 1B	A	4	4	16
Math 1	A	4	4	16
Math 215	P	n/a	(2)	n/a
		TOTAL	10	32

Now we have a total of 10 graded credits attempted and 32 overall quality points. Dividing 32 points by 10 credits gives us a grade point average of 3.2. Nice!

Common Challenges and Questions

My college changed from quarters to semesters after I left.

The semester system is far more popular in the United States, so it's no surprise that some colleges are transitioning away from the quarter system. If this occurred at your school, your transcript will likely include a note about the shift. Your transcript may show recalculated credits, in which case you will probably see unexpected decimals in your completed credits. It's also possible that your college will display your original quarter system credits so that your transcript continues to show the credits as they were calculated while you were enrolled. Don't be afraid to contact the college and ask how it handled this shift on your transcript.

The college I attended is not on either the quarter or semester system.

A few colleges out there operate on their own unique calendar systems. These credits can be more difficult to convert and evaluate accurately.

Sometimes these calendars are just semesters in disguise, such as the split-term system that divides each semester into two shorter sessions: term A and term B. If the overall calendar is still based on fall and spring semesters, these are most likely semester credits.

Other colleges have adopted a block schedule, where students take one class at a time for three or four weeks each. At these colleges, one class usually provides 1 credit, and it takes approximately 32 credits or classes to complete an undergraduate degree. Unfortunately, it isn't easy to convert these hours into semester credits accurately. For now, use an estimate of 3 semester credits per course.

Some of my classes are noted as "noncredit" or "nontransferable."

Community colleges frequently offer both credit and noncredit courses. Credit courses are usually academic classes designed for students who are working toward a degree.

However, not all students enroll at a community college to earn

Transcript Self-Evaluation   41

a degree. Some students may be preparing for a specific career that requires training but not necessarily a degree. These courses may be labeled as CTE, or Career and Technical Education, and are usually not transferable to a four-year university. Do not include these classes in your overall credit count.

If you have taken foundational math or ESL (English as a Second Language) courses, you must also remove those classes from your credit count. Universities usually do not accept these predegree preparatory classes for transfer.

How bad is a W on my transcript?

It's always better to withdraw and get a W than to stay and get a D or F. The W grade does not get factored into your GPA, while a D or F does. Let's revisit our GPA calculation example. The F in Art led the student to have an overall GPA of 3.2. If the student had withdrawn from that class instead, the grade would have been a W and excluded from GPA calculations.

Class	Letter grade	Grade points	Units attempted	Total points
Art 80	W	n/a	n/a	n/a
English 1B	A	4	4	16
Math 1	A	4	4	16
Math 215	P	n/a	(2)	n/a
		TOTAL	8	32

Now the student has only 8 graded credits and still has 32 quality points. Dividing 32 by 8 gives the student a GPA of 4.0.

However, a pattern of excessive unexplained W grades over multiple semesters might be a red flag for the university you wish to attend. So don't drop a course every time you feel academically challenged — challenge is an expected part of the college experience. Withdrawing from a class in the face of health challenges or a family emergency is perfectly understandable, though. If you have withdrawn from numerous courses for valid reasons such as these, you might want to write about the circumstances in your application.

Will my GPA transfer to the new school?

In most cases, your prior GPA will *not* transfer to the new school. The college admissions office will consider your GPA when deciding whether to accept you as a transfer student. Once you enroll, you will likely start fresh with a brand-new GPA.

CHAPTER 5

Alternative Credit Sources

Not all college credits come from college classes! You may be able to claim credits from other sources, such as test scores, prior work experience, or military training.

Think back to high school. Did you take Advanced Placement (AP) classes? Did you participate in an International Baccalaureate (IB) program? Both of these programs include course final exams that may provide you with college credit! Perhaps you self-studied for a CLEP or DSST exam. If you enlisted in a branch of the military, you may even have had free access to these credit-granting exams through DANTES. (These exams and programs are covered in detail below.) If you have been in the workforce, think about any certifications or training programs you pursued.

Even if you think a credential is too old or irrelevant, gather the details just in case. You want to claim every possible credit when you transfer to a new college so that you don't have to waste time taking classes on topics you have already mastered.

Tests

Are you a strong test taker? You may have some test scores from your past that will provide you with college credit now! You might even want to consider self-studying for additional tests to prove your knowledge in specific subject areas. Strategic use of college credit–granting exams can streamline your path to a degree.

The College Board: AP and CLEP

The College Board is best known as the organization behind the popular SAT college entrance examination. However, the College Board also offers two testing programs that can help students earn college credit outside of a traditional university setting.

Advanced Placement

The Advanced Placement (AP) program is a common source of college credit for high school students. AP tests are offered once each spring and are intended to act as final exams for College Board–approved AP high school courses. According to the College Board, 80 percent of American public high school students have access to five or more AP classes and exams at their schools.[1] In 2023, *The New York Times* reported that US students took 5.2 million AP exams in total.[2] Were you part of this growing trend during your high school years? If so, you may have college credits lingering in your College Board account. Log in and find out! Make a note of each test you took and the score you received. AP exams are scored on a scale of 1 to 5, with 3 being the minimum for transferable credit in most cases. Don't throw away those 1s and 2s, though! In some rare cases, universities will grant credit or waive prerequisite classes in certain subjects even if a student scores below the standard pass threshold of 3.[3]

College-Level Examination Program

If you didn't take AP classes and exams while you were a high school student, don't worry about them as a college student. The College-Level Examination Program (CLEP) is the more relevant testing program for you now. CLEP is also administered by the College Board but is intended for students of all ages. Unlike AP exams, CLEP tests are not aligned with specific curricula and don't need to be scheduled through your high school. Students can self-study and then register for an exam directly at a testing center. Students can even take CLEP tests online at home with remote proctoring.[4] It's never too late to self-study for a CLEP exam in an area of interest and earn college credit! Just make sure your potential future colleges accept CLEP credits. If you need help preparing for CLEP exams, look into the free online classes available from ModernStates.org.

DANTES Subject Standardized Tests

Designed initially for members of the military, DANTES Subject Standardized Tests (DSST) are now available to anyone seeking credit by examination. DSST and CLEP tests are quite similar, and some students take a combination of exams from both programs to earn credits in a variety of subject areas. While CLEP tests typically provide only lower-division credit, some colleges may offer upper-division credit for certain DSST exams. DSST is not as well known or widely accepted as CLEP, so research target schools carefully to see if colleges of interest accept DSST credits.

International Baccalaureate

The International Baccalaureate Organization (IBO) authorizes and supports schools worldwide that wish to offer IB programs and the accompanying tests. Although the IBO offers curricula starting at the primary level, the IB high school Diploma Programme and Career-related Programme are the most relevant for college transfer students. As of 2024, 934 high schools in the United States participated in the IB Diploma Programme. If you attended one of these high schools and completed an IB diploma or earned a score of 5, 6, or 7 on IB Higher Level exams, you may have transferable college credits on file with the IBO.[5]

Languages Other Than English

There are multiple test options for students who have learned other languages, either formally or informally. Many of the tests named above can be used to evaluate skills in several common languages. Students who have gained fluency in less frequently taught languages can take specialized language exams to verify their skills and potentially earn college credits. The American Council on Education (ACE) has reviewed several of these exams, including the STAndards-Based Measurement of Proficiency four-section test (STAMP 4s), Defense Language Proficiency Test (DLPT), and American Council on the Teaching of Foreign Languages (ACTFL) tests, and recommends that students receive college credit for passing scores. However, it is up to each individual college to decide how much credit, if any, will be awarded to students for particular scores on any given exam.

Case Study: Moe

Remember Moe, the reverse transfer student from chapter 1? Moe made excellent use of the College-Level Examination Program (CLEP) during his quest for a degree. A history buff, Moe read numerous books on various periods of American history in his spare time. He knew the required introductory US History course offered at his community college would likely bore him, so he decided to self-study for the History of the United States I and II CLEP exams. He registered online at the College Board website and arranged to take the exams at a local testing center a few days later. Each exam lasted ninety minutes, and Moe passed with flying colors because he had previously mastered the material.

Moe shared his official CLEP scores with his community college, and American history course credits were soon added to his official community college transcript. In just three hours of test time, he had earned six college semester credits. Moe went on to take additional CLEP exams in areas of interest and expertise, which facilitated his efficient AA degree completion.

Credit for Prior Learning

Learning happens everywhere. Although many universities award credits and degrees based only on seat time (hours spent in the classroom) and earned grades, there is a growing movement to recognize and certify other kinds of learning experiences. ACE is at the forefront of this movement with its credit recommendation programs.

ACE National Guide

On the ACE website, students can search the National Guide database for nontraditional learning experiences from various education and training providers, read descriptions of the expected learning outcomes of those experiences, and view the estimated number of equivalent academic semester credits.[6] The guide includes credit recommendations for internships through the Disney College Program, online classes from Coursera.com and Study.com, technical certificates from Google and Microsoft, Divemaster training from PADI (Professional Association of Diving Instructors), and many more. Check the database and see if you have any qualifying learning experiences that might be eligible for academic credit.

ACE/Credly Transcripts

Learners who complete ACE-recommended programs are eligible to earn digital badges through the credential network Credly. These badges can be shared on LinkedIn profiles or added to a mobile wallet on a smartphone. Students can also request official ACE transcripts through Credly. Remember, these transcripts indicate only credit recommendations. Your future university will decide whether or not to accept these recommendations and apply credit toward your degree.

ACE Military Guide

In addition to the National Guide, ACE also offers a Military Guide that provides details and credit recommendations for military training and occupation experiences. Veterans can even upload their military transcripts to the ACE Military Guide to receive a thorough explanation of their experiences in academic terms. If you have military experience, please read on to learn more about the credits that may be available to you.

Credit from Military Service

If you have served in a branch of the US Armed Forces, you probably have a transcript that details both your military training and occupation experiences. It may also list credits earned by exam if you took tests such as CLEP or DSST exams through the DANTES program.

48   Assessing Earned Credit

Military Transcripts

The Joint Services Transcript (JST) is available to active-duty, reserve, and veteran members of the Army, Navy, Marines, and Coast Guard. If you have served in the Air Force or Space Force, your transcript will come from the Community College of the Air Force (CCAF). Although these documents are referred to as transcripts, they are quite different from those issued by a college because the military does not provide academic credits the same way a college would. Instead, the military offers education programs and hands-on experience to prepare service members for active duty. Descriptions of those experiences have been standardized and translated into terms that civilians are more likely to understand. ACE then offers credit recommendations to help employers and colleges interpret those military experiences in terms of college-level academic credits.

Here is an example of a military training entry on a Coast Guard JST:

CG-1511-0002 V06   02-FEB-2015 to 02-MAR-2015
Chief Petty Officer Academy:
Coast Guard Training Center
Petaluma, CA

Upon completion of the course, the student will be able to plan, manage and control organizational and personnel programs; apply strategic human resource planning to support organizational mission and objectives; employ organizational behavior perspectives and practices to enhance individual and team development; produce effective communication documents; employ leadership techniques to influence, motivate and maintain a productive and diverse work environment; and demonstrate coherent, ethical communication principles in business and Coast Guard environments.

· Communication	3 SH	L
· Human Resource Management	3 SH	U
· Leadership	3 SH	U
· Organizational Behavior	3 SH	U

This veteran attended the Chief Petty Officer Academy at the Coast Guard Training Center in Petaluma, California. ACE recommends that this student be awarded 12 semester hours of academic credit for this training experience. To align with traditional educational systems,

ACE has divided this program into four 3-credit courses: lower-division Communication and upper-division Human Resource Management, Leadership, and Organizational Behavior.

It is important to note that these credits are advisory only. ACE is not a credit-granting institution of higher education, and neither is the Department of Defense. The student's future university will evaluate these credit recommendations and decide which credits, if any, can be applied to a degree at that school.

First-Year or Transfer?

Since your JST or CCAF transcript is really just a recommendation of credit, you may wonder if you are eligible to apply to colleges as a first-year or transfer student. Unfortunately, there is no easy answer to this question. Some colleges classify all military veterans as transfer students because of the recommended credits placed on the military transcript. Other colleges define transfer students as those who have taken college classes and earned a specific number of credits through coursework, so a veteran with primarily military and test credits would apply as a first-year student. Individuals must research application requirements for each university of interest to determine if a first-year or transfer application is most appropriate at that particular school. It's entirely possible that the same student will apply as a first-year to some colleges and as a transfer to others.

Although it is somewhat rare, a few colleges (notably, Wesleyan University and Brown University) now have specific applications just for veterans regardless of credit status or class standing. Instead of reading the fine print and choosing an application path, veterans interested in these schools can submit veteran-specific forms, send official transcripts, and let the colleges decide how to process the applications and award transfer credits.

A Note Regarding the GI Bill

Don't use your GI Bill benefits before you have to! GI Bill funding for college is capped by time, not by credits or cost.[7] So if you decide to go from the military to a community college and then transfer to a four-year university, save your GI Bill funds for the more expensive four-year institution. See if you qualify for a Pell Grant or state-based free community college program to pay for the less costly classes at the two-year college.

Here's an example of how you can maximize your funds: Most veterans get thirty-six months of GI Bill benefits after separation from active duty. Let's say you move back home with your family and attend a local community college for two years to build up your college transcript. Since you are living at home, the GI Bill housing allowance is unnecessary, and the community college tuition in your state is a mere $46 per credit, so you pay that directly. After those two years, you transfer to a private university that charges $65,000 per year in tuition. Your GI Bill benefits will cover 36 months of continuous enrollment at that private university — sufficient to complete a bachelor's degree after you transfer your existing college credits. Also, you can pause and restart your benefits at any time, such as during summer breaks or semesters off. So if you spend two years at community college and pay out of pocket, and then use GI Bill benefits to pay for two years at a private university to earn your bachelor's (nine months of benefits per year), you'd still have eighteen months of benefits left over — enough to also earn a master's!

Expert Help

Transfer admission is complicated. Transfer admission with credits from a JST or CCAF transcript is even more complicated. However, universities appreciate the diverse experiences service members bring to campus. They want to admit you, so do not be discouraged! Prior to separation, be sure to take advantage of the Transition Assistance Program (TAP) learning opportunities available at your base or online. Also consider requesting free assistance from a nonprofit organization committed to helping veterans transition from active duty to college study, such as Service to School (S2S).[8] Mentors and counselors with expertise in college admissions for veterans can save you time, money, and frustration as you navigate the path to a degree.

Case Study: Robin

Robin grew up in a military family, but she didn't initially plan to follow in her father's footsteps and enlist. Like most of her high school peers, she intended to pursue a traditional college path immediately after graduation. She had embraced challenging coursework, earned high scores on her AP exams, and confidently applied to her state's flagship university. However, Robin underestimated the selectivity of the school's computer science program and was not admitted, which forced her to completely rethink her post–high school plans just as the Covid-19 pandemic sent much of the country into lockdown. Joining the US Air Force suddenly seemed like a great idea.

Although Robin expressed interest in computer science and cybersecurity, her affinity for languages made her an excellent fit for the sixty-four-week intensive Chinese language program at the Defense Language Institute Foreign Language Center (DLIFLC) in Monterey, California. While there, she took some CLEP and DSST exams to earn additional general education credits that would make her eligible for an associate degree from DLIFLC. Two years after graduating from high school, Robin graduated from DLIFLC with highest honors and received the Command Sergeant Major Award. After some additional military intelligence training, Robin was ready to get to work as an airborne linguist, or Airborne Cryptologic Language Analyst, intercepting and interpreting Chinese naval messages.

College was never far from Robin's mind. Even while serving, she took online classes through Arizona State University to explore her interests in computer science and prepare for her eventual transfer applications. During the final year of her four-year Air Force contract, Robin applied to thirteen colleges as a transfer student in computer science.

Yale requested an interview. Arranging a virtual interview while deployed in Okinawa, Japan, was no small feat! By the time Robin was able to speak live with a Yale representative, she had rediscovered her love for East Asian cultures and languages in Japan and was eager to inform Yale that she had changed her mind about her major. Simultaneously, Yale's Eli Whitney program for nontraditional students had learned about Robin's story and invited her to apply to the program, even though she had been out of high school for only four years, rather than the usual five required for standard eligibility.

It was a perfect match. Robin's impressive background and passion for languages and global relations made her a desirable candidate for Yale's East Asian Studies major and the Eli Whitney Students Program. Yale accepted Robin, and she enrolled immediately after separating from the Air Force. While Yale did not accept any military training or test credits from Robin's CCAF transcript, they did accept all her language and general education credits from the DLIFLC, granting her second-semester sophomore standing. Robin is in no rush to graduate, though. She is enjoying the academic rigor of Yale classes and the camaraderie of the veteran and Eli Whitney communities at Yale, and she's looking forward to her upcoming internship with the US State Department. Thanks to her GI Bill benefits, she can afford to take her time.

Common Challenges and Questions

I took some tests many years ago. Can I still get college credits for my scores?

Maybe. It depends on the tests, when you took them, and the policies of the school where you hope to obtain credit. Most colleges will require you to send official test score reports to their offices directly. Even if a previous college gave you credit for scores and noted it on your transcript, there is no guarantee that the next college will accept scores that way. So you will most likely need to contact the College Board or other testing agency to have official scores sent again.

If several years have passed since you completed the tests, your scores may have been archived. The College Board, for example, archives AP scores after approximately five years, so when you access your College Board account, you may be unable to view or send older AP scores from the website. In that case, you must make a special request for scores to be retrieved from the College Board archives and sent to your college. In other instances, scores may expire completely and be unavailable for reporting after a specific date. Check with each testing agency to see if your scores are available.

How much credit can I earn just by taking tests?

Most colleges have policies outlining the maximum number of credits that can be transferred from other institutions or earned through tests and other nontraditional methods. The more prestigious and competitive the college, the less likely it is to accept a large number of test credits. If you are looking for the fastest and cheapest path to a degree, tests can be extremely useful at certain institutions! But if you hope to gain acceptance to a more selective university, your time will be better spent taking transferable college coursework. Demonstrating success in conventional college classes will boost your odds of transfer admission, and the credits you earn will more likely transfer to a broader range of schools.

What are "pass-along credits," and why is my college refusing to transfer them to my new transcript?

Pass-along credits are college credits that were transferred into a previous college, and then requested for transfer again to a future college without the original documentation. For example, if you earned college credit by taking a CLEP exam, your first college likely recorded those credits on your official transcript and may have noted course equivalencies available there. When applying for transfer to a different college, the new program is not obligated to accept the CLEP credits merely because they appear on your previous transcript. If the new school has a pro-CLEP policy, they may require a new official score report sent directly to them for verification and credit awarding. If the new college does not accept CLEP, you will not receive credit for your CLEP scores even though the credits were officially recorded on your previous college's transcript. Either way, these credits are considered "pass-along credits," and you must check with each college directly to see how they handle such credits for incoming transfer students.

PART III

SEARCHING FOR COLLEGES

The more frequently you transfer between colleges, the more likely you are to lose credits and extend the timeline for graduation and degree attainment. Therefore, it's important to make sure that your next college is the right match for you.

Obviously, there is no "perfect" college. Students always have to make compromises when selecting a school. There is no small liberal arts college with full-ride scholarships where you can major in engineering and intern with research-oriented faculty in a college town near the ocean with easy access to snowboarding facilities. That's a unicorn. It doesn't exist. To find the best fit, you will need to prioritize your college needs and preferences. Hold firm on the elements that are critical to your success, but be prepared to compromise on the bells and whistles.

Prioritize with Maslow

Let's get nerdy for a minute. Have you ever heard of Abraham Maslow's Hierarchy of Needs? It's a psychological theory that divides essential human needs into five or six categories, usually displayed on a pyramid to illustrate the idea that each need must build on the previous.

At the bottom of the pyramid, the most basic human needs are physiological. We need food, water, and sleep to survive. Next, we need safety and security. Once those most basic needs are met, we can begin to think about finding a sense of belonging in a community. Then comes esteem — a sense of achievement and feeling recognized for your work. Finally, Maslow positioned self-actualization at the top of the pyramid. The idea is that humans need all the elements of the first four levels of the pyramid before they can become the best versions of themselves. Maslow later added a sixth level to his pyramid — transcendence. Once a person becomes self-actualized, we might hope that they will use their skills to improve the world around them.

What does any of this have to do with the search for a college? Well, think about your goals for going to college and getting a degree. You might be thinking about careers and money on the surface, but college is much more than that. It can be a transformative experience where you explore new ideas, discover your passions, and then use your new-found knowledge and confidence to make your mark on society. That sounds a lot like self-actualization and transcendence, doesn't it?

When trying to separate the "must-haves" from the "nice-to-haves" of college qualities, think about this pyramid from the bottom up. For example, a university might offer amazing internships and research opportunities in your major, but if it doesn't offer the mental health support you need, you may not be able to take advantage of those opportunities. That's not to say that self-actualization cannot be achieved at a college unless every aspect of the lower levels is perfect! Just be mindful of how basic unmet needs might prevent you from ascending the pyramid and becoming your best self.

Self-actualization/ transcendence
Internships, research programs, career center

Esteem
Classes, majors, mentoring, awards, student government, credits

Belonging
Student clubs, demographics, inclusion initiatives

Safety
Campus crime rates, campus policies, state and local laws

Physiological needs
Location, campus housing, meal plan, physical and mental health, financial aid

The Transfer Dimension

As a transfer student, you also have another dimension to your college search. Your next college needs to be welcoming to transfer students and the credits they bring to campus. A transfer-friendly college should cultivate transfer students' sense of belonging, be generous in accepting transfer credit, and ensure that admitted transfer students are supported continuously through graduation.

Some colleges may achieve these goals better than others. What are your priorities? Are you willing to extend your graduation timeline for an ideal college environment? Or are you looking for the quickest path to a degree at any college that can get the job done?

CHAPTER 6

The Five P's for College Research

When it comes to researching colleges, transfer students have a distinct advantage. You likely know which characteristics of your previous college(s) helped or harmed you in the past. Personal experience from attending college can provide valuable insights as you define your ideal future university.

Reflect

Think about the following questions as you read this chapter:

- What did you like best about your previous college(s)?
- What did you like least about your previous college(s)?
- What support programs are necessary for you to succeed?
- What other programs are necessary for you to feel confident and comfortable?
- Was your last college too big, too small, or just right?
- How did you feel about the local surroundings of your previous college(s)?
- If you could change anything about your previous college experience(s), what would it be?

The Five P's

One way to organize your college research is with the five P's: Place, People, Pastimes, Programs, and Practicality. Try assessing your last college according to these traits. You can find a 5 P's worksheet and spreadsheet template at TransferSavvy.com/Book. How does that school fare when you examine it through this lens?

Place

How do you narrow down your choices when there are over four thousand colleges and universities in the United States? Location is often a good place to start. If you despise snow, need to be near a major airport, or plan to live with family or friends while attending school, you can quickly cross hundreds of colleges off your list. Then move forward with serious research on the remainder. The following are some factors to weigh when considering locations.

Temporary or Permanent Relocation

When considering college location, think beyond the next few years. Students are likely to find internships and make career connections near their universities. Recruiters from local businesses attend job fairs at nearby campuses. Many students also meet their significant others at college and choose to settle down in the same state or region after graduation. Choosing a college to attend feels like a temporary relocation, but it could turn into a much more significant decision.

Travel Budget

Remember that the college's total cost of attendance (as stated on the financial aid pages of its website) includes a line item for travel expenses. This number is just an average dollar amount that doesn't take an individual student's home address into account. If your family's home is an hour's drive away, you will probably spend less than average on travel when you ask your cousin to give you a free ride home for the holidays. If you'd rather attend college on the opposite side of the country, be sure to budget for the number of plane flights, taxis, and checked bags to get you back and forth throughout the year.

Local Surroundings

Small college town or big city internships? Walk to the farmer's market or take the train to the city? Think about the local amenities that will help you thrive in college. If you need a daily nature walk to clear your head in times of stress, look for nearby options at potential colleges. If you know that the distractions of city life will interrupt your study routine, consider a college in a more secluded area. College can be a wonderful time to spread your wings and try something new! However, if you already know yourself well, there might be some locations you should rule out early.

Campus Housing

Most colleges guarantee or even require campus housing for incoming first-year students. This is less common for transfer students. Although some colleges require or encourage transfer students to live on campus, most schools urge transfers to live elsewhere to preserve limited housing space for incoming first-years. Check if colleges of interest guarantee (or even offer) campus housing for transfer students. If college-owned housing is limited, research rental availability and prices in the community. You don't want to be surprised by unaffordable rent or a long commute once you enroll. Remember that safe housing is a basic human need, and even the threat of that need going unmet can hinder your success.

Regional Agreements and Guarantees

Investigate transfer agreements among colleges and universities in your local area. The best transfer opportunities, especially for community college students, often exist at four-year universities in the same state. Check for legislation guaranteeing the transferability of credits in your state and find out if there is a statewide database of transferable classes. Additionally, explore regional tuition reciprocity programs like the Western Undergraduate Exchange (WUE) or Academic Common Market (ACM), which aim to make participating out-of-state colleges more affordable by reducing nonresident tuition rates. These tools and agreements can streamline the transfer process and save you money on tuition. (See chapter 8 for more on partnerships.)

Student Safety

Safety is an often overlooked factor that students should be sure to consider during the college search process. Feeling safe and valued in your new college community means you can focus your attention primarily on academic endeavors. Look up recent crime statistics for the communities surrounding colleges of interest and compare those to the statistics from your hometown. You can also research campus crime rates in great detail thanks to the Clery Act.[1] Look beyond the numbers as well. For example, relatively high rates of certain crimes might not indicate that the college is a hotbed of criminal activity but instead that it is a safe space where victims and witnesses are encouraged to report incidents to campus police. Last, consider how state laws and campus policies might affect your comfort levels. In these times of extreme political division, students of various ethnic backgrounds, religious beliefs, gender identities, and sexual orientations may feel better protected in some locations than in others.

People

Humans are social learners.[2] We don't acquire knowledge in a vacuum, independent of others. Instead, we learn from those who have gone before us as we read textbooks and listen to lectures from experts. Then we wrestle with ideas in small groups, discuss concepts with peers over coffee, and pop into office hours to ask professors for clarification. And to do these tasks effectively, we need to feel a strong sense of belonging. So, as you research potential colleges, take note of the people in each prospective learning community. Who will surround you and cheer you on as you work toward your degree?

Campus Population

Big research university or small liberal arts college? Sure, that question refers to instructional methods and overall campus acreage, but it also asks students to estimate the size of their ideal learning community. Think about environments where you feel most comfortable and confident. Perhaps you thrive in a small community where you can't walk to the library without running into an acquaintance. Conversely, maybe you feel more confident when your voice is one among thousands, and you can avoid the spotlight. Will you work best in the intimate nine-hundred-person community of Cal Tech or the sprawling Texas A&M campus with 60,000 fellow undergraduates?

Class Sizes

Overall campus enrollment is an important factor to be sure, but average class sizes in your major will directly impact your day-to-day

62 Searching for Colleges

learning experiences. As you research prospective colleges, take note of statistics on class sizes and the number of employed faculty. Be careful when considering student-to-faculty ratios, though. A low ratio means that there are fewer students per faculty member on campus, which sounds like a promise of small class sizes and personalized attention. But do you know how many classes each faculty member teaches per term? At some universities, full professors might be so focused on research or publishing that they rarely have time to teach undergraduate courses at all. On the other hand, a teaching-focused college might have a higher student-to-faculty ratio but smaller class sizes because every faculty member is hired specifically to teach multiple classes each year.

In addition, class sizes can vary by level and subject. Popular introductory courses that serve as prerequisites for multiple majors often occur in large lecture halls that can accommodate hundreds of students. However, as a transfer student, you probably won't need to enroll in those classes. Ideally, you will use transfer credits from your previous college to satisfy common prerequisites and skip directly to specialized upper-division courses in your major at the new school. Ask college representatives specifically about average class sizes for juniors and seniors in your major.

You can also look up required courses on the college's current class schedule and see how many seats are available. Here's an example from the University of Oregon, a large public research university. The introductory human physiology course has a maximum enrollment of 192 students, as shown below.

BI 121   Intro Human Physiology — 4.00 cr.

	CRN	Avail	Max	Time	Day	Location	Instructor
Lecture	10749	0	192	0830-0950	tr	100 WIL	Lombardi V

Farther down the page, the course numbers increase to indicate upper-division courses. For example, this upper-division neurobiology class has a maximum enrollment of fifty.

BI 360   Neurobiology — 4.00 cr.

	CRN	Avail	Max	Time	Day	Location	Instructor
Lecture	10837	14	50	1400-1520	tr	229 MCK	Singh A

If you have completed the lower-division prerequisite classes at your previous college, you should be able to enter directly into upper-division courses, which are typically capped at a lower number of students, like the neurobiology class shown above.

Professors, Instructors, and Advisers

Find out who your mentors will be. Colleges employ a variety of part-time and full-time instructors to teach classes. You may take classes with graduate students who are paid hourly, part-time faculty contracted for one class at a time, or full-time tenured professors who hold regular office hours. Similarly, when you step into an advising office, you may get advice from peer mentors, have a drop-in session with the academic counselor on call that day, or sit down for a regularly scheduled appointment with your assigned major adviser. If you think you might need additional support to succeed in college, research the services available at the disability resource office, mental health facility, and tutoring center, too. Learn about the experts who will be by your side all the way to graduation, and make sure they are the right people to support you on this journey.

Demographics and Diversity

College is a great time to expand your social circles and meet new friends. It can also be a time for you to network with like-minded individuals who share a common background. Many students report feeling empowered by the camaraderie of an all-women's college, a Historically Black College or University (HBCU), a Hispanic-Serving Institution (HSI), or a faith-based educational institution. Other students enjoy the campus culture and extracurricular learning opportunities that accompany a diverse student body. Your learning will undoubtedly extend beyond the classroom, so think about what kind of community will challenge, engage, accept, and support you both in and out of the classroom.

Pastimes

"All work and no play makes Jack a dull boy." It probably also makes Jack tired, lonely, and stressed. While academic study is certainly a primary focus of the college experience, no one can study *all* the time. It's important to find a healthy balance between scholastic pursuits and leisure activities. Plus, students who feel a strong sense of belonging and human connection at their colleges have better academic outcomes, too!

Student Clubs

Colleges often proudly advertise the number of student-led clubs available on their campuses. Look for a directory and see if your favorite activities are represented. Check social media and see how active the clubs appear to be. Don't be afraid to message club contacts and ask about their experiences at the college. First-person reviews of student life can be valuable as you decide which college to attend.

Greek Life

Fraternities and sororities can be a polarizing aspect of college communities. Students who dislike single-sex social organizations can look for colleges that ban Greek life, have low participation, or prioritize mixed-gender professional fraternities. On the other hand, Greek life is an important feature of the traditional college experience for many students, and transfer students often benefit from seeking out additional social opportunities as they integrate into campus life. In most cases, transfer students should be able to participate in recruitment activities, or "rush," just like first-year students.

If you joined a sorority or fraternity at your former school, you might be able to transfer your membership to the chapter at your new school. The National Panhellenic Conference and North American Interfraternity Conference policies generally prohibit students from switching organizations once initiated, so verify that each prospective college has a chapter of your organization on campus, as this would be the only way for a current member to continue in Greek life.

Visual and Performing Arts

At some colleges, art programs are restricted to students studying in related major departments. For example, advanced dance classes might be restricted to dance majors only. Or the spring musical may only allow theater majors to audition. If art is an important part of your life, investigate your participation options in advance. Find out if nonmajors can participate in arts programs of interest and if there are alternative paths for more casual art lovers to hone their skills. Even if the main ceramics studio is closed to nonmajors, you might find pottery wheels and a kiln available at the craft center. Similarly, the activities and recreation center might offer dance classes and practice space for unofficial student dance teams.

Athletics

Competitive athletes must abide by additional transfer policies set forth by the National Collegiate Athletic Association (NCAA), the National Association of Intercollegiate Athletics (NAIA), or other collegiate sports associations. Often, applying for transfer while maintaining continuing eligibility for athletes revolves primarily around placement within the sport and must begin with the student's current college coach. Throughout the process, careful communication between athletes, coaches, and compliance administrators is required. Although digital tools like the NCAA transfer portal have streamlined the transfer process for athletes, it is still wise to do careful research and consider discussing your options with an expert before taking any action. The free resources available at CollegeAthleticAdvisor.com /Transfer can help you get started.

More casual athletes should research opportunities to play their favorite sports via intramural and club programs. Intramural sports are typically open to all students regardless of ability or experience. Club sports, however, can vary in both competitiveness and commitment. Especially popular club sports teams may require prospective athletes to advance through several rounds of tryouts and commit to extensive practice schedules before being added to the rosters. Research historical competition data to see how strong a club sport is at a particular school, and consider contacting the club manager, coach, or team members to inquire about the likelihood of joining the team. They may be able to tell you how many students tried out in recent years and how many of those hopeful athletes made the cut.

Case Study: Ashley

Ashley, a social butterfly, could not wait to transfer from her community college to a large four-year university. She was eager to meet new people who shared her interests in dance, theater, social justice, and philanthropy. At the club fair during welcome week, she searched among the tables for the student-led dance teams first and scheduled a series of auditions for the hip-hop and jazz-focused groups. She ultimately became a member of an all-female student dance troupe that focused on fun and camaraderie but also sought out performance opportunities on campus. A highlight of her first year on campus was participating in a halftime performance during a basketball game featuring the university's popular Division I team.

Seeking ways to participate in philanthropic efforts and connect with additional peers, Ashley also decided to rush a sorority. She received a bid from her first-choice chapter and was matched with a "big sister" who quickly became a close friend and confidante. Together, they raised funds for a local women's shelter and spoke out against domestic abuse. Ashley met a fellow transfer at the sorority house as well. This student had been a member of the same sorority at her previous four-year university on the other side of the country. When she transferred between universities, she was able to transfer chapters, too, and continued her sorority membership uninterrupted.

Programs

We've finally reached the heart of the college search process: finding the right academic, financial, and support programs to match your needs and interests.

Majors

First-year applicants are often undecided about their major area of study. They might guess at a possible major on the application, or they might apply for an exploratory program designed to help students discover new academic interests and pinpoint a degree path. Transfer applicants, on the other hand, are often expected to apply directly into a specific major. The assumption is that transfer students spent their first year or two of college completing general education requirements and exploring possible areas of interest. But that doesn't mean you can't change your mind about what to study! Just know that switching your major after admission might be challenging, especially if the new major is impacted (i.e., overcrowded) or requires additional preparatory coursework.

Students with multiple major interests may be able to plan strategically for admissions by major. For example, computer science is a notoriously popular and competitive major to enter, so students might want to prepare for transfer to data science as an alternative. Psychology is another high-demand major at many colleges, but students who love psychology might also enjoy sociology. As you look at potential majors, dig into the fine print. Look for a list of required classes or a sample student schedule. Do those classes sound interesting? Have you taken any classes that have similar descriptions?

Experiences

College is more than just your major, though. Many other experiences and opportunities can contribute to a student's overall growth. When researching potential colleges, find out if they offer internships, research opportunities, or co-op programs. If they do, are there any barriers that make it difficult for transfer students to participate? If you are interested in studying abroad, find out how common it is for transfers to participate. It's also important to ask if transfers are still able to graduate on time after participating in a study-abroad program. Sometimes the availability of short-term programs can make participation more realistic for transfer students who don't want to significantly extend their time in college.

Honors colleges and programs can provide additional opportunities

68   Searching for Colleges

for academic enrichment and community building. Especially at a large university, an honors program can feel like a small college within a college and can become a valuable resource for networking and developing friendships with classmates. Honors programs can also offer special benefits, such as priority class registration, research opportunities, smaller class sizes, specialized housing, and more.

Unfortunately, not all honors colleges are equally welcoming to transfer students. Some programs require specific honors course sequences that can be difficult to complete on a transfer timeline. If you are interested in participating in an honors college or program, ask specific questions about both student benefits and participation requirements, especially as they pertain to transfer students. Currently enrolled community college students should also check for any "honors-to-honors" agreements between their community colleges and connected universities, which can streamline the transfer process for honors students and facilitate the completion of honors requirements at both schools.[3]

Support Programs

What kinds of support programs will you need to succeed? Consider the supports you already took advantage of at your current or previous school, in your community, or at home. These could be formal and professional, such as accommodations approved and provided by the disability resource center at your school, or a regular weekly appointment with a trained therapist. Some supports might be more casual but are just as important to your success. Perhaps your current roommate is a math whiz who enjoys helping you with those pesky calculus problems. Or your mom watches your toddler while you attend classes and complete your homework. Who will provide such assistance when you embark on your next adventure as a transfer student? You can find a worksheet to help identify your necessary support programs at TransferSavvy.com/Book.

Students who are neurodivergent or have previously been diagnosed with learning disabilities should be particularly mindful of the accommodations and programs they may need to perform at their best. Each college's disability resource center or accessibility services program will likely offer a unique combination of support options, ranging from the bare minimum of legally required accommodations to full-service assistance (often for an additional fee). Contact these programs early to gain an understanding of what may be available to you and how to apply for services. If their in-house services seem insufficient for your needs, ask if they can recommend outside providers to supplement your support team.

Don't forget about your mental and physical health, too! Find the student health center and learn about their services. Do they accept your current health insurance, or would you be better served by the student health insurance plan? In case of emergencies, where is the nearest hospital, and how do students get there? Be sure to ask about options for therapy, counseling, and other mental health services. Many universities are understaffed these days and have trouble meeting the mental health needs of their students in a timely manner. Find out who provides the majority of counseling services — peers or professionals. Then ask how long the average wait to see a mental health professional on campus is. Be wary of a college that cannot provide timely mental health services to students in need.

Even if you have never used such programs before, you might benefit from learning-support or mental health services in the future. The transition to a new university is a common trigger for stress, which can lead to mental and physical health challenges, diminished executive function, increased dependence on caffeine or other substances, and more. As you adjust to a new learning environment, fresh challenges will arise, and you shouldn't have to face these challenges alone.

Financial Savings Programs

While it can be fun to window-shop and imagine yourself at the college of your dreams, it's also important to think about any financial constraints you may have. Universities vary widely in the amount of financial support they provide to transfer students. Look for colleges that offer transfer-specific net price calculators on their websites, meet 100 percent of demonstrated financial need for both first-year and transfer students, and perhaps even offer merit-based scholarships for transfers. Some schools have separate financial aid policies for first-year and transfer applicants, so read the fine print carefully.

Tuition reciprocity agreements may offer affordable college options in nearby states.[4] Generally speaking, students considering public universities will find the lowest tuition rates at schools within their states of residency. However, colleges that participate in tuition reciprocity programs agree to charge in-state, or greatly reduced out-of-state, tuition for students from neighboring states. For example, the largest tuition reciprocity program in the United States is the Western Undergraduate Exchange, whose 170 member institutions have agreed to offer tuition rates ranging from in-state to 150 percent of in-state for students who reside in one of the eighteen member states and territories. (See chapter 8 for more information on tuition reciprocity agreements.)

Individual states may offer savings programs independently, too. In Ohio, the Forever Buckeyes program enables high school graduates who leave the state to claim in-state tuition upon their return.[5] Students with grandparents residing in Florida can apply for the Grandparent Waiver to pay in-state tuition rates.[6] Several states offer tuition discounts or waiver programs for Native American students who are enrolled members of federally recognized tribes.[7]

Case Study: Grace

Grace had been homeschooled since kindergarten. Like many homeschoolers, she took classes at her local community college as part of her high school curriculum. She loved the variety of courses available in every discipline — the course catalog was so much more extensive than the list of online high school classes she had selected from before. Grace could specialize in theatrical costume and makeup design while fulfilling her biology and physics requirements with unique classes like physical anthropology and astronomy.

Although she began as a dual-enrolled student, receiving both high school and college credit for each class, Grace quickly realized that community college was a great fit for her and wanted to go full-time. Homeschooling gave her the flexibility to graduate from high school early and enroll as a regular student at Foothill Community College in California. As a high-achieving student, Grace was encouraged to apply for the Foothill Honors Institute and eventually earned an associate degree with the Honors Scholar distinction noted on her diploma.

When it came time to apply for transfer, Grace prioritized applications to transfer-friendly universities with honors programs. She was torn between the University of California, Irvine, and the University of California, Davis, both of which offered her generous merit scholarships as well as admission to their honors programs. Grace ultimately chose UC Davis and enrolled in the University Honors Program. She took seminars with the dean of undergraduate education, was offered an internship with a graduate student, and completed a research project with a tenured professor, all perks of the honors program.

Practicality

Although the first four P's above can help you identify potential colleges that match your preferences, additional practical questions must be addressed as well:

- Can I get in?
- Can I afford it?
- Will my family support it?

Likelihood of Admission

If you are planning for transfer well in advance, you have time to prepare so that you can meet the minimum eligibility requirements before you apply. However, eligibility factors must define your college search if your transfer needs are more urgent. Locate a college's minimum transfer eligibility requirements on its website and compare them to your academic history. For example, have you completed enough credits? Have you taken the required classes? Is your college GPA above the minimum needed?

72   Searching for Colleges

While we generally think of eligibility requirements as minimums, it's important to look for maximum credit restrictions as well. Most universities require students to complete a minimum number of credits at their institution ("in residence") to earn a degree there, so excess credits, especially upper-division credits earned at a four-year university, may be discarded upon transfer. Although it is somewhat rare, having taken too many college classes could also completely disqualify you from transfer admission at some selective universities. Be sure to note the exact rules for maximum credits at each college — some credits, such as those earned via AP exams, high school dual enrollment, or lower-division community college courses, may be excluded from the maximum credit count.

Remember that eligibility does not equal admissibility. Colleges often have minimum requirements that are well below the averages of admitted students. For example, the University of California, Los Angeles (UCLA), requires a minimum college GPA of 3.2 for transfer applicants, but the average GPA of admitted transfer students is above 3.5.[8] Transfer students admitted to competitive majors at UCLA, like computer science, typically have GPAs closer to 4.0. Search for additional statistics on a "transfer student profile" document on college websites. Many colleges share GPA and earned credit ranges for admitted students to help you assess your admissibility. Be realistic about your admissions chances and look for schools where you are an average or above-average applicant. Including only "reach" schools on your college list usually results in disappointment.

Affordability

Your dream college cannot become a reality if you don't have a plan to pay for it. Calculate a college budget before you begin your college search, and stick to it. If you aren't sure how to estimate a yearly budget for college tuition and expenses, start with a FAFSA (Free Application for Federal Student Aid) calculator. FAFSA is the primary tool used to calculate a family's financial need for college. You don't have to wait for the current year's official FAFSA to become available to get an estimate, though. Many FAFSA calculators are available online, but the US government hosts an official Student Aid Estimator on its website. With a few basic pieces of financial data, the Federal Student Aid Estimator will calculate an estimated Student Aid Index (SAI) within a few minutes. The SAI was previously known as the Expected Family Contribution (EFC). Colleges use this number to calculate your eligibility for need-based financial aid by subtracting the SAI from the average total cost of attendance (tuition plus average housing costs, books and materials fees, travel expenses, etc.). You can use this number as a starting point for a realistic yearly budget. The SAI is probably more than you feel comfortable paying each year, but think about how you can leverage savings, work-study funds, and loans to get close to this number.

Many colleges also require completion of the CSS (College Scholarship Service) Profile to determine financial need, but unfortunately, the CSS Profile does not offer an online estimation tool. Each college is afforded a high degree of customization on the CSS Profile, so accurate estimates cannot be calculated without the unique formulas used by each individual college. For schools that rely on the CSS Profile, the net price calculator hosted on the school's website may be the most reliable source of financial aid estimation.

What is a "net price," anyway? The short answer is that the net price is the total cost you (and your family, if applicable) are expected to pay each year to attend that college. To arrive at the net price, the calculators estimate the grants and scholarships likely to be awarded based on both financial and academic data entered. These grants and scholarships are then subtracted from the total cost of attendance to arrive at the net price estimate that will be the student's responsibility to pay each year. If this estimate is significantly more than your SAI or your planned budget, the college may not be a realistic option financially.

It's important to note that many colleges do not provide accurate data for transfer students in their net price calculators. Federal law requires colleges to provide accurate net price calculators for "first-time, full-time undergraduate" students only.[9] In other words, there is no legal requirement for colleges to provide net price calculators that accurately predict the net price for transfer students. That said, many transfer-friendly institutions choose to include transfer data in their standard net price calculators or offer separate transfer-specific calculators on their websites. Read the fine print carefully to understand if this estimate is trustworthy for you as a transfer.

Family Support

If you depend on family members for financial support, are in a committed relationship, or have family responsibilities that influence your college decisions, consider the needs and preferences of your loved ones, too. Your parents may have additional financial constraints to consider. Sometimes divorce settlements dictate college budgets and payment responsibilities. Perhaps your significant other doesn't want to relocate to certain regions, or your teenager doesn't want to change high schools. Talk explicitly with your family about your college options before setting your heart on a particular college.

Common Challenges and Questions

Is it possible to transfer to an online college so that I don't have to worry about geographical constraints?

Many universities now offer fully online degree programs, especially in common undergraduate fields of study. While the sudden shift to emergency remote learning during Covid-19 certainly posed difficulties, it also helped to normalize online education. After a rocky transition, some students and faculty discovered that they actually preferred learning and teaching online and could achieve equivalent or better success through distance learning. Since then, online learning has grown in both popularity and respect.

That said, enrolling in a fully online college program may not be a wise decision.[10] Transfer research shows that students who transfer into predominantly online institutions are less likely to graduate with their bachelor's degrees in a timely manner.[11] On the other hand, students who cannot commit to consistent on-campus attendance may not be able to complete a degree without online classes. Some studies of online learning at the community college level revealed that there is a sweet spot for most students, where taking no more than 40 to 50 percent of their classes online resulted in the best overall outcomes.[12] With a mix of online and on-campus classes, students enjoyed the sense of belonging that accompanies in-person learning but were able to use online courses to juggle competing demands on their time.

If you decide to pursue online learning, consider enrolling in a nearby college that will allow you to attend in-person classes as well. Even if you seldom take classes on campus, you will be able to connect with the school community and avoid feeling isolated. If there are no compatible programs nearby, research respectable colleges that have developed their own online programs. Check for accreditation and nonprofit status, and ask if the classes are developed and taught by the same faculty who work on campus. Degrees earned online should be essentially equivalent to those earned on campus.

Can I join the dance/hockey/cheer/baseball team as a transfer?

Maybe! If you are a competitive athlete, be sure to consult your supervising sports association (such as the NCAA or NAIA) first. There are very specific rules that athletes must follow to maintain continuing eligibility through the transfer process.

Recreational participants in arts and sports programs have much more flexibility. It would be unusual for an intramural or recreational team to have a policy explicitly excluding transfer students from participating. You may not be able to audition for a team until you arrive on campus, though. If you made the team at your previous school, you may have to take a leap of faith when you transfer and hope that your skills, interests, and experiences will be a good match for a similar team at your new school.

Can I transfer to a military service academy?

It is possible to apply to a military service academy after beginning college at another college, as long as you still meet the age eligibility requirements. If you have been participating in an ROTC program at your current college, you may even have an advantage because your nomination can come from an ROTC professor. However, every new recruit starts at the beginning of the four-year program at a service academy, regardless of prior college experience. While you might be able to transfer some credits from your previous college to fulfill prerequisite or general education requirements, you won't be able to accelerate your progress toward a degree. If you are interested in a senior military college, such as The Citadel or Virginia Military Institute, the transfer process is similar to that of other nonmilitary universities. The Citadel even offers specialized "2+2" degree programs that allow students to begin at a community college and finish at The Citadel!

CHAPTER 7

Qualities of a Transfer-Friendly College

What makes a college transfer-friendly or transfer-affirming?[1] Although nearly every college in America allows transfer students to submit applications, not all colleges truly welcome transfers to their campuses and have policies in place to help new transfer students integrate into their communities.

Most data reported on public college research sites is collected only from traditional first-year students. The data that pertains to transfer students might be very different. For example, the six-year graduation rate typically reported on college websites is based on the number of full-time first-year students who graduate within six years of entry. Part-time and transfer students are not usually included in that statistic. To understand how well a college supports its transfer students on the path to degree attainment, deeper research is required.

Admissions Requirements

Visit a prospective college's website and navigate to the main admissions or application page. Is information for prospective transfer students presented alongside information for first-years? Or does it feel like transfer admission is an afterthought? Compare the sections on transfer admission with the sections on first-year admission and look for similarities in structure and content. It should be just as easy to locate deadlines and requirements for transfer applicants as it is for first-year applicants.

78   Searching for Colleges

Although many colleges continue to offer test-optional and test-free admissions, some selective institutions have reinstated their test requirements since Covid-19. If the college requires test scores from first-year applicants, see if it also requires test scores from transfer applicants. Mandating SAT or ACT scores from transfer applicants can often create a barrier to entry, especially for older students who may have attended high school and taken standardized tests many years ago, so look for possible exceptions and alternatives. If none exist, you should feel empowered to contact the admissions office to inquire about their requirements and learn how you can best fulfill them.

Most universities have specific course requirements that must be completed prior to transfer. There may be additional recommended courses for students in specific majors. A transfer-friendly school will be transparent about these requirements and recommendations. Look for a list of academic requirements, qualities of successful transfer applicants, and specific details that will help you prepare a competitive application. By browsing the admissions section of a college's website, you should be able to determine your eligibility for transfer and get a sense of how strong an applicant you will be.

Within the admissions section of the website, some schools provide a list of admissions counselors and representatives who are assigned to serve various geographical regions and/or student groups. If the university in question has such a page, look for a counselor who is specifically assigned to transfer students. At some larger transfer-friendly schools, there may even be multiple transfer admissions counselors who are assigned to various community colleges and geographic regions. The presence of admissions counselors who are specifically trained to assist transfer applicants can be a sign of a college's commitment to transfer students.

Colleges that value their transfer students typically provide straightforward access to transfer application requirements on their website and extend a welcoming invitation to learn more and apply online. Contact admissions and ask any questions that you may have about the transfer application process. The speed and clarity of the response may provide you with additional insights regarding the college's commitment to transfer students.

Transfer Credit

Before you go to the effort of applying for admission, you should know how likely it is that your credits will transfer. Many students assume that typical college classes will transfer anywhere. Unfortunately, this is often not the case. The faculty of each college decides which elements of a class are most important for future success within a program. If a course you've completed lacks an element the faculty has deemed critical, your course may not transfer. But how can you know this in advance? Transfer-friendly universities provide tools to assist you.

Transferology Database

The largest common repository of transferable coursework is currently Transferology.com. This website allows potential transfer students to input courses completed at nearly any college in the US. They can then search for other colleges that have previously approved those courses for transfer. Students can also enter AP exams, dual enrollment courses, and military experience to understand their transferable credits fully. Clicking through to a university provides more details on how a specific course will transfer — either as equivalent to a particular course or as an undefined elective.

In the Transferology example below, the student has entered two economics classes taken at Boston University. Both classes are transferable to the college being researched and will be considered equivalent to Econ 2022 and Econ 2012 at this school. This represents the best possible transfer scenario.

Boston University

- CAS EC101 INTRODUCTORY MICROECONOMIC ANALYSIS 2024 → ECON2022 👍
- CAS EC102 INTRODUCTORY MACROECONOMIC ANALYSIS 2024 → ECON2012 👍

The following example from Foothill Community College shows that a chemistry course will transfer, but only as a lower-division elective in the chemistry department. This school does not judge the Chemistry 12A class as equivalent to any of its own chemistry classes.

Foothill College

- CHEM12A ORGANIC CHEMISTRY 2023 → CHLD ⓘ

Notes about the transfer rule for CHEM12A
CHLD: Lower Division elective in the department indicated.

The "misses" and "maybes" tabs offer additional insights into why a particular course did not appear as transferable at this school. It might be that the school simply has not had the opportunity to evaluate a course listed as a "maybe" before, so providing documentation could result in transfer credit. If a class is truly nontransferable, notes on the "misses" tab may help you understand why.

The example below shows "misses" from De Anza Community College. In this case, it is clear that these art and literature classes will not transfer to the school in question.

De Anza College

Does Not Transfer

These courses will not transfer to this school. Contact the school for more information.

- ARTS37A SCULPTURE 2022 → NONCRDT
- ELIT38 UTOPIAN/DYSTOPIAN LITERATURE 2022 → NONCRDT

However, in the case below, Spanish 1 *might* transfer if the student takes additional classes in the series. UC Santa Cruz operates on the quarter system, and this student is attempting to transfer to a school on the semester system. A single ten-week quarter of Spanish does not cover enough material to be equivalent to a fifteen-week semester of Spanish. Therefore, the student must take an additional quarter of Spanish to earn credit for an introductory semester of Spanish at the new university.

University of California-Santa Cruz

Additional Courses Required

These courses will transfer to this school, if you complete additional coursework (shown as italicized). Contact the school for more information.

- SPAN1 FIRST-YEAR SPANISH 2024 , *SPAN2* → SPAN001

Other Transfer Credit Tools

Unfortunately, only about four hundred universities currently provide full data access to Transferology. While you can enter courses you have taken at thousands of colleges, some universities may not share their credit review outcomes with the Transferology database for public access.

Transferology is not the only tool for determining potential transfer credit, though. Colleges that work with a high volume of transfer students may host their own databases on their websites. This may be in addition to or instead of participating in Transferology. Some colleges, especially small private colleges, may be willing to do a "pre-read" of a student's transcript. You can send the college a copy of your transcript, and they will review it unofficially to provide an estimate of your transferable credits.

Tasseled.com is a new website designed to help students plan their community college coursework in advance to maximize both credit transferability and cost savings. Enter a target university and desired major into its Pathways Planner, and Tasseled will generate a term-by-term list of transferable classes to take at a nearby community college. The example below shows four classes that a community college student hoping to transfer to Texas Tech University (TTU) could enroll in. Each community college class is shown with its equivalent at TTU and indicates how much the student can save by taking this class at the more affordable community college.

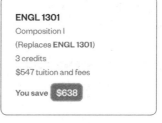

The AI Transcript Transfer tool at Tasseled is helpful for students who have already accumulated college credits elsewhere. Upload an unofficial transcript to discover the most efficient pathways to degree completion with estimated costs and time to degree.

Building on its success with the City University of New York (CUNY) Transfer Explorer, the education nonprofit ITHAKA has recently launched a new nationwide Transfer Explorer (TransferExplorer.org). The core tool, Map My Journey, functions almost like a reverse Transferology. Rather than inputting classes and then searching for "matches" among colleges that have previously accepted those course credits, students begin by selecting a target four-year university to see how their completed and planned courses apply to specific degree programs at that institution. In the example below, a student at Central Carolina Community College is planning for a biology degree at Lander University. In the general education section of the report, the Lander two-course requirement in Behavioral and Social Perspectives is shown. The student's PSY-150 course at Central Carolina CC is equivalent to PSYC-101 at Lander, fulfilling half of the two-course requirement. The student will need to take one additional course in this area to complete the full requirement.

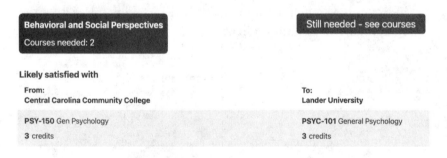

In some states, community colleges and universities have joined forces to create a statewide database of transfer equivalencies. For students on a planned transfer path from a community college to an in-state four-year public university, these regional databases provide critical details to assist students with efficient planning. (See chapter 8 for more details on partnerships such as these.)

Several states also have common course numbering (CCN) policies so students can easily understand which classes are equivalent across institutions. In Florida, for instance, Colonial American History is AMH 110 at every public postsecondary institution that offers that class. Thus, University of Florida, Florida State University, University of Central Florida, Hillsborough Community College, and so on all use AMH 110 to designate this commonly required history course. Private Florida colleges can also opt to participate in the CCN system if they wish to align their curricula to Florida standards and smooth the transfer process for in-state transfer students.

Transfer Credit Evaluation Report

Upon admission, you should receive a full transfer credit evaluation report from the college. If you have been able to preview transferability with a tool like Transferology, this report should not be too surprising. If you want to take a chance on a university without a mechanism for preevaluating your transfer credits, make sure that you will receive the transfer credit report immediately upon being admitted so you have time to review and appeal if necessary. Check the school's website for a timeline regarding its transfer admissions process. A college that does not provide a transfer credit report until after the enrollment deposit deadline is not proactively supporting its transfer students.

Financial Aid

Transfer students complete the same FAFSA or CSS Profile forms as first-year applicants and can qualify for federal aid, such as the Pell Grant. However, institutional financial aid policies for transfer students sometimes differ from those for first-year applicants. Even a college that proudly advertises that they cover 100 percent of demonstrated financial need may have a footnote clarifying that only first-year students are subject to that policy. Or a university that is "need-blind" (i.e., does not consider financial need in the first-year admissions process) might be "need-aware" for transfer applicants. Read the fine print carefully to see if a school's stated financial aid policies apply to both first-year and transfer applicants. If they do not, ask why.

84   Searching for Colleges

Net Price Calculators

Federal law requires colleges to provide net price calculators on their websites. These interactive online tools allow students and their families to enter basic financial data and receive a breakdown of their projected college costs, including the amount of financial aid they are likely to receive, instantly. Unfortunately, the law only requires colleges to provide these net price estimates for first-year students. When colleges don't provide accurate net price estimates for transfer applicants, students and families may have difficulty deciding which colleges are going to be affordable.

Colleges that voluntarily choose to include transfers in their net price calculators reveal their commitment to affordability and transparency for transfer students. Some colleges provide a completely separate transfer calculator or determine transfer status via a question early in the calculator form, while others offer equivalent financial aid packages to first-year and transfer students (and note that on the calculator). If you cannot discern whether the net price calculator is accurate for transfer students, reach out to the college for more information. Don't assume the calculator provides accurate information for transfer students unless the college explicitly indicates that it does.

Merit Scholarships

There is a long-standing myth that transfer students cannot obtain merit scholarships. That's simply not a standard truth anymore. Many universities see the value that transfer students bring to their campuses, so they entice high-achieving transfers to attend their institutions by awarding merit scholarships. Unfortunately, transfer-specific scholarships are often valued at lower dollar amounts. For example, the University of Southern California (USC) published a scholarship guide for the 2024–25 academic year that included top merit scholarships for incoming first-year and transfer students.[2] The top scholarships for first-year students are the Trustee and Presidential scholarships, covering full and half tuition, respectively. The most valuable scholarship for transfer students covers one quarter tuition. Worth approximately $17,000 per year, this scholarship is one of the most generous available to transfer students attending a prestigious private university, but it still is not equivalent to the scholarships awarded to first-year students.

Explore university websites to view the scholarships available for first-year and transfer students. If no merit scholarships are available for transfer students, consider why. If the college doesn't offer any merit scholarships at all, then that's just their policy. But if the college offers generous first-year scholarships but has nothing available for transfer students, you should wonder how much you will be valued on their campus.

Housing Options

Not all transfer students want to live in campus housing. However, living within the student community is a surefire way to meet your fellow students and integrate yourself into campus life. If you are relocating from afar, having a guaranteed place to live on campus can relieve some of the anxiety associated with making such a significant transition.

Availability

Many colleges face a housing shortage due to increasing enrollment and limited capacity to expand accommodations on campus. This housing deficit is especially problematic in urban settings. When residential living space is limited, most colleges prioritize incoming first-year students, who tend to be inexperienced and require the support services available in traditional residence halls. This tendency does not relieve colleges of their duty to safely house transfer students, though.

Transfer students should proactively inquire about housing options early in the research and application process. It's crucial to ask not only if campus housing is available for transfers but also whether it's guaranteed. Many institutions only offer housing to transfer students on a space-available basis, which can be incredibly unpredictable. You may be placed on a waiting list that can leave you in housing limbo for months. Clarify housing policies early so that you can identify colleges that will help make your transition to campus life as smooth as possible.

Transfer-Specific Housing

Some universities offer transfer-specific housing options. Learn about the features of these accommodations and why they are particularly suitable for transfer students. For example, colleges recognize that transfer students are more likely to have prior experience living independently and probably prefer quieter living areas with more privacy. Therefore, transfer housing is often designed to resemble a shared apartment rather than a traditional residence hall or first-year dormitory. There may be trade-offs, though. As universities have expanded housing facilities to accommodate larger numbers of students, transfer students are sometimes placed in buildings located on the outskirts of university-owned land, necessitating bus or shuttle rides to campus each day.

Still, the opportunity to live in transfer-specific housing is likely to be worthwhile. Simply living with other new transfer students can help prevent the social isolation that sometimes accompanies a move to a new campus. When colleges add support services and social programming relevant to transfers, a residential community can become especially valuable. The University of Oregon, for example, offers a "Transfer Scholars Residential Community" in one of its residence halls.[3] It consists of apartment-style accommodations within a larger building restricted to upper-division students. Shared lounges, study rooms, and music practice rooms invite students to collaborate, while single bedrooms offer privacy. Transfer advising sessions and community events designed just for transfers provide additional value. Similarly, at UC Berkeley's Helen Diller Anchor House, completed in 2024, transfer students can live in a conveniently located modern apartment building that includes intentional community spaces designed to nurture a sense of belonging.[4] The building houses satellite offices of the Cal Transfer Student Center, as well as fitness facilities, private and communal cooking areas, and a rooftop vegetable garden. Some areas are open to nonresident commuter transfer students as well, further demonstrating the university's commitment to transfer student success.

New Student Orientations

New student orientations play a vital role in acclimating students to their new academic environment. For first-year students, these orientations also introduce them to college life in general. The orientation needs of transfer students are different, since they have already experienced college life to some extent. Transfer-friendly universities acknowledge these diverse needs and tailor orientation experiences accordingly.

Fall Orientations

Transfer students who enroll at the beginning of the academic year may participate in orientation activities alongside first-year students. While this can foster connections with the broader community, it can also be inefficient for transfers who require more targeted information. Orientation programs that incorporate transfer students should at least provide breakout sessions with content tailored specifically to their needs.

Some colleges operate entirely separate transfer orientations, which allows for highly relevant programming and the facilitation of authentic peer-to-peer connections. Even when academic orientation programming is altogether separate, fall-start transfer students should still be able to participate in schoolwide social events such as club involvement fairs and welcome-week festivities.

Midyear Orientations

Winter or spring transfers often receive entirely different orientation programming. Due to the smaller transfer cohort size and possible lack of first-year students, midyear entrants are less likely to experience full-scale orientations. Colleges might only provide abbreviated orientations with minimal social and community-building events at this time of year.

Ongoing Support for Transfer Students

The need for support doesn't end when you complete orientation and settle into your housing accommodations. Transfer-friendly universities continue to support transfer students socially and academically throughout their enrollment.

Transfer Advising and Registration

Transfer students need transfer advisers — advisers who not only understand how transfer credits can clear prerequisites and apply to a degree but also respect and value each student's prior experiences. Ideally, academic advising will begin long before transfer students arrive on campus. Since transfer students have usually completed some number of general education and prerequisite courses, they cannot simply choose from a selection of generic breadth courses for their initial term the way first-year students might. Transfers need to participate in advising sessions on a timeline more like that of returning upper-division students. That might mean a fall transfer student needs access to an academic adviser the spring before.

Early advising and advanced class registration are especially important for transfer students seeking entry to popular classes that tend to fill up early in the registration period. Some universities reserve seats in classes that transfer students commonly need. For example, several University of California campuses reserve a percentage of seats for incoming students at both the transfer and first-year levels. New students are the last to register, so a selection of open seats is held until initial advising sessions and subsequent course enrollments have been completed. In future terms, transfer students may be grouped together with other upper-division students for course registration dates by seniority, or they may enjoy priority registration dates that allow them to select the specific classes they need most before seats begin to fill.

Community-Building Resources

Students who feel a strong sense of belonging in their educational communities are more likely to persist in college and successfully earn their degrees. Developing this sense of belonging is especially important for transfer students, who may initially feel like outsiders or impostors on campus. Transfer-friendly colleges understand this and provide opportunities for transfer students to connect with others and become integrated into the larger student community.

Many universities have a physical transfer student center on campus where students can gather for study groups, social events, drop-in advising, and more. The programming options and facilities vary by school, but they usually provide at least an informal space for transfer students to meet and socialize. On some campuses, transfer centers also incorporate services for veterans, reentry students, and other nontraditional students.

Some transfer students may experience transfer shock or impostor syndrome. Transfer shock refers to the challenging transition period when transfer students sometimes see a dip in academic performance as they adjust to new academic expectations. This dip is often accompanied by feelings of inadequacy as new transfer students feel like impostors who don't deserve to be on campus. Several recent studies have confirmed the value of peer mentors in alleviating these problems while simultaneously contributing to an overall sense of belonging for transfers. Peer mentors also provide transfer visibility on campus and offer a low-stress avenue for transfer students to ask questions. Most symptoms of transfer shock are temporary, and facilitating a strong peer-to-peer support network can encourage quick recovery.[5]

Wraparound Support

Additional types of support may be necessary in certain situations, depending on the student's stage of life. For instance, students with spouses or children may require family housing options and/or childcare to enable regular attendance at in-person classes. Low-income students might need access to affordable textbooks, healthy food pantries, free healthcare, technology rentals, and so on. Students aged twenty-six and older, who cannot remain on parental health insurance plans, likely need inexpensive healthcare options. Universities dedicated to transfer student success have established resources to support the entire transfer student.

Transfer Enrollment and Outcomes

As noted at the beginning of this chapter, graduation rates reported in mainstream media and general college guides rarely include transfer data. The vast majority of widely publicized college statistics are based on first-time, full-time students, not transfer students. In fact, the National Center for Education Statistics did not reliably collect transfer data and graduation rates until 2016.[6] Even though transfer data can be challenging to locate, it is available and can be used to find universities that offer robust support systems to help transfer students reach graduation.

90   Searching for Colleges

Admission and Enrollment Figures

It's difficult to have a robust transfer community at a college that enrolls very few transfer students. So it's wise to check on transfer student admission and enrollment numbers early in your research. The vast majority of universities report information like this via the Common Data Set (CDS). Visit a college's website and do a search for "Common Data Set." Look for a page listing links to CDS files from recent years. Universities often share these reports via their "Institutional Research" department or similar.

Once you have access to a CDS file, scroll down to section D2. You should find a table like this one from New York University (NYU) reporting on the fall 2023 entering class:

D2. Fall Applicants: Student Counts

Provide the number of students who applied, were admitted, and enrolled as degree-seeking transfer students in Fall 2023. If your institution collects and reports non-binary gender data, please use the "Another Gender" category.

	Applicants	Admitted Applicants	Enrolled Applicants
Men	4697	1557	1068
Women	5876	2373	1591
Another Gender			
Total	10573	3930	2659

As you can see here, NYU had 10,573 transfer applicants for fall 2023 and admitted 3,930 students. Of those, 2,659 enrolled. So by dividing the admitted applicants number by the applicants number, we find that NYU had a 37 percent transfer admission rate that year and has a fairly large transfer student community with 2,659 entering in a single semester.

Because transfer enrollment at some schools can vary drastically from year to year, it's important to check multiple files to look for trends. Here is additional data from the fall 2022 NYU CDS count:

D2 Provide the number of students who applied, were admitted, and enrolled as degree-seeking transfer students in Fall 2022. If your institution collects and reports non-binary gender data, please use the "Another Gender" category.

	Applicants	Admitted	Enrolled
Men	3,396	532	248
Women	4,965	1,180	550
Another Gender			
Total	8,361	1,712	798

In fall 2022, the NYU transfer admission rate was 20 percent, and 798 students enrolled. Since most transfer students require at least two years of study to complete a bachelor's degree, it's probably safe to assume that in any given year NYU has at least 3,000 transfer students on campus. NYU has a total undergraduate population of approximately 30,000 students, so transfers represent about 10 percent of enrolled undergraduate students.

By the numbers, it seems that NYU has a solid transfer community, but before we make that determination, let's check some additional historical data. Fall 2020 and 2021 were unusual due to the Covid-19 pandemic, so let's skip those years and view the data for fall 2019:

D2	Provide the number of students who applied, were admitted, and enrolled as degree-seeking transfer students in Fall 2019.		
D2		Applicants	Admitted Applicants	Enrolled Applicants
D2	Men	3,463	641	350
D2	Women	5,047	1,222	593
D2	Total	8,510	1,863	943

The admission rate for fall 2019 was just under 22 percent, and 943 students enrolled. Either fall 2023 is an anomaly, or the admission of transfer students to NYU is trending upward.

Transfer enrollment numbers can also be found via the US government's College Navigator site.[7] Comparisons between colleges are more easily done at this site because it compiles statistics from all US colleges in one searchable location, but data is only available for the most recent academic year. In addition, the "transfer-in" population cited accounts only for new transfers entering that year. Continuing transfers are absorbed into the overall undergraduate enrollment number.

Here's the fall 2023 College Navigator entry for the California Institute of Technology (Caltech):

⊝ ENROLLMENT	
FALL 2023	
TOTAL ENROLLMENT	**2,463**
Undergraduate enrollment	1,023
Undergraduate transfer-in enrollment	5

Only five students transferred in that year. If we assume that five students transfer in every year — and it takes two or three years to graduate — we would have a total of perhaps fifteen transfer students on campus at any given time. With 2,463 undergraduates enrolled in fall 2023, that means less than 1 percent of the undergraduate students at Caltech are transfer students. It could be difficult to find peers and connect with other transfer students with such a small population.

College Navigator Outcome Measures

Remember that getting accepted to a college is only the start of your journey. The college you attend must offer the kind of environment and support systems that you need to succeed and ultimately graduate with your bachelor's degree. An additional data point to consider is the college's graduation rate for transfer students.

Graduation rates are an imperfect measure of student success, as they are highly dependent on preexisting factors outside the college's control. More selective colleges tend to have higher graduation rates because they admit fewer students facing external challenges. In contrast, colleges that strive to expand access to higher education opportunities may report lower graduation rates because they consistently admit students who encounter obstacles on the path to degree completion (e.g., first-generation students or those from low-income communities). That said, comparing the graduation rates of first-year and transfer students can provide valuable insights into a college's commitment to transfer initiatives.

College Navigator shares data on graduation rates for first-time, full-time students and outcome measures for all others. Search for a college of interest, then scroll down to the section on outcome measures. Find the charts for non-first-time students, with either full-time or part-time status. These non-first-time cohorts are primarily comprised of transfer students but can also include small numbers of students who changed their degree-seeking status while enrolled. Here's the chart representing the eight-year graduation rate for UC Berkeley's full-time, non-first-time degree-seeking students:

Qualities of a Transfer-Friendly College   93

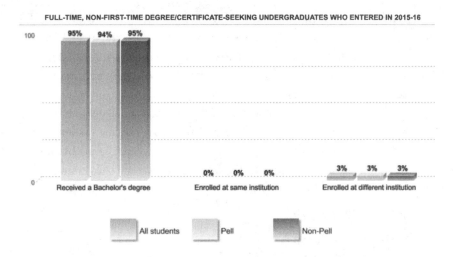

Eight years after entering, 95 percent of non-first-time (mostly transfer) students have earned their bachelor's degrees from UC Berkeley, including 94 percent of Pell Grant recipients, who would likely be considered low-income and therefore face more obstacles when pursuing higher education. These degree-completion rates are very similar to Berkeley's six- and eight-year graduation rates for first-year entrants.

At the University of North Texas (UNT), College Navigator shows that 1 percent of full-time, non-first-time students are still enrolled eight years later, 26 percent have transferred to a different college, and only 68 percent have earned a bachelor's degree from UNT within eight years:

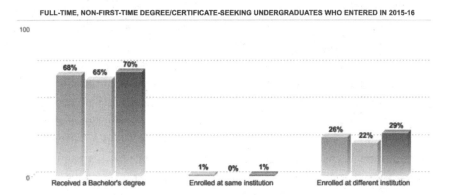

However, these rates must be considered within the context of the college as a whole. The eight-year graduation rate for first-year entrants is only 62 percent. At least according to these numbers, transfer students appear to be *more* likely than first-years to earn their bachelor's degrees within eight years.

Remember that this metric tracks student progress *eight years* after enrollment. Most students hope to complete degrees in far less time. Graduation rates for shorter timelines may be available within other publicly accessible government databases, but this data is not available on the College Navigator website.

Case Study of a College: UT Austin

The state of Texas has long supported higher education access through its network of community colleges and state universities. So it's no surprise that its public flagship university, the University of Texas at Austin, offers a robust Transfer Year Experience Program, modeled after successful first-year experience programs offered at UT Austin and nationwide.[8] Students can choose from a buffet of support services, transfer-specific student clubs, transfer-only course sections, a living-learning community, and leadership opportunities just for transfer students.

All UT Austin students must complete a Signature Course as part of the university's graduation requirements. These interdisciplinary courses introduce incoming students to academic expectations and resources at the university. Since transfer students already have some college experience, UT Austin offers transfer-specific Signature Courses in a small seminar setting, as well as transfer-only discussion sections for select courses in a large lecture format. Through these courses, transfer students can build academic skills to help reduce transfer shock while connecting with their peers.

Participants in Transfer-Year Interest Groups (TrIGs) register for one or two classes in areas of interest alongside other members of their TrIG cohort. Academic advisers help students find TrIG courses that will fulfill degree requirements so students aren't burdened with taking additional classes that don't apply to their degree plan. TrIG cohort members attend classes together, meet regularly with peer mentors and staff facilitators, and build communities of like-minded transfer students. There is also a TrIG designed just for nontraditional students, guided by a peer mentor who previously entered the school as a nontraditional transfer student.

Extensive transfer programming like UT Austin's Transfer-Year Experience is a sure sign of a transfer-friendly institution.

Common Challenges and Questions

What about rankings? I want to go to the "best" university!

No university can truly claim to be the "best," despite what published rankings might say. Each student's needs and priorities differ, so a university that is the best for one student may not be a good fit for another. The methodologies behind these rankings focus on specific college features that may or may not be relevant to your needs as a transfer student. For example, *U.S. News & World Report* prioritizes graduation rates in its college rankings. That sounds great, but when you read the fine print, you see that transfer students are not included in those graduation rate calculations.[9] In contrast, *Money* magazine's Best Colleges list includes transfer students in its graduation rates. As you might expect, *Money* places a greater emphasis on affordability in its ranking methodology, but the primary factor in *Money*'s affordability measure is the net price of a degree as estimated for first-year entrants.[10] No affordability metric for transfer students is included. Published lists of best colleges may sell magazines, but they cannot definitively state which college will be the best fit *for you*.

Do I have to live on campus?

While it is somewhat unusual for colleges to require transfer students to live on campus, some do so — especially those that require first-year students to live on campus for multiple years. University residence halls are excellent places to make new friends and integrate into campus life. Campus residents are also likely to be closer to amenities and services designed to help students succeed. Living off campus can separate new transfer students from the larger campus community and hinder access to resources. However, if you truly wish to avoid living on campus, check each university's policies carefully. Even schools that require all students to live on campus might make exceptions for older students, military veterans, and students with spouses or children, for instance.

CHAPTER 8

Partnerships

Partnerships between postsecondary educational institutions simplify and streamline the transfer process, while tuition reciprocity agreements provide new pathways to tuition savings across state lines. These collaborations break down barriers to transfer and build clearer pathways to degree attainment.

These agreements not only make education more affordable but also give students the flexibility to choose universities that best suit their academic and career goals, regardless of state boundaries. They can be particularly beneficial for students seeking specialized programs or those living in border regions.

The names and details of transfer partnerships and state-to-state tuition agreements vary by region, but all programs aim to broaden educational access. Search for the opportunities available in your state or region.

Transfer Articulation Agreements

"Articulation" is a fancy word to describe the process of colleges and universities lining up their classes to decide which ones are equivalent. Many classes can be considered transferable between institutions, but that does not mean they are *articulated* to specific classes or requirements. A transfer articulation agreement is a formal document that describes the course equivalencies (usually from public two-year to public four-year institutions) that have been reviewed and approved by the consenting institutions. Sometimes these agreements simply show course-to-course articulations, but they can also show groups of classes for general education, major preparation, or entire degrees.

Students can use articulation agreements to plan efficient transfer paths from community colleges to four-year universities. These agreements help students focus on taking required classes and avoid taking unnecessary ones, thereby removing the guesswork and uncertainty from course planning. Having a detailed and accurate plan also reduces the stress associated with transfer preparation and ensures that students don't waste time and money taking random classes that won't apply to a degree.

Associate Degree for Transfer

More than thirty states now have approved "associate degree for transfer" programs that guarantee transferability of specified associate degrees from the state's community colleges to in-state public universities.[1] The details of the guarantee vary by state, but most include confirmation that earning an approved associate degree will fulfill the general education requirements of the affiliated four-year universities and allow associate degree holders to transfer with junior class standing. Some associate degrees for transfer also include required major preparation, which ensures that students can seamlessly enter directly into their intended majors. Note that these degrees only guarantee transferability of coursework, credits, and class standing. Unless explicitly stated, associate degrees for transfer do not necessarily guarantee that a degree holder will be accepted into a particular university.

General Education Blocks

General education (GE) requirements frequently look quite similar across colleges nationwide. Wouldn't it be nice if everyone could agree on a single set of requirements to create a transferable block of GE courses accepted everywhere? The Interstate Passport program tried to do just that. The last cohort included sixty-nine institutions in twenty-nine states that had agreed to accept the same set of GE courses as a transferable block. Unfortunately, the Interstate Passport was discontinued in 2023.

Thankfully, several states have established their own transferable GE blocks, some of which are also accepted in neighboring states. Here are a few common statewide GE blocks:

- The University System of Georgia's Core IMPACTS
- MassTransfer (Massachusetts)
- Intersegmental General Education Transfer Curriculum (IGETC; California)
- Ohio Transfer 36 (OT36; formerly the Ohio Transfer Module)
- Washington 45
- Texas Core Curriculum (TCC)
- Arizona General Education Curriculum (AGEC)

Keep in mind that states with associate degree for transfer programs may have incorporated common GE requirements into their transferable degree programs. An associate degree typically comes with additional benefits, such as priority admissions consideration and guaranteed junior standing, so weigh your options carefully.

Major Pathways

It is also possible to take classes in preparation for transfer into a specific major without completing either an associate degree or a GE block. Articulation agreements of this nature are often referred to as major pathways, major transfer maps, or simply transfer guides. It is often advisable to complete GE requirements alongside major prerequisites, but students on an abbreviated transfer timeline or those pursuing prerequisite-heavy science, technology, engineering, and mathematics (STEM) majors may find that major preparation is the highest priority. It is wise to check with a transfer adviser to learn which course tracks are most important to complete if it is impossible to finish them all.

California maintains one of the most extensive databases of statewide major course equivalencies at Assist.org. Students can select the California community college they currently attend and then choose a target university — either a University of California or a California State University campus. From there, students can select a major to find a list of required and recommended prerequisites at the four-year university and their equivalents, if available, at the two-year community college.

Here is an excerpt from Assist.org showing the major articulation agreement between Moorpark College and UC Berkeley for the statistics major:

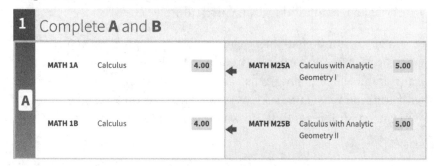

Two semesters of Calculus are required for admission to this major. At UC Berkeley, these classes would be numbered Math 1A and 1B, worth four semester credits each. The approved equivalent courses at Moorpark are named and numbered differently and worth a different number of credits, but because they have been preapproved and listed in the Assist.org database, Moorpark students can confidently enroll in these classes and know that they are fulfilling the requirements for transfer into the statistics major at UC Berkeley. If they decide to take classes at a different community college, or aim for admission at a different university, they can simply select different colleges from the menus and view an updated course list.

Transfer Admission Guarantees

Transfer admission guarantee programs are powerful agreements that provide eligible community college students with a clear road map to assured admission at a participating four-year university.[2] While earning guaranteed admission requires careful planning and sustained dedication to fulfill comprehensive requirements, the peace of mind afforded by such a guarantee makes the effort worthwhile. For many students, the clearly defined goals and timelines of guaranteed admission pathways alleviate the stress that can accompany the transfer journey. Additionally, meeting the criteria used to determine eligibility for a transfer guarantee often makes a student a strong candidate for transfer admission at other universities as well.

Requirements

A typical guaranteed admission agreement outlines specific requirements that must be satisfied along with deadlines for critical elements of preparation. Although requirements vary by school and major, some common qualifications include:

- minimum grade point average (GPA)
- minimum grades earned in specific classes
- completion of introductory math and writing courses
- completion of general education requirements
- minimum number of credits earned
- satisfactory progress toward major prerequisites
- completion of key prerequisites prior to specified deadlines (i.e., not planned or in progress at the time of application)
- completion of associate degree

Some transfer guarantee programs have an additional application process. This secondary application might be due upon completion of requirements or alongside the main transfer admission application. In some cases, students must apply to participate in a guarantee program early in their community college journey so that advisers can monitor their academic progress.

Joint-admission programs — also known as dual admission or co-admission — require the most forethought, as students usually need to apply directly to the target university and its community college partner at the beginning of the college journey. Once admitted, co-enrolled students can access classes and services at both schools immediately. This early connection allows students to seek guidance from advisers at the four-year university even as they begin their studies at community college.

Check for guaranteed admission programs in your state and read the details carefully to determine when and how to access these programs.

Restrictions

While transfer admission guarantee programs offer tremendous benefits, students must carefully review all requirements and restrictions before committing. Some programs have limitations that can make the guarantee difficult to use effectively or may exclude popular campuses or competitive majors. For example, the University of California offers a Transfer Admission Guarantee (TAG) program for just six of its nine undergraduate campuses, and students can only apply for guaranteed admission at one of these. The most selective campuses, UCLA and UC Berkeley, are excluded, as are UC San Diego and some of the most competitive majors, like computer science and engineering. However, applying for guaranteed admission through the UC does not limit other transfer opportunities. Students can still apply to any UC campus through the regular admissions process and pursue guaranteed admission programs at universities outside the UC system. Although the scope of the UC guarantee is limited, it is flexible enough to allow students to benefit from the guarantee agreement while keeping their other transfer options open.

Tuition Reciprocity

Tuition reciprocity agreements are partnerships between states or public universities that allow students to attend out-of-state institutions at in-state (or greatly reduced out-of-state) tuition rates.[3] Public universities are partially funded by state taxes, so they frequently double or even triple the tuition bill for students from other states. These agreements make crossing state lines for higher education more affordable, often dictating a maximum out-of-state tuition rate of no more than 150 percent of in-state, thus expanding students' transfer options beyond the borders of their home states. While each program has its own specific terms and conditions, they all share the common goal of making higher education more accessible and affordable for residents of nearby states.

Eligibility

Each regional group sets minimum requirements for student eligibility, and then individual colleges may further refine the conditions for participation. In the most straightforward reciprocity programs, eligibility is automatically determined by the student's residence as indicated on the application for admission. In this case, students don't need to apply for tuition reciprocity and may not even be aware that the program exists until they receive a financial aid award letter with a discount. When additional requirements are present, they often take the form of minimum GPAs or additional applications. Schools that want to limit the number of regional discounts provided may also implement earlier application deadlines or treat the tuition discount like a scholarship awarded to high-achieving students.

Restrictions

Not all colleges (or all campuses of a college) within a region participate in regional tuition reciprocity agreements. Of those that do, certain high-demand majors may be excluded. Nursing, engineering, and computer science are examples of popular majors that may not be covered under some regional tuition reciprocity programs. In the most restrictive programs, the only majors eligible for tuition discounts are those that are unavailable at public universities in the student's home state. Additionally, some programs might be limited to first-year applicants and unavailable for transfer, or vice versa. Reading the fine print on any tuition reciprocity program of interest is critical. Not only will you learn how to obtain a tuition discount upon enrollment, but you will also discover how to maintain the reduced rate for the remainder of your undergraduate career.

Popular Tuition Reciprocity Programs

There are four main multi-state tuition exchange programs covering more than forty US states. (Only a handful of states do not participate in any kind of tuition reciprocity agreement.)

- Academic Common Market (primarily Southern states)
- Midwest Student Exchange Program
- New England Regional Student Program (also called Tuition Break)
- Western Undergraduate Exchange

Individual colleges and smaller subregions may also have tuition discount programs. These are most commonly found at colleges near state borders. For example, Southern Oregon University in Ashland offers in-state tuition to transfer students from three of the northernmost California community colleges. Similarly, the University of Nebraska Omaha offers residents of neighboring Iowa the opportunity to pay deeply discounted nonresident tuition rates.

Case Study: Lauren

In high school, Lauren's sister was known as the "smart one." While Lauren focused on friends and fun, her older sister took early college courses and studied for AP exams. Lauren didn't see how she could possibly live up to her sister's academic reputation, so she decided not to try. But when her sister went off to college at the University of California campus of her dreams, Lauren realized she wanted that life, too.

As she began her senior year of high school, Lauren was motivated to work harder in her classes. It was too late to recover from the low grades she had earned in previous years, though. Her best hope was to attend a community college and then transfer to a university. As a California resident, Lauren could take advantage of the streamlined transfer agreements between her local community college and the University of California (UC).

Ideally, Lauren wanted to transfer to the beautiful UC Santa Barbara campus. It's a selective school, and her 2.8 high school GPA made her ineligible to apply as a first-year student. However, if she enrolled at her local community college and planned her courses carefully, she could participate in UC Santa Barbara's Transfer Admission Guarantee (TAG) program. She reviewed the detailed requirements on the TAG matrix[4] and created an account on the UC Transfer Admission Planner (TAP)[5] site to track her courses. Each semester, she carefully selected community college courses to satisfy not only the TAG requirements but also general education requirements and prerequisites for her planned economics major. She also had to make sure that her course grades and overall GPA remained above the minimum required for TAG eligibility.

Fulfilling the TAG agreement required Lauren to complete certain courses during her first year of community college and apply for transfer several months in advance, so she was glad she planned ahead! She submitted a separate TAG application in September of her second year, followed by the full UC transfer application in November. Both applications required her to list planned and in-progress courses that would meet the rest of the TAG requirements. If she dropped or failed any of those classes, she risked cancellation of the TAG contract, so she had to be proactive in her planning and communication.

After two years of carefully planned community college coursework, Lauren earned an associate degree with a 3.6 GPA and secured guaranteed admission to her top college choice — UC Santa Barbara.

Case Study: Martin

Martin grew up just a few blocks from his state's flagship public university. His budget-minded family assumed that attending the local public college while living at home would be the most affordable way for him to earn a bachelor's degree. Although attending the university in his hometown felt anticlimactic, Martin was willing to give it a try.

Living at home certainly lowered the cost of university attendance, but it also reduced Martin's opportunities to engage with the campus community. By winter break, he wanted to drop out. He was on a path to earn a degree inexpensively, but he was missing out on the full college experience. His parents, realizing that the value of college is not limited to the diploma earned and the money saved, agreed to let Martin seek out transfer opportunities as long as he kept the family budget in mind and continued to make progress on his degree at his current college while he researched other options.

Martin's first stop was the Savings Finder database on the Western Undergraduate Exchange (WUE) website.[6] He selected his status as a transfer student, narrowed his search to states with warmer weather, and checked the box for his major, astrophysics. The Savings Finder delivered exactly one result: the University of New Mexico (UNM). UNM had not been on Martin's radar, but it offered everything he wanted in a college. Better yet, UNM offered guaranteed admission to transfer students who had earned a C average or higher in previous college courses and a full WUE tuition discount for students who maintained a 3.0 or higher GPA throughout college. A strong student, Martin was eligible for both. He immediately applied and was accepted for the coming fall semester.

The WUE discount reduced Martin's UNM tuition to the in-state rate, which was even less than his previous home-state college tuition. Additionally, the lower cost of living in New Mexico made student housing more affordable as well. Ultimately, the total cost of attendance at UNM was only slightly higher for Martin, and the opportunity to fully experience college life was well worth the price.

Common Challenges and Questions

What if I have not met a requirement for a transfer guarantee program?

Is it worth extending your time at the community college to complete this requirement and earn the guarantee? Would staying longer push you into high-unit territory? It's unfortunate that a minor oversight disqualified you from the guarantee program. However, you don't need a guarantee to apply for transfer and be accepted to a university. In most cases, it doesn't make sense to delay transfer for the sake of the guarantee program. Create the strongest applications you can, and submit them to multiple universities. If your records were strong enough to almost qualify for a guarantee, you probably have a strong enough application to be admitted to several colleges without a guarantee.

Can articulation agreements exist with private and out-of-state colleges?

Sure! Many private colleges and universities choose to participate in transfer articulation agreements with select community colleges or state systems. Curry College has agreements with some Massachusetts community colleges, and several members of the Association of Independent California Colleges and Universities accept California associate degrees for transfer, for instance. Some out-of-state public universities may also accept general education blocks from nearby states. For example, Oregon State University and the University of Oregon both accept California's IGETC. New collaborations emerge all the time. Watch for new agreements in your area!

PART IV

PLANNING

Successful transfer requires careful research and preparation. If you are taking a planned transfer route through a community college, your planning should begin as early as possible. Exploring transfer requirements early allows you to be efficient with your community college coursework. When you know which classes are required or recommended at universities of interest, you can design your course schedule each term to optimize your chances of admission.

Even if you unexpectedly find yourself wanting or needing to transfer laterally, you can start preparing as soon as you begin to consider transferring. You may not have as much time to arrange your classes to meet specific transfer requirements, but you can take steps to improve your transfer admission chances. This might be as simple as switching out one of your planned classes for the next term, or it could be as significant as planning a detour through a community college while you prepare to transfer to a new four-year university.

Regardless of your transfer path, thorough planning is key to a smooth transition. Start now!

CHAPTER 9

Minimum Eligibility Requirements

Every university has a set of general eligibility requirements for transfer. These requirements commonly include a minimum or maximum number of credits earned, minimum GPA, or completion of specific courses. You may also find conditional eligibility requirements, such as students with fewer than twenty-four college credits needing to submit high school transcripts or standardized test scores. Requirements might also vary by major program.

If you start early, you may be able to attain eligibility for transfer admission if you don't already meet the minimum requirements. In some cases, though, you might find that the eligibility requirements are not possible for you to achieve, thus eliminating certain schools from your list. For example, many universities have a maximum number of units that transfer students can earn prior to enrolling at their school. If you have already earned more than the specified number of credits, there may be no viable path to admission for you at that school. It's essential to discover these requirements early so that you can inquire about policy exceptions or find other schools that better fit your needs.

Pay special attention to the deadlines for meeting eligibility milestones. Some schools state that a minimum number of units must be completed prior to submitting an application, while others require completion of those units by the end of the term before you intend to transfer. There may even be different deadlines for some requirements at some schools. For example, you may need to complete required math and English courses by the end of the fall term before transfer, but you have until the end of spring to complete the overall required number of credits.

Remember that these are *minimum* eligibility requirements (i.e.,

Planning

this is what you must achieve to even be considered for admission). Fulfilling these requirements does not guarantee admission. In fact, you may find that the minimum requirements are considerably lower than what most admitted transfer students have achieved. If the college publishes an admitted student profile for transfers, you can see what the average statistics are for past successful transfer students.

Earned Course Credits

When identifying potential universities for transfer, begin by looking for their definition of a transfer student. It's common for universities to define a transfer student as someone who has taken classes at a college after high school graduation or has earned a specific number of college credits since high school graduation. In some cases, if you don't meet their definition of a transfer student, you might be eligible to apply as a first-year student. In other instances, you may simply have to wait until you achieve the requirements for transfer eligibility.

Next, look for the minimum and maximum earned units required for transfer. The average number of credits required to apply for transfer admission typically ranges from 24 to 60 semester credits, or 36 to 90 quarter credits. Some colleges will consider transfer applications from students with as few as 12 or as many as 90 semester units, but this is somewhat rare. Read each college's description of maximum unit limitations carefully. Some colleges will not consider applications from transfer students who have more than the maximum number of earned units. Other colleges will still review applications from high-unit transfers but won't apply all the credits to a degree program at their school.

As you read the details of required units at each college of interest, look for answers to the following questions:

1. Are AP/IB/CLEP credits included in the minimum unit count?
2. Are dual enrollment college credits earned during high school included in the minimum unit count?
3. What is the minimum grade that must be earned in a class for the credits to be included in the minimum unit count?
4. What is the deadline for earning the minimum required units?

Since the answers to these questions may vary from school to school, so might your eligibility for transfer admission. Read carefully and ask questions if any requirements are unclear.

Case Study: Hugo

Hugo graduated from high school in 2020 in the throes of the Covid-19 pandemic. He didn't know exactly what he wanted to do after high school, so he enrolled in a few general education courses at the local community college, with a plan to transfer to the local public university. When the fall term began, he realized that classes were still being held online rather than in person. He had found remote learning challenging during the last few months of high school, so he was not excited about the prospect of starting his college career online, but he decided to give it a try.

Halfway through the semester, he was struggling with both the material and his mental health. His grades were dropping so low that he felt it would be impossible for him to finish the term with passing grades. Rather than accept the low grades, he decided to withdraw from all his classes and try college again at a later date. At this stage of the term, he could still withdraw from classes, but the record of his enrollment in them would not be erased. Hugo's transcript would include a list of courses attempted, each with a grade of W for Withdrawal.

A few W's with good explanations are generally not problematic for transfer admission. However, in Hugo's case, this record of attempted courses made him ineligible for admission at the nearby state university. He could have returned to the community college to retake those courses and prepare for transfer. But after spending some time in the workforce, he had a better idea of what he wanted to study and felt ready to apply directly to a four-year school. Unfortunately,

114   Planning

Hugo learned that he could not apply to the local university as a first-year because he had begun building a college transcript — albeit one with zero earned credits — after graduating from high school. He was also ineligible to apply as a transfer student because he had not earned the minimum number of units required to apply.

Hugo had two choices: return to community college to gain transfer eligibility or apply to other four-year universities with more flexible requirements. He opted to reenroll at the community college and pursue a transfer pathway that would lead to admission at his desired local university.

Grades and GPA

The second most common transfer eligibility requirement (after units earned) is a minimum college GPA. The vast majority of North American universities require transfer students to attain a GPA of at least 2.0 to be eligible for admission. More selective universities often set a GPA requirement of 3.0 or higher. Individual majors and transfer guarantee programs may also establish higher GPA minimums. While meeting the minimum GPA requirement is a strong starting point, keep in mind that aiming for a higher GPA can significantly improve your chances of admission and open doors to more opportunities at your desired institution.

If your current GPA is near the minimum required for transfer at a desired college, it would be wise to focus on raising your GPA as much as possible before applying for admission. You might also want to postpone your application submissions until you have completed additional classes with higher final grades. Also, consider taking an accelerated two-to-three-week January intersession course to get an additional GPA boost between full terms. If you are preparing for a March 1 application deadline, earning an A in a winter intersession course could improve your GPA and provide evidence of an ongoing upward trend in academic performance.

Please note that the minimum GPA requirement most likely refers to the average of *all* your college grades, including classes taken at other colleges or via high school dual enrollment programs. If you have college credits from multiple schools, average all the grades together to determine your cumulative GPA. (See chapter 4 for more information on calculating your transfer GPA.)

Required Courses

Institutions often require students to complete specific courses prior to transfer. The most common requirement is first-year English composition. Many universities also require completion of a college-level mathematics course. Some institutions, like the University of Oregon, require second language proficiency as well. The University of Virginia has one of the most extensive lists of prerequisites, with thirty semester credits in designated subject areas beyond the English, math, and second language requirements: twelve credits in natural sciences, six in social sciences, six in humanities, three in history, and three in non-Western perspectives.

Ideally, you will be able to verify that courses available at your current institution are considered equivalent to the required classes at your target university by using a tool like Transferology, Tasseled, or the college's own transfer equivalency database. If you cannot locate confirmation of course equivalencies, do your best to search for classes that have features similar to those of the required courses at your target school. For example, most colleges offer a two-course series in English composition with similar learning outcomes. Introductory courses in mainstream subjects like psychology, biology, and history are likely to fulfill the same general education requirements or major prerequisites.

Whatever courses you choose, be sure to save every syllabus. If the textbook is not already listed on the syllabus, make a note of the text, author, and edition, too. If your future university is unsure whether a class you took is equivalent to one it requires, you will need to submit documentation to obtain credit.

Online Course Ineligibility

Watch out for online courses! Some colleges do not accept online courses for transferable credit. Look for a detailed transfer credit policy that describes the university's position regarding online coursework.

Since Covid-19, many colleges have become more flexible about accepting online courses, but there are often still restrictions, such as science labs or world language courses that must be in person.

High School GPA and Completion

High school may feel like a distant memory, but your records might become part of your transfer application. Most universities require transfer students to obtain a minimum GPA at their former colleges, but a few will also ask students to show proof of a minimum GPA earned in high school. The inclusion of high school requirements often depends on how many college credits have been earned prior to transfer. In general, the more college credits you have, the less likely it is that your high school record will factor into the transfer admissions decision. If your high school GPA is less than ideal, you will want to identify universities that do not require high school records for transfer or ensure that you earn enough college credits to negate consideration of the high school GPA in transfer admissions.

Even colleges that don't include high school transcripts in the admissions review process may require proof of high school graduation. This might be in the form of a transcript, diploma, or General Education Development (GED) certificate. If you did not graduate from high school, you may need to pass the GED exam to become eligible for transfer admission at some schools. If you have earned an associate degree, or are able to earn one before you transfer, seek out universities that will waive the high school graduation requirement for transfer students who have completed associate degrees. Alternatively, you can restrict your college search to universities that do not require high school completion for transfer students. This will limit your options significantly, though. If you decide to pursue transfer admission without a high school diploma or GED, you should plan on doing additional research regarding financial aid eligibility. Access to some funds may be contingent on showing proof of high school graduation.

Good Standing

Many four-year colleges require transfer applicants to be "in good standing" at their previous institution, but what does that mean?

Without additional context, it can be difficult to decipher this requirement, but the generally understood meaning is that transfer applicants must be in good *academic* standing at their current or most recent institution. In other words, you should not attempt to apply for a transfer while on academic probation or suspension at your current college. You must first resolve any outstanding academic issues — either by returning to your previous college to satisfy the terms of academic renewal or by successfully completing classes at a community college to create a new academic record that demonstrates your good academic standing.

The term "good standing" can also sometimes refer to behavioral or disciplinary issues. This may be clarified by the inclusion of a phrase such as "eligible to return" to a previous college. This statement from the University of Oregon addresses both academic and disciplinary standing: "To be considered for admission as a transfer student, you must be in good standing at your most recent institution and eligible to return to any previously attended institution."[1]

In this example, the first mention of good standing refers to academic standing at the current or most recent institution. Note that applicants are not required to be in good academic standing at all previous institutions — only the most recent one. Thus, if you struggled academically at a former university, but then attended a community college to strengthen your transcript, you would only need to prove your good academic standing at the community college.

The next phrase, regarding eligibility to return to prior institutions, refers to the secondary requirement concerning disciplinary issues. Unlike the previous statement about academic standing, this section does require good disciplinary standing at all prior institutions. If you have been dismissed from a university for inappropriate conduct, you are likely ineligible to return to that university, and therefore also ineligible to apply for transfer to the University of Oregon and other schools with similar policies. Improving your disciplinary standing is not as straightforward as simply building a strong academic record at a community college, although that can help! Overcoming an adverse disciplinary history can be challenging and may require significant patience and extensive additional dialogue with university officials who have the authority to make exceptions to eligibility requirements when warranted.

118   Planning

Common Challenges and Questions

What if I want to leave my current college before I earn enough credits to be eligible to apply as a transfer student?

Each university sets minimum eligibility requirements for transfer student admission, including a minimum number of credits earned. The university may stipulate that the required number of credits be earned prior to application, enrollment, or some other stated deadline. If you will not meet the minimum unit requirement for a desired university, you have a few options:

- Consider staying at your current school for another term.
- Temporarily transfer to a community college to earn the needed credits.
- Contact the prospective university's admissions office and ask if they ever make exceptions to their minimum unit policy. (Exceptions are rare, but it can't hurt to ask!)

My GPA is currently below the minimum required for transfer, but I'm working hard to improve it! My GPA will be high enough by the end of the semester, but transfer applications are due before then. Can I still apply?

Maybe. Very selective universities may have strict requirements for achieving minimum GPAs. Less selective universities might be more forgiving and may ask for your final end-of-semester transcript before making an admissions decision if your current GPA is close to the required minimum. When in doubt, contact the admissions office and ask.

Can I retake a class to replace a bad grade?

Maybe. Some colleges have academic renewal policies that allow students to repeat a class, replacing the old grade with a new one. However, not all universities acknowledge these policies from other schools. It is entirely possible that when you retake a class, one university will only consider the new grade in your GPA calculation, while another will average the two grades together. If you earned a D or F in a class and have the opportunity to retake it, it is always wise to do so. Even if the college you are trying to transfer to won't accept the new grade as a replacement, enrolling in the class demonstrates your commitment to learning the material and recovering from past mistakes.

CHAPTER 10

General Education

Most colleges include a series of general education (GE) courses in their degree requirements. These classes are designed to give students a broader education beyond the major subjects they have chosen and establish some basic skills and knowledge that the college believes all graduates should possess. Exact GE requirements are defined by each individual college or system of colleges and can be described by various names, such as breadth pattern, common curriculum, and baccalaureate core, to name a few.

Whatever they are called, these classes are often intended to be taken in the first two years of a bachelor's degree program, which offers the added benefit of exposing new college students to a range of subjects before they must declare a major. As a transfer student, you are expected to have completed some of this exploration through GE courses at your previous college. Even if completion of specific GE coursework is not required for admission, it's wise to work toward some common GE requirements prior to transfer for a few reasons:

- Classes that fulfill GE requirements are often introductory or "survey" classes, and thus they are more likely to receive credit at other universities because course equivalencies are easily identified.
- Completing common course requirements, such as writing and math, allows transfer applicants to demonstrate college-ready skills that admissions officers find desirable.
- Early exploration of multiple subject areas allows transfers to focus on major requirements upon arrival at the next university, leading to timely graduation.

If you have a target university in mind, research its degree requirements to identify potential GE course equivalents at your current college. If you aren't sure where to apply yet, focus on taking classes within some of the common breadth areas defined in this chapter. Don't forget to try classes in subject areas that might lead you to your major!

Last, if you are attending a community college that offers associate degrees for transfer, find out what that means in your region. These degrees are often designed to fulfill general education requirements at partnering four-year institutions. Earning an associate degree for transfer can simplify your planning process because you can focus on the degree requirements at your current school, knowing your classes are guaranteed to fulfill GE requirements at partner institutions.

English Composition

Writing classes are among the most commonly required general education courses. Even universities that don't have a traditional GE program often require evidence of writing proficiency. Brown University is famous for its Open Curriculum, which allows students to design personalized pathways through courses of interest. Although Brown students are not required to take specific GE courses, they must demonstrate competency in writing by successfully completing two "writing-designated" courses before graduation.[1]

Every student should take at least one, preferably two, writing courses before transfer. Look for classes at your college described as "first-year composition" or similar. These core classes are often offered in a series, titled "English 1a/1b" or "Writing 101/102," and are explicitly designed to help college students strengthen their writing skills for the academically rigorous college coursework that lies ahead. Expect to write and revise several essays in these classes as you hone your skills. Completing these classes early in your college journey will help you succeed in many other courses and will demonstrate your proficiency in a key academic skill.

Mathematics

Math, or some form of quantitative reasoning, is a common degree requirement. Precalculus, calculus, and statistics classes often satisfy a math-related GE requirement, but other, more creative options may also be available. At many universities, computer science courses can now fulfill quantitative reasoning requirements, and math-heavy sciences, such as physics, can also sometimes do so.

At Boston University, general education requirements are called the "Hub." One class in quantitative reasoning is among the Hub's course requirements.[2] Students can choose from a long list of math-adjacent classes, such as "Cosmic Controversies" and "Puzzles and Paradoxes," in addition to standard math classes like Calculus, to complete this requirement. The College of Arts & Science at New York University (NYU) offers a rotating list of seminars that can be taken to fulfill its quantitative reasoning requirement.[3] Recent offerings include "Great Ideas in Mathematics" and "From Data to Discovery." Such niche classes are unlikely to transfer and fulfill specific requirements at other universities, though, so be cautious.

If you want to take a class that is most likely to transfer and potentially satisfy a math GE requirement, a standard calculus or statistics course is likely the best choice. You may be required to take a placement test before enrolling in a math class, so investigate your options early. If you are placed into a lower-level math class, it may take more than one term for you to become eligible for the level of math needed for transfer.

Alternatively, some colleges have been experimenting with adding support classes to Calculus and other high-level math.[4] Instead of requiring students to take a remedial math class in preparation for Calculus, these colleges allow students to enroll directly in Calculus with an additional tutorial class as a corequisite. This approach enables students to work through the Calculus curriculum while filling in gaps in their math knowledge along the way. If you plan to take a math class this way, you must leave room in your schedule for this additional one- or two-credit math support class.

World Language

Not all colleges require proficiency in a second language, but those that do may define proficiency in one of several ways. Some schools may accept two to four years of high school language classes as evidence of second language proficiency. Others may require a passing score on an AP (or similar) language test in order to use high school records to fulfill the college's language requirement.

At the college level, completing two to four terms of classes in the same language will usually clear the requirement. If you wish to start learning a new language this way, begin early so that you can achieve some level of proficiency prior to transfer. Since sequential world language class curricula don't always align neatly, you may be required to take a language placement test at your next university to continue your studies.

Last, you may be able to satisfy a language requirement with a proficiency exam. Some universities offer in-house tests or interviews on campus, or they might provide a list of acceptable exams that students can take independently. If you have attained fluency in another language outside of a traditional college classroom, a proficiency exam may be the most efficient way to fulfill a GE language requirement. You may also want to consider demonstrating your fluency by earning the Global Seal of Biliteracy.[5] An increasing number of colleges award credit or waive second language requirements for students who hold this credential. It's also a valuable certification in the professional world.

Other Courses

Universities with robust general education programs may require additional courses across various subject areas. If you have selected some target universities for transfer, you may be able to take classes that are likely to fulfill their requirements in advance. If you haven't chosen any potential transfer schools yet, it might be difficult to guess which classes will satisfy requirements post-transfer. Be careful about taking courses with no intended goal in mind — you may wind up spending unnecessary time and money on classes that won't apply to the degree you pursue at the next college.

Case Study: California IGETC

The University of California (UC) and California State University (CSU) systems have defined a comprehensive general education sequence for transfer students that is standardized across all thirty-two undergraduate campuses statewide. This eleven-course sequence is called the Intersegmental General Education Transfer Curriculum (IGETC). Although each campus has established its own unique set of GE requirements for first-year entrants, transfer students who choose to complete the full IGETC sequence are exempt from those individual campus GE requirements.

IGETC completion is not required for transfer admission to a UC or CSU, but it can strengthen an application because it shows that the student has finished a comprehensive general education program and is prepared to focus primarily on major requirements upon enrollment at the new university. Such a student is on a clear path to timely degree completion and is therefore an attractive applicant. Acknowledging the strength of the IGETC program, several private colleges in California[6] and non-California public universities[7] now also accept the IGETC and waive GE requirements for transfer students who enter with a complete IGETC sequence.

Even if you have no plans to transfer to a college that recognizes the IGETC, loosely following the general GE guidelines it establishes will likely set you on a strong path for transfer admission while simultaneously encouraging you to explore new academic subjects.

IGETC Subject Area Requirements

- English communication: two classes
- Mathematical concepts and quantitative reasoning: one class

- Arts and humanities: three classes from different areas
- Social and behavioral sciences: two classes from different areas
- Physical and biological sciences: two classes, at least one with a lab
- Language other than English: demonstrated proficiency
- Ethnic studies: one class

Alternative Ways to Fulfill GE Requirements

Traditional college classes aren't the only way to fulfill general education requirements. You may already have completed several GE requirements if you have AP or IB scores from high school! If you want to use tests to start clearing GE requirements now, see if your potential transfer universities accept CLEP credits. You may be able to self-study for a few CLEP exams if they do. Not everyone can effectively self-study, though. Many students benefit from the support and materials available for free through ModernStates.org, a nonprofit organization committed to reducing the cost of college by helping students earn college credit by exam. Online videos, readings, and self-check quizzes help you master the material needed to pass the associated CLEP exam successfully. Upon completion of the free course, ModernStates.org will provide you with a voucher to take the CLEP exam for free.

Another inexpensive way to earn college credits that are likely to fulfill GE requirements is through Study Hall, in collaboration with Crash Course and Arizona State University (ASU).[8] Perhaps you are already familiar with the Crash Course YouTube channel, the brainchild of Hank and John Green. They produce high-quality educational videos on a variety of high school and college subjects. In 2023, Crash Course partnered with ASU to develop videos that align with courses available through the ASU Universal Learner program. After paying a nominal fee to gain access to the class, students can earn college credit by watching YouTube videos and completing assignments and tests from ASU. If they earn a passing grade, they can pay an additional fee to place the course credit on an official ASU transcript. If the class doesn't go well, there is no permanent record of the student's enrollment in the course. It is a risk-free way for students to restart a college career, make up lost credits, and earn transferable college credits that are likely to fulfill many common GE requirements. Just make sure that your target schools accept transfer credits for online courses.

Case Study: Jade

Jade wasn't sure she wanted to go to college. But as all her high school friends began sharing their college acceptances, she decided she wanted to attend after all. Given the timing, Jade had few options available for last-minute applications. She selected a nearby Christian college with a high acceptance rate, applied, and was accepted.

Although Jade had been raised in a Christian family, she was not prepared for the intensely religious atmosphere on campus. And as the months wore on, she became increasingly uncomfortable with the anti-LGBTQ+ rhetoric she heard from her peers. It seemed that many of her fellow students believed that Christianity was incompatible with support for the LGBTQ+ community. As Jade was simultaneously discovering her own queer identity, she felt like an outcast and knew she would not feel safe coming out in that environment. She withdrew.

Several years later, Jade wanted to give college another try. She was nervous about returning to school after more than five years in the workforce. The Universal Learner Courses at Arizona State University (ASU) gave her the opportunity to try online college classes risk-free. Registration was only $25 to start, and she was not obligated to put the class and grade on an official ASU transcript if she didn't want to. If this new college experiment failed, she could simply pretend it never happened, and she would only lose $25. But she did not fail — she thrived!

Jade's confidence continues to grow as she chips away at GE requirements, one class at a time. Buoyed by this success, she is now preparing to transfer to ASU Online as a fully enrolled student so that she can complete her bachelor's degree.

Common Challenges and Questions

I've been studying American Sign Language, but I don't know if that will satisfy the second language requirement when I transfer. What can I do?

Although American Sign Language (ASL) is gaining acceptance as a second language at the college level, many universities still do not allow students to fulfill their second language requirement with ASL. Even if your selected college accepts ASL to fulfill the language requirement, you may have difficulty proving your proficiency. There is no AP or CLEP test for ASL, and many schools do not have ASL instructors on the faculty who can interview students to determine fluency. Ideally, your courses will transfer to the new university and be applied directly to your degree in fulfillment of the world language requirement. If not, the burden is on you to demonstrate your language skills. Investigate ASL testing options, such as the Avant STAMP for ASL assessment or the American Sign Language Proficiency Interview (ASLPI) by Gallaudet University. Ask potential colleges if they will accept one of these tests to fulfill their language requirements.

I have a language-based learning disability and struggle to learn other languages. My second language requirement in high school was waived for this reason. Can I get the second language requirement waived in college?

Probably not, but you may be able to ask for a substitution. Consider seeking out a university that does not have a second language requirement or a school that offers degrees in certain majors that do not require language proficiency — bachelor of science and bachelor of fine arts degrees sometimes fall into this category. If you fall in love with a college that has a second language requirement, peruse the website to see if there is a stated policy on substitutions for language classes. If you don't find a clear policy, contact the disability resource center or accessibility office to inquire. That office cannot guarantee that *you specifically* will get approval for a substitution request, but they may be able to tell you how common such accommodations are at that school.

CHAPTER 11

Majors and Prerequisites

When you apply for transfer admission to a university, you often apply directly to a major or area of concentration. While a few colleges allow transfer students to enter undeclared, they are less common. Low-unit transfers may have more opportunities to apply and enroll without a confirmed major, but junior-level transfer students are almost always expected to have a major in mind and to have completed some prerequisite courses. Students pursuing selective majors must complete many major prerequisites and likely also need a higher-than-average GPA to gain admission to the major. Although the popularity of specific majors varies from school to school, here are a few of the majors most frequently cited as selective.[1]

- Computer science
- Engineering
- Business
- Health (pre-med/nursing)
- Psychology
- Biology

Even if you are planning to transfer into a less competitive major, universities often expect to see some introductory classes in the subject on your transcript if they are available at your current college. Many transfer applications ask students to write short essays about their planned majors and future career interests. Those essays are difficult to write if you have no classes or work experience in the subject area!

Prerequisites for the Major

Universities assume that you will take most of the specialized upper-division classes for your major after you transfer. Each school takes a unique approach to organizing the curriculum for a major, so it's unlikely that you will find the exact same pattern of major coursework at multiple colleges. Unless you can identify preapproved equivalent courses at your current school, it's best to focus on broad major prerequisites.

Prerequisite Details

Remember those articulation agreements from chapter 8? This is where they become really useful. If you are attending a college that has established major pathways, transfer guides, or articulation agreements with four-year universities, you should plan your classes around those approved course maps for your intended major. If you aren't sure where to find such maps, search the internet for the name of your state and "transfer articulation agreements" or "transfer guides." This will bring up statewide databases of articulation agreements, like MassTransfer A2B Pathways for Massachusetts and Assist.org for California.

Read each agreement carefully to make sure you catch all the details! You might find that some prerequisite courses are required for transfer, while others are just recommended. Also, look for a date or year the agreement becomes effective. Sometimes, a new agreement will have been drafted, but students who began their studies earlier can continue using the previous plan so that they don't have to change their class schedules mid-degree.

Deadlines

Pay special attention to deadlines for the completion of required major prerequisites. In most cases, prerequisites simply need to be completed by the end of the term before you intend to transfer. Students can usually apply for transfer with some prerequisite courses for the major in progress or planned for an upcoming semester.

Some selective majors may have earlier deadlines for key prerequisites. For example, impacted nursing programs frequently require students to complete critical science classes like biology and anatomy before submitting a transfer application. In-progress courses may not satisfy the requirements, so students aiming for popular majors might need to focus on required classes for the major early and plan to take some general education requirements during the last term before transfer.

GPA

While there is often an overall minimum GPA required for transfer admission to a university, some majors, particularly in competitive fields like engineering, business, or computer science, may have higher GPA requirements. This could mean an overall higher GPA is required for entry, or it could mean that a separate "major GPA" must be calculated. To determine your major GPA, first research which prerequisite courses the target university includes in the major GPA calculation. Then, check your transcripts for the grades you earned in those classes, and average them according to the instructions in chapter 4 (pages 38–39). Additionally, some colleges require students to earn higher minimum grades in specific classes. For example, a math-heavy science major may require that students earn at least a B in each required calculus class, although the overall university policy states that credits are transferable when the student earns at least a C.

Even if it's not explicitly required, you should focus on excelling in the prerequisite courses for your major to improve your odds of admission. These classes often carry more weight in the admissions decision, and achieving high grades in major coursework demonstrates your dedication to the subject. If you're struggling to maintain a high GPA for your first-choice major, you may want to look for related majors that are less competitive but still align with your interests.

Preparing for Multiple Options

Most students don't apply to just one college unless they are participating in a transfer guarantee program. If you don't have assured admission to a desirable university, you likely want to apply broadly. Transfer admission can be unpredictable, so it's wise to avoid putting all your eggs in one basket. Unfortunately, applying for transfer to multiple institutions complicates the process. Universities frequently have completely different course requirements for entry into the same major. You must start early, plan ahead, and remain flexible.

Overlapping Courses

Start by researching the major requirements at each potential transfer destination, paying close attention to required prerequisite courses, optional courses, GPA requirements, and any specific program admission criteria. Create a comprehensive spreadsheet or chart that compares these requirements side by side, as in the example shown below. (You can also find a downloadable template at TransferSavvy.com/Book to complete your own comparison.)

Requirement	Target University A	Target University B	Target University C
Minimum GPA	2.5	2.0	3.0
Minimum Credits Completed	12 semester credits	24 semester credits	60 semester credits
English Composition	1 course completed or in progress before application	Not required prior to transfer	2 courses completed before enrollment
Math	1 college-level math course completed or in progress before application	Not required prior to transfer	1 college-level math course completed before enrollment
Second Language	Proficiency through second semester college level completed or in progress before application	Not required prior to transfer	Proficiency through third semester college level completed before enrollment
Major Prerequisites (Biology)	Intro to Biology Chemistry 1	Intro to Biology (recommended)	Intro to Biology Calculus 1 Calculus 2 Chemistry 1 Microbiology

Look for courses that satisfy requirements across multiple institutions, prioritizing those that are the most widely accepted. For instance, if five out of six of your prospective universities require organic chemistry, but only two require microbiology, focus on chemistry first. As you move through classes, discover your interests, and earn grades, you might add or remove colleges from this chart. Then, you can choose courses of secondary importance. It's entirely possible that you will not meet all the major requirements for every school. At some point, you may be forced to choose between classes. In that case, select courses required by the schools you favor and the schools that are the most practical to attend.

Double-Duty Major and GE Courses

You can also optimize your transfer process by prioritizing courses that fulfill both general education and major prerequisites whenever possible. As you research the major prerequisites at your target transfer institutions, look for classes at your current college that are also designated as GE courses or seem likely to fulfill GE requirements at your target schools. If you can occasionally check two boxes with one class, your path to transfer becomes much more efficient.

Case Study: Sara

Sara had always wanted to become a nurse. In high school, she even took two dual enrollment classes at her local community college that fulfilled nursing prerequisites to get a head start. She then enrolled in a local university's pre-nursing program, transferred in her dual enrollment credits, and began volunteering at a nearby hospital. She loved nursing, and she was good at it. There was just one problem. Sara's progression from the pre-nursing major to the bachelor of science in nursing (BSN) program was not guaranteed. Sara had to complete an additional nursing application halfway through her undergraduate program to be eligible to continue. Since her university typically received three hundred nursing applications for only twenty-five spots, Sara decided to apply for transfer to other colleges with BSN programs, just in case.

Since nursing is an impacted major at many colleges, the competition for admission is fierce. A successful transfer application requires completion of several nursing-specific prerequisite courses with above-average grades, a passing score on the Test of Essential Academic Skills (TEAS), and evidence of healthcare-related work experience. Each nursing school sets its own requirements and deadlines, so gaining eligibility for transfer to multiple colleges is unusually challenging.

Unfortunately, Sara did not realize that transfer requirements for nursing programs could vary so widely. She followed the recommended path through prerequisites at her current college and assumed that the requirements would be similar at other schools. As she began researching other colleges in-depth, she was disappointed to learn that she was ineligible to apply to several colleges of interest. These particular schools required completion of a microbiology course no later than December of the year prior to transfer. Unfortunately, Sara planned to take that course in the spring, and she was too far into the fall semester to add a course to her schedule.

Sara's list of potential colleges dwindled from an initial fifteen to just four where she was eligible to apply. She submitted her applications, crossed her fingers, and started making backup plans. If she was rejected from all the colleges, including the nursing program at her current school, she had two choices: remain at the current college and complete a different major or take a gap term after completing prerequisites and reapply next year.

Ultimately, Sara was admitted into the full BSN program at her current university and was able to continue her degree without needing to transfer. She withdrew her applications to other colleges and happily committed to completing her degree on her current campus.

Common Challenges and Questions

What if I'm not sure about my major yet?

Some colleges will accept transfer students who apply with "undecided" or "undeclared" majors. However, it is most common for transfer students to apply to a specific major, or at least general department, at the new college. Generally speaking, the more credits you have already earned, the more you are expected to apply to and be prepared for a specific major.

If you find yourself in the position of having to select a major for a transfer application before you feel ready, try to choose a major that interests you and aligns with the classes you have taken so far. The following tools and quizzes online may help you narrow your interests as well:

MyMajors.com
Me3.careers
CareerExplorer.com
O*NET Interest Profiler (see MyNextMove.org/explore/ip)

Research any potential major at your prospective future colleges to make sure there are no additional application requirements that might complicate your transfer process. Also, contact the colleges and ask if it is difficult to change your major after you enroll. Ask about impacted majors and programs for transfer students. There may be some areas of study that can only be accessed by direct entry, such as nursing or computer science. If you are interested in one of those impacted majors, you might need to apply directly to that program to have a chance at studying for that particular degree.

Last, remember that your undergraduate major does not define your entire career. Students often change majors in college and then go to work in completely unrelated fields. Some go to graduate school or earn vocational certificates in a new field to pivot to new careers. The major you choose now is not necessarily in the same subject area as the job you will have for the rest of your life, so don't overthink this choice.

My major requires a yearlong chemistry sequence. I took Chemistry 1 at a community college near my home, but I want to take Chemistry 2 at a different community college near my work. Is that OK?

Be careful! Yearlong sequences may use different textbooks and are not always divided evenly into terms. One college may complete units 1 through 5 in the first semester, while another college begins the second semester with unit 8, leaving you with a knowledge gap. Whenever possible, it's best to complete an entire sequence of courses at the same school. That improves your chances of succeeding in the course and also increases the odds that your next university will accept your credits for transfer. This is especially important if you are considering transfer between schools on the quarter and semester systems. Chemistry 1 at one college combined with Chemistry 2 at a different college will not necessarily add up to a Chemistry A-B-C sequence at a quarter-system university. When in doubt, contact universities of interest to learn about their policies.

CHAPTER 12

Transfer Timeline

You have already read much about two-year community colleges and four-year universities. In reality, the term "four-year university" is a bit of a misnomer. Fewer than 50 percent of entering first-year students complete a bachelor's degree at the same institution in four years,[1] and it's even less common for transfer students, who attend two or more institutions, to earn a bachelor's degree in that timeframe.

At community colleges, many students dream of a "2+2" transfer plan that results in an associate degree after two years, followed by a bachelor's degree two years after transfer. This dream is not impossible to achieve, but it does require careful planning and research from the start.

Students transferring from one four-year university to another may have more difficulty planning an efficient timeline. Because they are more likely to be transferring unexpectedly, these students have less time to prepare. They are also unlikely to be able to take advantage of articulation agreements and other transfer planning tools that can streamline the process.

As you map out a timeline for your transfer plan, consider your college goals and priorities. You may have to choose between needs and wants, or efficiency and enjoyment. You are not in a race to earn your degree. There is no extra credit for finishing college first. Take the time you need (and can afford) to pursue a meaningful journey through your undergraduate education. There is no perfect path through college. Everything requires compromise, and only you can decide what matters most in your educational journey.

"Four-Year" Degree

Let's break down exactly what goes into a typical bachelor's degree to better understand the expectation of completion within four years.

The average bachelor's degree requires approximately 120 semester or 180 quarter units to complete. With two semesters or three quarters in each academic year, taking 15 units each term results in degree completion at the four-year mark. The average student loses about 13 semester credits through the transfer process, which puts the average transfer student half a year behind on the path to a degree. Avoiding credit loss through preplanning, careful school selection, and post-acceptance credit appeals can help keep students on track.

Making up for lost credits is another way to speed up your degree plan. If earning 15 units per semester leads to a 120-unit degree in four years, then what would happen if you took 17 units per semester plus 5 units during each summer? That adds up to 156 units, giving you an extra 36 units of wiggle room. If you take a gap term, participating in one that offers college credit through language learning abroad or a credit-bearing internship can make your "time off" work toward your degree. Taking CLEP tests in areas of interest can give you additional units and potentially fulfill general education requirements at some schools, too. Of course, by now you know that not all credits are equally transferable, but if you choose courses and programs carefully, earning some additional credits will likely give you more flexibility as you proceed along your degree path.

Entry Timing

Some universities only accept transfer applications for fall entry. Others offer transfer students the opportunity to begin study at the start of every term. So when is the ideal time to transfer? There are pros and cons to every option, and the best answer for you depends on your personal circumstances.

Fall Entry

Many universities offer only fall admission for good reason: Fall is often the best time to transition to a new college.

138   Planning

Socially, it's easier to meet other students in the fall. First-year students are eager to make new friends as they arrive for orientations and dorm move-in. Continuing students have been busy with a variety of activities over the summer and are returning to campus with fresh enthusiasm. With housing assignments shuffled at the start of the academic year, suitemates and floormates are beginning to bond in their new living spaces. New faculty members and graduate students are also joining the community.

Whether the college offers transfer-specific orientations or includes transfers in the first-year orientations, programming is usually more robust in the fall when a greater number of students enter. Similarly, student clubs and teams usually recruit new members primarily in the fall. Integrating into the campus community is easier on multiple levels.

Academically, fall is often the best time to begin study at a college because sequenced courses usually begin during the first term of the year. Large universities may offer the first class of a sequence during every term, but smaller schools may only be able to offer each level once per year. For example, if you must take Physics 1 as a prerequisite before enrolling in Physics 2, you may only be able to complete the full sequence during a single year if you begin in the fall.

Winter or Spring Entry

Acceptance rates for winter or spring terms can be higher or lower depending on the school and intended major. Sometimes, midyear acceptance rates are simply inconsistent and unpredictable. Consider contacting the admissions office or a transfer counselor at a target college to ask about the differences in historical acceptance rates.

Transfer applications for winter or spring terms are usually due in the fall. If you are in your first year of college and wish to transfer to a new school for the coming winter or spring term, your first-term college course grades will most likely not be available to include with your application, so universities will need to base their admissions decisions on your high school records. Students attempting to transfer from one four-year to another at this stage might also raise concerns in the admissions office — a student who wants to leave a college so soon after arriving may not have the tenacity to succeed at the new institution either.

Also, many new friendships are formed during the fall term. By January, roommates and housemates have settled into routines, study groups have been meeting for months, and newcomers might find it difficult to break into social circles. Even the most extroverted students can struggle to make friends when it seems that everyone else already knows each other. That said, midyear entry may be necessary for students who have run out of useful classes to take at their current college and want to continue making progress toward a degree.

Summer Entry

Joining a new university during the summer term comes with its own set of benefits and challenges. It can offer a gentle transition for some. Summer classes typically have smaller sizes, which allows new students to interact more with professors and peers. Since fewer students are on campus during the summer, it can be easier for new transfers to learn how to navigate the campus and access facilities in this calmer environment. However, this reduced campus population also has a potential downside: fewer students to interact with. Summer terms are often condensed as well. Classes that might be spread over twelve to sixteen weeks in a regular semester might run for only six to eight weeks in the summer. If a new student enrolls in too many challenging classes, it can be easy to feel overwhelmed.

Gap Term

As you weigh your options for application deadlines and entry terms, consider incorporating a gap term into your timeline. Taking a semester or quarter away from traditional college classes can be particularly useful if your completion of transfer preparation doesn't align with your planned entry to a new university. For example, if you are on track to complete an associate degree in December but prefer to enter your new university for the fall term, a spring gap semester might allow you to continue working toward your education and career goals through an internship or language immersion program. It might also provide a much-needed break after years of hard work to become transfer-ready.

Sample Transfer Timelines

Every student's timeline is unique, but here are a few sample timelines for common transfer scenarios.

California Community College to University of California Planned Transfer

YEAR ONE	
Summer	• Enroll in community college. • Send AP/IB scores and dual enrollment transcripts to community college and request that credits be added to your community college transcript. • Register for fall classes, prioritizing English and Math in the first year.
Fall	• Meet with a CC adviser to learn more about GE requirements, associate degrees, and transfer guarantee programs. • Create a tentative two-year CC plan. • Create your Transfer Admission Planner (TAP) account. • Save all course syllabi.
Spring	• Meet with an adviser to review progress on GE requirements. • Using the tools at Assist.org, select GE classes that also satisfy prerequisites for potential majors of interest. • Take a full course load (usually at least 12 units) and improve or maintain your GPA.
YEAR TWO	
Summer	• Consider taking a summer course to ensure that all transfer prerequisites can be met on time. • Update your TAP account.
Fall	• Meet with an adviser to make sure you are on track to complete the requirements for your planned transfer pathway. • Apply for a Transfer Admission Guarantee (TAG). • Apply for UC admission.

Spring	• Submit the Transfer Academic Update [a requirement specific to California state schools] online in January. • Apply for graduation with associate degree. • Meet with an academic adviser to have completion of your GE plan formally approved.

YEAR THREE	
Summer	• Review your admission offers and select the UC campus you wish to attend. • Submit your Statement of Intent to Register (SIR) and deposit. • Apply for housing. • Attend transfer orientation. • Send official copies of all transcripts and test scores to UC.
Fall	• Begin classes at the UC! • Meet with your new adviser to create a plan for degree completion. • Review your UC transcript to ensure that all transferable courses and credits have been correctly documented.
Spring	• Continue working on required coursework. • Meet regularly with your adviser.

WHEN READY
• Apply for graduation when you near completion of your degree. • Celebrate your achievements!

142   Planning

Lateral Four-Year to Four-Year University Unplanned Sophomore Transfer

YEAR ONE	
Fall	• Begin classes at first university with an open mind. • Join clubs, participate in activities, attend office hours, and maintain GPA. • Save all course syllabi.
Winter	• Consider the pros and cons of sophomore-level transfer. • Review transfer eligibility requirements at colleges of interest.
Spring	• Apply for transfer. • Request letters of recommendation from current professors. • Check applicant portals and upload or request required documents as needed. • Review admission offers, transfer credit evaluations, and financial aid offers. • Submit Statement of Intent to Register (SIR) and deposit. • Apply for housing. • Withdraw from current university.
YEAR TWO	
Summer	• Confirm on- or off-campus housing. • Send final official transcripts and test scores. • Attend transfer orientation.
Fall	• Meet with your new adviser to create a plan for degree completion. • Review your new transcript to ensure that all transferable courses and credits have been correctly documented.
Spring	• Continue working on required coursework. • Meet regularly with your adviser.
WHEN READY	

- Apply for graduation when you near completion of your degree.
- Celebrate your achievements!

Swirling Due to Academic Suspension at Four-Year University

ORIGINAL UNIVERSITY	
Initial term	• Academic warning from university.
Subsequent term	• Academic suspension from university.
When ready	• Enroll in community college, full- or part-time as needed to establish success.
COMMUNITY COLLEGE	
Term 1	• Send official transcripts and test scores to community college and request that transferable credit be added to your CC transcript. • Meet with a CC academic adviser to select appropriate courses. • Seek courses that are equivalent or similar to those failed at original university. • Save all course syllabi.
Term 2	• Work up to a full load (typically 12 or more units) while improving GPA. • Prioritize math and English courses, in addition to repeating previously failed courses. • Meet regularly with CC adviser to select courses and plan for transfer. • Consider transfer options: Will you be a strong candidate after just one term of CC classes? • Consider applying for reinstatement at original university as an alternative to transfer.
Term 3 and beyond, as needed	• Continue working toward a strong GPA and full-time course load to demonstrate transfer readiness. • Research universities of interest with admitted student profiles in your GPA and credit range.

When ready	• Apply for transfer. • Request transcripts from *all* colleges and universities, including the original dismissing university. • Request letters of recommendation from current CC instructors. • Check applicant portals and upload or request required documents as needed. • Review admission offers, transfer credit evaluations, and financial aid offers. • Submit Statement of Intent to Register (SIR) and deposit. • Apply for housing. • Attend orientation.
NEW UNIVERSITY	
Term 1	• Meet with your new adviser to create a plan for degree completion. • Review your new transcript to ensure that all transferable courses and credits have been correctly documented.
Term 2	• Continue working on required coursework. • Meet regularly with your adviser.
When ready	• Apply for graduation when you near completion of your degree. • Celebrate your achievements!

Case Study: Eva

Colorado native Eva had always dreamed of attending an elite liberal arts college in the Northeast, but when her father was diagnosed with terminal cancer, she knew she wouldn't be happy living so far away from him. Instead of applying early to colleges in the fall of her senior year, she took the GED and dropped out of high school to spend as much time as possible with her dad. She then enrolled in her local community college to keep moving forward with her education.

Although her dad's timeline was uncertain, Eva wanted to begin applying to four-year schools right away so she could transfer at the sophomore level. As long as her dad held on, she wanted to be by his side. But she also wanted to be prepared to move on to the next phase of her life as soon as he passed. Ultimately, she applied to nine selective liberal arts schools and was admitted to seven of them. She accepted a space at her dream school in May, with plans to begin her studies that fall. Miraculously, though, her father's health stabilized over the summer, and doctors predicted that he would live for several more months — well into Eva's first term away at school.

Eva submitted a deferral request to her new college, which was quickly granted. Understanding her extraordinary situation, the college administrators tried to be as flexible as possible to offer Eva what she needed during a difficult time. They also granted Eva's request to continue taking community college classes during her deferral period. So Eva enrolled in a couple of courses to keep her mind active while she waited for the inevitable.

When her father succumbed to cancer in late December, Eva didn't feel ready to hop on a plane in just a couple of weeks to begin a new adventure. Instead, she extended her deferral and took a gap semester in the spring. She needed time to grieve and heal, but she also traveled and immersed herself in the Spanish language and South American cultures. By August, she felt ready to begin the East Coast liberal arts education she had long imagined. Although she was a year older than most of her fellow sophomores, Eva embraced her unique path and timeline, approaching life and academics at her own pace and savoring each experience along the way.

Common Challenges and Questions

Should I finish an associate degree before I transfer, even if that means staying longer at a community college?

This answer depends on the type of associate degree and the transfer agreements your community college has made with universities. Strong transfer-focused associate degree programs offer many of the following benefits at partner universities:

- Guaranteed transfer admission
- Guaranteed transfer of credits
- Automatic completion of GE requirements
- Direct entry into intended major
- Priority consideration of application

If the associate degree you are working toward does not include any of these benefits, it may not be worth staying longer at the community college just to complete the degree. Consider a few additional factors:

- The transferability of individual courses required for the associate degree — don't accrue useless credits!
- The value of an associate degree in your intended career for the short term, before you earn your bachelor's degree, or in the event that your circumstances change and you don't ultimately complete a bachelor's
- Availability of fall and spring transfer admission opportunities

It's also important to note that the 2024 Community College Research Center's Tracking Transfer reports revealed a positive correlation between completion of associate degrees and bachelor's degrees. More research is needed to determine if associate degree completion actually *causes* students to be more likely to persist until they attain a bachelor's degree,[2] but it's worth taking this data point into consideration as you make your decision.

If I don't get in this semester, I can just apply for next semester, right?

Maybe, maybe not. Some universities have policies that limit the number of times you can apply within a stated timeframe. For example, Brown University states that "Transfer students may only submit one application per intended calendar year of entry."[3] In other words, if you apply to Brown for January transfer admission and are not admitted, you will be ineligible to apply for September admission of that same year. On the other hand, if you are not admitted to the fall term, you *may* reapply for spring admission because the spring term begins in January of the following calendar year. In this case, you might not want to rush into a Brown application for the spring semester if you would be a better candidate by the time applications are due for fall.

Virginia Tech has a completely different policy: "Students may apply for Spring term admission and subsequently for Summer OR Fall term admission in the same cycle, but should not apply for both Summer and Fall."[4] Applying to Virginia Tech for spring entry does not disqualify you from applying for the very next term, as long as you don't apply to both summer and fall of the same year.

Also, remember that many universities only offer transfer admission once a year, in the fall.

PART V

APPLICATION

You've planned. You've prepared. Now it's time to actually apply! But how? Let's break the transfer application down into three main steps:

1. **Data entry:** You will need to type in a lot of information about yourself, your previous school(s), your outside activities, and so on. This part is tedious, but it isn't especially difficult.
2. **Writing:** This is your opportunity to describe your educational journey. You may need to write one long essay, several short essays, or maybe a combination of the two. If you dislike talking

150   Application

about yourself, this part may make you feel uncomfortable, but a variety of tactics can help you successfully approach this task.

3. **Additional documentation:** Most colleges will request formal proof of your academic abilities and character. At this stage, you may need to request recommendation letters, official transcripts, and other bits of paperwork. The hardest part of this task is keeping everything organized and double-checking that important documents are delivered.

The three chapters in this section will help you work through each of these steps. Remember to be honest, thorough, and accurate throughout the application process. Be careful now to avoid problems later.

CHAPTER 13

Data Entry

To begin the application process, you must first find out how each of your desired colleges accepts transfer applications. Many colleges use a third-party service, such as the Common App or the Coalition App. States with large university networks, like California and Texas, may use state-specific applications. Some colleges create their own transfer application forms and host them on their individual websites. If you are applying for reentry to a college you previously attended, there may be a special application for that purpose. Check each college's website to learn which application system(s) they use.

Just because a college uses a particular application service for first-year admission does not mean it uses the same service for transfer admission! Don't assume — check the college websites to be sure.

If a college offers multiple options, choose the format you like best — colleges review all transfer applications equally. If you are planning on applying to multiple schools, look for the system that hosts a majority of schools that interest you — storing all of your educational data in one place can save you time and keep you organized.

Next, create an account with each service you plan to use this application season. Consider acquiring a new email address just for this purpose. It can be helpful to know exactly where all your college communications will land and then check that mailbox often. Maybe even set up automatic forwarding to a friend or family member who is helping you with the application process to ensure that nothing is overlooked. Be sure to check spam folders occasionally, too — you never know what might be incorrectly marked as spam.

Last, keep a list of important application websites with your usernames and passwords. You can use an app to save passwords, if you like, or simply write everything down on paper and store that document somewhere safe.

Now, go get all those transcripts you analyzed in chapter 3! It's time to put them to use.

Application Forms

Third-Party Applications

More than six hundred universities in the US use the Common App for transfer students, so that is a great place to start. As the name implies, the Common App allows students to answer certain questions that a majority of college transfer applications have in common. These questions cover basic personal data, such as name, birthdate, home address, previously attended schools, and so on. There may also be optional sections for entering specific coursework and standardized test scores. Some colleges require these sections, and others do not. Once you have selected all the colleges to which you wish to apply (called "programs" within the Common App), the application form will clearly state whether or not these sections are necessary.

If you used the Common App to apply for first-year admission, you might wonder if your data can just roll over into the Common App for transfer. As of this writing, the first-year Common App and the Common App for transfer are entirely separate systems, and no data is shared between the two.

The Coalition for College also offers a centralized application form, but Coalition member schools are significantly less common. Unlike the Common App, the Coalition App has tight integration between its first-year and transfer applications. A series of questions at the start will determine your status and conveniently direct you to the transfer portions of the application if you meet the transfer criteria defined by each Coalition school.

Students interested in applying to Historically Black Colleges and Universities (HBCUs) should check out the Common Black College Application (CBCA). This application allows students to apply to over sixty member institutions for one low application fee. The CBCA is similar to the Coalition App, in that it has a single application for both first-year and transfer students. Students identify themselves as transfers early in the application and then list their top four preferred college choices. Ultimately, the application will be shared with all member institutions, so students may receive admission offers from a number of HBCUs.

It's extremely rare for a student to need accounts with all three of these application services. Nearly every college that accepts the Coalition App also accepts the Common App, for example. Check your colleges of interest and see if a majority accept one or the other. Most students end up completing the Common App along with some state- or school-specific applications. However, colleges can change their application processes each season, so check the college websites when you are ready to apply. A school that used the Common App last year might be using the Coalition App this year!

Statewide Application Hubs

Some larger states with numerous universities offer a central hub for applications. For example, ApplyTexas allows prospective students to use a single account to apply to any Texas public university or community college as well as several private colleges. It's a one-stop shop for higher education within the state of Texas! Many of these Texas colleges are on the Common App or Coalition App as well.

California has three statewide college application systems. The state's 116 community colleges are available through CCCApply. Students who are interested in the California State University system can use Cal State Apply. Finally, the nine University of California undergraduate campuses accept the UC application. All three groups of California campuses are generally not accessible via any other application system.

The State University of New York (SUNY) has a single application that students can use to apply to most SUNY campuses, with a few exceptions. The City University of New York (CUNY) also has a common application for all CUNY campuses. These systems are unique because they include both two-year community colleges and four-year universities. So some students may end up using the same application to apply for transfer that they used to enter a community college originally.

You don't have to be a resident of Texas, California, or New York to use these statewide application hubs. While some of the application sections might be specialized to allow state residents to more easily enter state-specific information, anyone can apply via these forms.

Individual School Applications

Some colleges host their own individual applications on their websites, either in addition to or instead of using a centralized application service. If a college only accepts transfer applications via its own website, students must complete that web form to apply. Schools that also participate in a common application service provide students with a choice. Often, an individual college application form on a college's website is simpler than a common program that must accommodate a multitude of questions to satisfy all member institutions. Therefore, students applying to just one or two schools may find completing each individual college application more straightforward than using a central application service. Conversely, students applying to several schools will likely discover that a common application form is more efficient. Colleges review all application submissions equally, so students should choose the application path that suits them best.

Third-Party Mobile Application: Edvisorly

Edvisorly is a free mobile application designed specifically for community college students planning to transfer to a four-year university. It includes numerous features to help students assess their transcripts, plan class schedules to meet selected goals, explore transfer-friendly universities, and chat with university representatives. Several universities have also opted to participate in Edvisorly's mobile application process, which allows students to quickly send their application details to universities of interest. Even better, Edvisorly leverages AI to analyze uploaded college transcripts to simplify and expedite credit transfer evaluation.

Direct Admissions

In recent years, colleges have begun experimenting with direct admissions, which flips the traditional college admissions model upside down. Instead of applying to multiple universities, students can create searchable profiles and express interest in certain types of schools. Then colleges can proactively offer admission (and sometimes scholarships) to students who match the school's eligibility requirements and enrollment priorities. Some states, such as Minnesota and Idaho, have taken direct admissions a step further by skipping the student profile requirement. In these states, colleges automatically offer guaranteed admission to students who meet certain GPA requirements. Although it is still in an experimental phase, direct admissions is growing in popularity for first-year applicants. Transfer students have not been included in these initial pilot programs so far, but organizations like Niche are actively working to develop a direct admissions platform for transfer. After seeing how successful direct admissions programs have been for first-year applicants, many universities are eager to implement similar programs for transfer students.

Common Data Entry

Now that you have identified the application form(s) you need, it's time to start entering the common data that most colleges will request.

Contact Information

The exact wording may vary, but every college will want some basic information about you: name, email, phone number, address, and so on. These kinds of questions are pretty straightforward and serve practical purposes. For example, you may be asked to enter your address and, optionally, your *permanent* address. What's the difference? Well, if you are currently attending a university and live in the residence halls, you may want your dorm address to be used for any urgent documents. But how long will you live there? It would be wise to include a secondary address (perhaps a family home to which you return regularly) for future communications.

Snail mail is probably not your primary form of communication, though. Your email and phone number will be used much more frequently. So some questions will likely ask you to give permission for college representatives to contact you via these methods. If you communicate by text frequently, be sure to check the box to allow colleges to send text messages to your cellphone so you don't miss important alerts!

Personal Details

Some questions may feel invasive — sex, gender, race, religion, income level, and so on. Why do colleges need to know? Are the answers really that important? It depends. Colleges are required to collect some demographic information so that they can file federal reports about the general makeup of the campus population each year. Admissions officers may not even see many of these details about you. Other responses may be used to better understand who you are as a three-dimensional person or help colleges select candidates who satisfy their current institutional priorities and increase the variety of students enrolled in their programs.

Family Background

Colleges may also want to know about your family and the levels of education that your parents and other close relatives have attained. If you are applying to a school that a family member previously attended, you may have legacy status. If you are the first in your family to attend college, you might receive some special support for first-generation applicants.

Depending on your age, details about your parents may also affect your residency status and eligibility for financial aid. Traditionally aged college students are usually considered financially dependent on their parents, so changes in parental income or state residency can affect student eligibility for financial aid and state-based tuition discounts. Read carefully and consult your parents if you are unsure of the correct answers in this section.

Academic History

Do you have those transcripts handy? You will need to reference them as you work through this section. You might want to ask a friend or family member to help you as you enter schools, classes, credits, and grades. A second person can double-check your work to help you avoid errors while also alleviating some of the boredom of data entry. Consider having your friend read off courses from your transcript as you type them in or vice versa, then switch roles and check your work.

High School

As a transfer student, you might think that high school is irrelevant. Maybe it is, but you still need to answer each question fully. College admissions officers will decide whether or not your high school records are relevant. Some colleges just want to know when you graduated from high school or earned a GED. Other colleges may evaluate high school transcripts in conjunction with college transcripts, especially when considering low-unit transfers who have short college records.

Colleges Attended

List every college you attended, no matter how brief your enrollment. If you took college classes as a dual-enrolled student during high school, include those colleges here as well. For each school, start typing the name slowly and see what appears in the drop-down list. Carefully scroll through the options and ensure you select the *exact* school you attended. Many colleges have multiple campuses in different cities and online, so verify both the name of the college and the location provided.

Below is an example for Arizona State University in the Common App. If this student attended the main ASU campus in Tempe, Arizona, the second option from the top would be the correct one.

* **What college or university did you attend?**

arizona state

ARIZONA STATE UNIVERSITY - DOWNTOWN PHOENIX ...
Arizona, United States

ARIZONA STATE UNIVERSITY - TEMPE
Arizona, United States

ARIZONA STATE UNIVERSITY AT THE WEST CAMPUS ...
Arizona, United States

ARIZONA STATE UNIVERSITY POLYTECHNIC CAMPUS ...
Arizona, United States

⑦ Can't find your school?

It's rare for a college not to be listed in application drop-down menus such as this. If you have searched for a college and cannot find it, double-check your spelling, then try variations on the name. Is it St. Mary's or Saint Mary's? Berkeley or Berklee? Miami University or University of Miami? In the very unusual event that a college you attended is truly not listed in the drop-down, select the option labeled "Can't find your school?" or similar to manually enter the name and location of the school you attended.

Courses and Grades

Some schools require students to enter every class from every college ever attended. Before you begin typing in each and every detail, check to be sure your prospective colleges actually require this information. If they do, set aside plenty of time to complete this step slowly and accurately. The colleges that request this section will use your input to evaluate your preparedness for transfer to their institutions. However, when it is time to enroll, they will require you to send a final official transcript directly from the college(s). The courses, grades, and credits on that official transcript *must* match your course and grade entries on your application. Any discrepancies will likely trigger an audit, which could lead to the college revoking your admission offer.

If you have attended multiple colleges, your most recent college transcript probably lists classes you took elsewhere and then transferred in. Do not enter these courses in the section for your most recent college. Each college you attended will have a separate section on the application for courses taken at that school. It's best to copy your courses and grades from the original transcript created by the college where you took the courses. The college that accepted your transfer credits probably didn't include the grade you originally earned and may have adapted the course names and credits to align with their own terminology.

Here is an example from a transcript listing a psychology class taken online at the University of Phoenix. On the original transcript, the class is listed as "Psy/205T Life Span Human Development" with a grade of A-, as shown on the next page.

Mo/Year	Course ID	Course Title	Grade	Credits Attempted	Credits Earned	Quality Points
UNIVERSITY OF PHOENIX						
11/2020	PSY/205T	Life Span Human Development	A-	3.00	3.00	11.01

When the student transferred that class to his local community college, the registrar added it to the student's transcript as "Psych 116 Developmental Psych: Lifespan," which is the name of an equivalent course at the community college. Instead of A-, the grade listed here is T for Transfer.

Applied Toward School - Arts, Hum & Soc Sci Program
Institution: Univ Phoenix

Course		Description	GR	UE
PSYCH	116	Developmental Psych: Lifespan	T	3.00
		Transfer Totals:		3.00

During the transfer application process, the student did not include this psychology class as part of his community college record. Instead, he had a separate entry in that section for the University of Phoenix and entered Psy/205T with a grade of A-.

In-Progress and Planned Courses

Your future college also wants to know which classes you are currently taking as well as which classes you plan to take in future terms prior to your transfer date. Read the application instructions carefully to find the correct place to list these classes. Most applications will instruct students to list current and future courses alongside completed courses, simply replacing the grade with IP for In-progress and P (or PL) for Planned.

If you are not currently taking any college classes, that's OK, too! As long as you have enough completed credits to meet the college's minimum transfer requirements, you can safely skip this section.

160   Application

Test Scores

To test or not to test? Many colleges were test-optional for transfer students long before Covid-19 made test-optional admissions a more standard practice. However, even if test scores aren't required for admission, some transfer students might wish to share their scores anyway. Strong standardized test scores can not only help students gain admission but also provide proof of subject mastery, indicate language fluency, or determine placement in a leveled course series, such as math.

High School Tests

The SAT and ACT are the most commonly required tests in first-year admissions, but some colleges have introduced more flexible test policies that allow students to submit scores from other testing programs in lieu of the SAT or ACT. Yale's recently revised test policy for both first-year and transfer applicants states:

YALE'S TEST-FLEXIBLE POLICY

Yale requires all first-year and transfer applicants to submit standardized test scores. Applicants choose which scores to include from four options:

- ACT
- Advanced Placement (AP)
- International Baccalaureate (IB)
- SAT

Applicants who choose to meet the requirement with AP or IB scores should include results from all subject exams completed prior to applying. Applicants who choose to meet the requirement with ACT or SAT scores may also include any AP or IB scores of their choosing.[1]

In this case, applicants can choose which tests to use to fulfill Yale's testing requirements. However, if you didn't take any of these exams while you were a high school student, it might be challenging to access them after graduation. For example, AP and IB tests can only be scheduled through high schools where students typically take the corresponding classes. Students of any age are eligible to register for exams directly with the ACT and SAT organizations, but the testing sites are often high schools filled with teenagers. Understandably, transfer students may feel uncomfortable testing in these environments. If test requirements present a barrier to admission for you, don't be afraid to contact the college's admissions office and ask if your application can be considered without test scores. Sometimes colleges make exceptions for students applying to specific programs designed for nontraditional students, those who have earned a minimum number of college credits, or students with especially high college GPAs.

Other Subject Exams

Transfer applications often have additional spaces for students to enter test scores from other kinds of exams. For example, since transfer students frequently take CLEP exams, most applications will provide a space to enter CLEP scores. Although the SAT Subject tests (previously known as SAT II) have been discontinued, students returning to college after an absence may have old scores on file with the College Board. International students, even if they have been studying at a US university, may be asked to submit TOEFL or IELTS scores to prove English fluency. There are so many academic exams available — no application could possibly list them all individually. However, if you have taken a test that is not listed and you think your score accurately represents your academic potential, you should feel free to enter it on your application in one of the additional information boxes.

Choosing to Submit Scores

When given the opportunity to select specific test scores to send, or none at all, do a little research first. Search for reports of the average test scores submitted by successful applicants to that school. Sometimes these details can be found in a college's "admitted student profile" or Common Data Set. If your scores are above average for that test, submitting your scores will likely improve your chances of admission. If your scores are below average, it might be better to apply test-optional or, if required, send only the highest scores you have available.

162 Application

If you can't find useful historical data on the average test scores of admitted students, think about how your scores will look within the context of your overall application. Do test scores support your application or detract from it? If you think your GPA is not an accurate reflection of your abilities, strong test scores can show your potential. Conversely, if you are a straight-A student but suffer from test anxiety, admissions officers could wonder if comparatively low exam scores mean that your GPA is simply a result of grade inflation. Don't agonize over this decision, though. Remember that no single factor will make or break your application.

Extracurriculars: Experiences and Achievements

What do you do outside the classroom? Anything beyond your regular academic work counts as an extracurricular activity. You are more than just your GPA. Colleges want to know who you are as a complete person. Although the activity list is not nearly as important for transfer as it is for first-year admissions, it still offers a chance to share some pieces of your life that make you the interesting, complex individual you are and give potential colleges a glimpse of the student they might invite to campus.

The extracurricular section also helps admissions officers understand your classes and grades in context. A student who maintains a high GPA while working thirty hours a week probably has a strong work ethic and great executive function skills. That student's GPA is even more meaningful with this added context. That doesn't mean a heavy list of activities will excuse low grades, though. A student who becomes overburdened with commitments to multiple school clubs, sports teams, and music ensembles isn't showing mastery of important college-ready skills like time management and prioritization.

Your Extracurricular Timeline

Think back through the last couple of years. Which activities have been most influential or meaningful for you? Where have you spent the most time? Which experiences shaped you or led you to your planned career? If you were active in high school activities, it might be tempting to list your accomplishments in varsity sports or student government.

However, if you have been out of high school for more than a year or two, colleges don't care as much about your high school activities and awards. They want to know more about who you are now, so stay focused on the post–high school years. If you are a recent high school graduate and feel that an activity or honor from your senior year is especially impressive or relevant, it might make sense to describe it in this section, but only if you have plenty of space.

Describing Activities and Experiences

Each activity or experience entered on your application must include a few important details. Usually, you will be presented with a drop-down menu to categorize the activity as employment, volunteer work, family responsibility, and so on. The form will then ask for information about the organization, your role, and dates of participation. Don't worry if your activity wasn't part of a formal organization. It's OK to put "independent" or "family" as the organization if that makes the most sense. Then provide a brief description of the activity and your responsibilities. Be sure to mention any examples of your leadership, growth, and achievements related to this activity. Think of the description as an entry on your résumé — use strong verbs and focus on "transferable skills" that might indicate your ability to succeed in college or a future career.

Describing Honors and Achievements

Most transfer applications also have a section for students to enter any awards or honors they may have received. If this doesn't apply to you, it's OK to skip this section. Not everyone has access to the kinds of activities that lead to public recognition of their achievements. However, if you have won an award, published an essay or research paper, made the dean's list, or joined an honor society like Phi Theta Kappa, this is your chance to shine. Don't be shy!

The description boxes for these activities can be quite short — often between three hundred and six hundred characters. It can be difficult to visualize how little space you have to explain your achievements, so you might find the downloadable worksheets available at TransferSavvy.com/Book helpful. These worksheets include filler text

164   Application

of the maximum correct character counts so you can clearly see the limited space you will have to write your descriptions.

Letters of Recommendation

Not all colleges require or even accept letters of recommendation. Be sure to follow the application guidelines and submit only what the college requests. If the college requires two letters of recommendation, don't send three. You may think you will impress the college with extra support, but in reality, the college will assume you didn't read carefully or don't care about following the rules.

Academic Recommendations

When a college wants to read letters of recommendation, they most likely want to know what past teachers and professors thought of your academic potential. If you are currently enrolled in (or just recently left) a college, ask some of your favorite instructors if they would be willing to write strong letters of recommendation for you. The best academic recommendations will probably come from instructors who taught you in multiple classes, gave you high grades, and/or seemed to enjoy speaking with you during office hours or after class.

At some universities, students have very little individual contact with their professors. Standing at the front of a five-hundred-seat lecture hall does not give a professor the opportunity to get to know students well on a personal level. Such large classes usually have teaching assistants (TAs) who interact with students in smaller discussion sections and grade student papers. If you have developed a good relationship with one of your TAs, it is perfectly OK to request a recommendation letter from them. A strong personalized recommendation letter from a graduate student TA is better than an impersonal form letter from a lecture professor.

Professional or Other Recommendations

In some cases, a college may offer the opportunity to submit non-academic letters of recommendation. If you have been in the workforce, consider having a supervisor or business owner write a letter that describes your skills and work ethic. If you have been involved in community service or an ongoing hobby or pastime, perhaps a fellow volunteer or organizer can vouch for your abilities. However, potential recommenders outside the world of higher education may not know how to write a proper college letter of recommendation. You may need to help them understand their role in your transfer application process by providing them with sample letters and instructions for submission. You can find some examples and templates at TransferSavvy.com/Book.

Timeline

Ask for recommendations *early*! As soon as you know you are planning to apply for transfer, begin asking prospective recommenders if they are willing to write letters for you. Ideally, you should aim to provide your recommenders with four to six weeks of lead time for writing. However, some instructors, managers, and colleagues who are eager to support you will be willing to write a letter when asked at least two weeks in advance. Last-minute requests are frowned upon.

Once you know who is willing to write your letters, ask them what you can do to make their task easier. Offer to provide a copy of your résumé, a written explanation of your desire to transfer, or a list of memorable projects and activities you completed under the recommender's guidance. Some seasoned recommenders will ask you specific questions and might even give you a form or worksheet to complete so that they will know exactly what to say about you.

FERPA and Privacy

Do not ask to see the completed recommendation letter! If the writer wants to provide you with a copy of that letter, you may graciously accept. You should be prepared for these letters to go directly to the college admissions office without ever reading them yourself. In fact, when you enter the names and emails of your recommenders on the application, you will probably be asked to waive your FERPA (Family Educational Rights and Privacy Act) rights or your right of access. Signing this waiver means that you will not be able to review the recommendation letters or other confidential materials in your application. It is possible to say no to the waiver question, but many recommenders will refuse to write letters without this waiver on file. Furthermore, prospective colleges like to know that the letters they receive are authentic and truthful. The lack of a signed waiver can raise concerns about the legitimacy of the recommendation.

Disciplinary Questions

As you move through your transfer application, you may encounter questions about disciplinary violations and/or criminal history. Both the Common App and Coalition for College have removed such questions from their core applications in an attempt to increase college access and equity. However, individual colleges may still include questions about applicants' prior experiences with high school and college disciplinary action, as well as interactions within the larger criminal justice system.

Because each college writes its discipline questions independently, you may find that the phrasing is unique for each school. It is important that you read the exact wording carefully and answer honestly. Let's look at a few examples.

School Discipline

Some colleges continued using the same school discipline question that had initially appeared in the Common App or Coalition App. For example, the Brown University transfer application uses an abbreviated version of the former Common App question:

> Have you ever been found responsible for a disciplinary violation at any educational institution you have attended from the 9th grade (or the international equivalent) forward, whether related to academic misconduct or behavioral misconduct, that resulted in a disciplinary action?

New York University, on the other hand, completely rewrote the question to focus primarily on violence and physical harm:

> Have you ever been found guilty of or responsible for a disciplinary violation, or withdrawn with disciplinary charges pending, at your previous high school, college,

or university for any act, including attempted acts, involving violence, physical force or the threat of physical force, a sexual offense, stalking, use or possession of a weapon, kidnapping, arson, any hate or bias incident, harassment, hazing, or any offense which caused or attempted to cause physical harm to another person?

Notice that Brown's question includes academic misconduct, but NYU's does not. A student who had been found guilty of academic dishonesty, such as cheating on an exam or plagiarizing a paper, would mark "yes" for Brown but "no" for NYU. A student who was disciplined for physical violence would need to mark "yes" in both applications.

Criminal History

Similarly, some colleges continue to use the same criminal history question that was previously included in the main portion of the Common App or Coalition App. Berry College, for example, still uses the exact same wording:

Have you ever been adjudicated guilty or convicted of a misdemeanor or felony? Note that you are not required to answer "yes" to this question, or provide an explanation, if the criminal adjudication or conviction has been expunged, sealed, annulled, pardoned, destroyed, erased, impounded, or otherwise required by law or ordered by a court to be kept confidential.

Harvard's application has a much more detailed question that allows applicants to withhold information about convictions under certain circumstances:

Have you ever been convicted of, or pled guilty or no contest to, any felony or misdemeanor, other than:

- An arrest or other detention that did not result in a conviction, or in which a conviction was vacated;
- A first conviction for any of the following misdemeanors: drunkenness, simple assault, speeding, minor traffic violations, affray or disturbance of the peace; or

168   Application

- Any misdemeanor conviction that occurred more than five years before your application for admission, unless you were also sentenced to imprisonment, or were convicted of any additional offense within the five year period.

Note that you are not required to answer "yes" to this question, or provide an explanation, if the criminal adjudication or conviction has been expunged, sealed, annulled, pardoned, destroyed, erased, impounded, or otherwise ordered by a court to be kept confidential.

The first question from Berry is very broad. Almost any run-in with the law would need to be disclosed, no matter how minor. Harvard's question is much more nuanced. First offenses and older convictions for common misdemeanors can be overlooked. Harvard is mainly concerned about recent or repeated infractions.

Both of these examples include a note that students are not required to disclose criminal history if the conviction has been expunged, as is common in cases involving juveniles. If a court record has been sealed, the student is not obligated to acknowledge or explain the situation. If there are any questions about the terms of a conviction or court record, it's best to consult a lawyer before submitting an answer to any criminal history question.

Provide an Explanation

Answering "yes" to a school disciplinary or criminal history question will reveal a text box to allow the student to provide details about the incident and surrounding circumstances. It's best to start with a straightforward explanation of the facts. Try to remain neutral and describe the situation objectively — this is not an opportunity to protest a disciplinary action or plead innocent. Don't attempt to justify inappropriate behavior, but do provide context to help admissions officers understand the underlying factors and motivations. As much as possible, take responsibility for your actions and show how you have grown and changed since the incident occurred. Everyone makes mistakes, and teens and young adults are especially prone to risky behaviors and rash decisions. A mature and transparent explanation of events can alleviate a college's concerns about troubling past conduct.

Document Upload

Some applications offer students the opportunity to upload supporting documents — some optional, some required. For example, you may be asked to upload your personal statement as a separate document, as described in the next chapter. Here are some other commonly requested documents:

- **Résumé or CV:** If you have significant work experience, it may be easier to fully illustrate your skills and career path via a traditional résumé or CV than through the activities section of the application.
- **Military papers:** Military-connected applicants can upload details of service, such as discharge papers, a Joint Services Transcript (JST), or a Community College of the Air Force transcript.
- **Unofficial transcripts (high school and/or college):** Colleges will eventually require official copies of your transcripts, but for initial admissions review purposes, many colleges will accept the free unofficial copies that can be downloaded from your school's student portal.
- **Course catalog descriptions:** Proactively providing course descriptions can aid in timely transfer credit review. Locate your college's online course catalog, copy the entire course description for each class you have taken, and paste them into a separate document.
- **Writing sample:** Any academic or professional paper you have written can provide proof of your ability to communicate in writing.
- **Test score reports:** If you are sharing test scores, unofficial reports provide admissions officers with additional information about your abilities in specific subject areas. Note that you may be asked to send official score reports directly from the testing agency later.
- **Portfolio:** Students applying to artistic and creative majors may need to share a portfolio of their work. Depending on the college, this may be done by uploading documents, providing a URL to a public portfolio, or using a connected service, such as SlideRoom.

Common Challenges and Questions

What if I haven't been in school for a long time and don't have a professor to ask for a recommendation?

If the application asks specifically for an academic or teacher recommendation, the college is signaling that they want a third party to assess your skills and abilities as a student. Can you think of anyone in your life who could provide that information in a letter? Perhaps a manager or trainer from work? If you feel uncertain about the appropriateness of a recommender, contact the university's admissions office and ask a transfer counselor for suggestions. They probably have seen students like you before and can offer advice to help you overcome this hurdle in the application process.

What if a university does not require letters of recommendation but offers space for optional letters? Should I send some?

If you believe that your recommender(s) will write overwhelmingly positive reviews of your academic abilities and work ethic, then go ahead. Additional evidence of your college potential can only help! However, if you aren't sure how strong a letter might be, look at how well your GPA aligns with the college's average transfer student GPA. If you are already a good match for this school, a mediocre recommendation letter won't improve your application — it could even weaken it. If you choose to send optional recommendation letters, make sure they are written by your most enthusiastic supporters!

Is there an advantage to applying on the school's website instead of via the Common App?

No. In fact, when colleges join the Common App, they agree to abide by the Common App policy that prohibits member institutions from showing preference for one application format over another. You should complete the application that makes the most sense for you.

What if I don't have any extracurricular activities?

Extracurricular activities don't carry nearly as much weight in transfer applications as they do in first-year applications. Transfer admissions decisions are based primarily on courses taken and grades earned. That said, don't leave the section on extracurriculars blank! Be sure to enter any activity that you do outside class, no matter how mundane it seems. Perhaps you taught yourself a skill by watching videos online or coordinated a weekly gathering of friends for Dungeons & Dragons. Everything counts!

CHAPTER 14

Writing

Tell your story! A transfer student's journey is not easily summarized in grades and test scores. Written statements and responses to short-answer questions provide much-needed context for college admissions officers. Plan to take advantage of every opportunity to showcase your personal and academic growth, explain your motivations for transferring, and demonstrate how your past experiences have shaped your academic and professional goals. Sharing your perspective can help admissions readers better understand both your previous journey and your future potential. Writing in your unique voice brings your application to life, allowing the readers to imagine you as an enrolled student on campus. Even if you don't think of yourself as a writer, remember that you are the expert on your own experiences and have a valuable story to tell!

Here are a few tips before you begin writing:

- Remember that these writing components are not like academic essays or résumés. Allow your creativity and personality to shine.
- Always write in a separate document, then copy and paste it into the application. It's easier to count words, track changes, catch mistakes, and save each version in a dedicated word-processing tool.
- Don't rely on ChatGPT or other AI tools. The large language models used to build these AI programs are, by definition, trained on others' writing samples, so they cannot write like the unique human you are. Plus, each university decides its own policies around AI, and you don't want to run afoul of a college's policy before you even enroll.
- Get help with proofreading, but don't let "too many cooks in

the kitchen." Your essay should still sound like your voice after editing.

- If you choose to name prospective colleges in your writing, be *very* careful to match each essay with the correct application. There is nothing more embarrassing than telling Purdue how much you want to attend Columbia.

Remember, your narrative is what sets you apart from other applicants with similar academic backgrounds. It can be challenging to write something so personal, but it's worth the effort to let potential colleges have a peek at the real you.

The Personal Statement

Many colleges request a personal statement from aspiring transfer applicants. Colleges that use the Common App for transfer are likely to offer a 650-word space with prompts that may resemble the first-year Common App prompts. In fact, if you wrote a personal statement for first-year admissions, you may be tempted to recycle that essay. Resist that temptation! The transfer personal statement has a different job to do.

The Objectives

What exactly is the job of a transfer personal statement? Your main objectives are to:

1. briefly describe your educational journey thus far.
2. explain why you feel the need to transfer now.
3. predict how enrollment at the selected school (and in the selected major, if applicable) will help you achieve your goals.

This doesn't mean you can't get creative with your writing, though! An intriguing opening hook and engaging storytelling style will help your reader become invested in your story. But before you write the next great literary memoir, determine which facts are most important to share and verify the instructions provided by the college. While 650 words may be the standard length of a personal statement, each college can define its own unique parameters in word or character limits. You don't want to be caught off guard when your 650-word essay doesn't fit into the 500-word text box!

174   Application

Prompt and Length

Let's examine a few sample prompts from universities utilizing the Common App for transfer. First, we have a very traditional transfer personal statement prompt from the University of Southern California (USC). Note the length suggestion of "approximately 650 words." However, the text box shows a limit of 6,500 *characters*. If you were to completely fill that text box, you would probably have closer to 1,000 words. It's OK to share an essay that is a little more or less than 650, but don't fill the entire box just because the system technically allows it.

> * Please provide a statement that addresses your reasons for transferring and the objectives you hope to achieve. You can type directly into the box, or you can paste text from another source. (Approximately 650 words)

0 word   0/6500

The next example is from New York University (NYU). The question is quite similar to USC's above, but NYU asks you to state the ways in which NYU specifically can support you. Even if other universities don't ask for this, you may want to consider including unique details like this for each college. In this case, the maximum length is stated only in characters, and the 2,500 maximum stated in the prompt matches the limit in the text box. This is much shorter than the limit for USC, so if you want to use the same essay, you will need to edit it down.

> * Please provide a statement that addresses your reason(s) for seeking transfer and the objectives you hope to achieve. How can NYU and the particular school, college, program, and/or area of study you are applying to support those goals? (2500 character maximum)

0 word   0/2500

Last, we have a prompt from Beloit College. Although Beloit is also using the Common App, this prompt does not offer a text box for your essay. Instead, you would need to upload a document. This means there is no automatic counting of words or characters, and you could technically submit an essay of any length. However, colleges will be most impressed by students who read and follow directions carefully, so use your word-processing software to track the word count and stick to the suggested 250-to-500-word range.

Personal Statement Prompt:

The personal essay is an important factor in the decision for admission to Beloit College in that it reveals a part of you that objective data like grades, curriculum, or test scores do not. This essay gives the application a voice - your voice! - and allows us to gain additional insight into the way you organize your thoughts, your preferred writing style, who you are, and who you might become.

Required topic for transfer students:
Please provide an essay (approximately 250-500 words) discussing your educational path. How does continuing your education at a new institution help you achieve your future goals?

All three colleges are asking for similar details in your personal statement. You should feel free to write one main personal statement and adjust it for each individual school. Obviously, you will need to add or cut words to meet the length requirements, but you also want to ensure that each version answers the specific questions in the school's prompt and includes any relevant details for that particular college.

Brainstorming Activity 1: Content

Before you begin writing, jot down short responses to any of the following questions that you find relevant. Your answers will likely reveal some of the most important facts about your educational background. Consider creating a timeline of your path through college to use as a reference while you write.

- How did you choose your first college?
- If you went directly from high school to community college, why did you choose a two-year over a four-year school?
- If you have attended multiple colleges, why did you move from school to school?
- What have you learned from your previous college experience(s)? Think about academics as well as life lessons.
- How have you grown since you first entered college?
- If your educational journey includes low grades, withdrawals, or academic probation, what went wrong? What did you learn from these challenges?
- How is your current college a mismatch for you? Try not to list what is "wrong" with your school — think about how it is just not a good fit for you personally.
- What are you looking for in your next college?
- What have you learned about yourself that makes your next college choice clear?
- How are you prepared to succeed at your next college? If past mistakes prevented your academic success, how do you know you won't make those mistakes again at the next college?

You probably won't be able to answer all these questions in detail as you write your personal statement, but it's wise to keep these ideas in mind as you work. Don't lose sight of the objectives of your transfer essay!

Brainstorming Activity 2: Creative

If you were to start writing with only the notes from brainstorming activity 1 to guide you, your personal statement might resemble a résumé or autobiography. Instead, let's get creative and show off your personality and writing style!

Your personal statement should take the reader on a journey. The content brainstorming questions above helped you establish the map and pinpoint a destination. Now, you need a vehicle to get your reader there. This could be a car, a bike, a bus, or a plane! Any vehicle can take your reader to the intended target. Which method of travel will be the most enjoyable and memorable? Let's look for a symbol, metaphor, or anecdote to weave into your story.

- What is an object you always keep with you? Why is it meaningful?
- What is your favorite animal, hobby, song, or possession? Why do you love it?
- Do you collect anything? What? Why?
- Walk around your room or home. What items do you see? Do they tell a story about you?
- Do any of the above objects and ideas lend themselves to a metaphor about your life?
- Do you remember a specific moment when you discovered your major?
- Do you remember a specific moment when you realized you needed to transfer?
- Do you have a series of parallel memories? For example, visiting libraries in various locations throughout your life.
- Do you have a pair of relevant before-and-after memories? For example, traveling to your first college dorm vs. withdrawing from college and moving home.

Compare your notes from these two brainstorming sections and look for possible connections. Maybe an object that you carry with you for good luck is also a reminder of your values and your future college goals. Mementos from past vacations might help you tell a story about becoming an international relations major. Once you have a couple of ideas, ask yourself how an admissions reader might fill in this blank after reading your essay: "Wow, this student sure is _____!" Or imagine how they will refer to you when discussing which students to admit: "Remember the student with the _____?" Write the story that fills in the blanks with the words you like best.

Case Studies: Creative Essay Topics

Haley: Water Bottle Stickers

Like many environmentally conscious teens, Haley carried a reusable water bottle wherever she went. Over the years, it became a convenient canvas for her social activist sticker collection. She purchased stickers to support her favorite causes, received free stickers as thanks for donations, and saved stickers from activism events and protests. A tour of her stickers was a tour of her values and illustrated her interest in pre-law.

Trinity: Sewing

As a self-taught sewing enthusiast, Trinity faced numerous challenges while learning new stitches and techniques through trial and error. When it came time to write about being ready to transfer from community college and face the challenges that would come with attending a large public research university, Trinity utilized sewing as a metaphor. Sewing had instilled patience in her and helped her make peace with failure. Just as she did not give up on her hobby, Trinity would not give up on her education.

Brad: D&D

Brad's main hobby was playing Dungeons & Dragons. He described getting into character and interacting with his role-playing friends, both as themselves and as their characters. Seeing how people revealed aspects of their personalities in D&D sparked Brad's curiosity and inspired him to study psychology, with an eye on graduate school and future research.

Annika: Worry Stones

Annika came from a family of worriers. Growing up, she had regularly experienced anxiety, and her family supported her with access to therapy and their own tales of struggle. In a show of solidarity, several family members gave her worry stones, both to remind her of her support system and to provide comfort during stressful times. Naturally, she took them to college, her most stressful transition to date. But as she grew in confidence and realized she craved a more rigorous academic experience, she used them less and less. While she plans to bring her worry stone collection to her next college, she intends to use them only as dorm room decor, to remind her of how much she has grown.

Kevin: Three Journeys

Kevin had a difficult first semester of college, which led to a complete withdrawal from the school by January. To explain the changes in his life, from enrollment to withdrawal to rebuilding at a local community college, Kevin compared three journeys in his pickup truck. First, he shared the excitement of packing up and traveling with his family on move-in day. Then, he described the sadness and shame of driving back home as a "failure." Finally, he discussed the new routines and coping skills he developed at community college, as illustrated by the regularity of his daily commute.

Organize and Draft

In most cases, transfer students should plan on writing an essay in loose chronological order. The goal is to describe your college journey, so it usually makes sense to begin at the beginning and end in the present moment, perhaps with an eye toward the future. That said, sometimes it can be effective to use an interesting "hook" in the first paragraph to lure the reader into your essay. Since the most memorable moments of your life may not have happened in a convenient chronological order, you may need to use a flashback after your introductory paragraph to get back on track with your timeline.

The middle section of your essay should focus on your growth and development over the last few years. Colleges want to know about the kind of student you are now, so stories from kindergarten probably aren't relevant. Consider making an outline or list of events and anecdotes that illustrate your journey. Jot down some details about each major idea on your list, including not just plot points, but also your reflection on the event and how it affected you. Then cut the oldest events and see if your story still makes sense. Try to include only enough background to place your current story in context. When you feel you have a compelling set of ideas to share in your essay, arrange them into an outline that you can use as a guide for writing your first draft.

If you choose to share some of the challenges you have faced, remember that the most important element of an "overcoming a challenge" essay is the part about overcoming. As writing instructors often tell their students, write from your scars, not your wounds. Colleges want to know what you have learned from your mistakes and how you achieved success despite difficult circumstances. If you feel that your former college is to blame for any of the challenges you faced, find a way to describe the situation neutrally, then focus on how you grew from the experience. There is no need to relive traumatic events as you write. Instead, focus on the courage, strength, and determination that helped you move forward.

Wrapping up a personal essay is often the most difficult part of the writing process. If you have written your story in chronological order, it might make sense to use your conclusion to look toward the future. If the rest of the essay tells the story of how you got to the present moment, perhaps the final paragraph can show how you intend to take everything you have learned and apply it to your next adventure at a new university. Some students like to personalize their essays in the last paragraph and share specific goals they have for their time at the new college. Since most transfer applications have separate writing sections for each university, you should be able to customize each conclusion. Just be sure to double-check the details in every one of your applications before you submit!

Revise and Edit

Once you have written a complete draft, set it aside for a few days. You need a little time to forget what you wrote so you can read your essay again with fresh eyes. Read carefully, paragraph by paragraph, and ask yourself what each section reveals about you. Any sentences that don't have a clear purpose or don't contribute to your overall message should be edited or deleted. Then look for holes in your essay. These might be places where more context is needed or where clearer transitions could connect the dots between elements of your story. Keep an eye on your word and character counts, and make sure you are within range of your goal. Finally, make sure your essay meets the objectives listed at the beginning of this chapter.

When you feel satisfied with the content of your essay, it's time to proofread and make any final edits. Here are a few tips to help you polish your writing:

- Utilize spelling and grammar checkers, but don't blindly accept every suggestion. Take the time to research highlighted grammar elements so that your essay will be a strong example of your writing skills.
- Read your essay aloud to a friend, a pet, or even a stuffed animal. The act of reading aloud forces you to slow down and notice awkward phrases and typos, even if no one is listening.
- Copy your text into a free word-cloud application. Words that appear more often in your essay will be displayed in a larger font in the word cloud. Do the largest words accurately reflect your essay's main ideas? Or are you overusing some stale vocabulary?

182 Application

- Create a duplicate copy of your document and hit return at the end of each sentence. Look for patterns and variety in the lengths of your sentences. If all your sentences are roughly the same size, your essay will probably sound monotonous to your reader. Shake it up!

Unfortunately, there is no perfect essay. You could tinker with your sentences for months and never be fully satisfied. Just do the best you can with the time you have, and remember that the overall explanation of your educational journey is the most important factor. No one was ever rejected from a college over a stray comma or misplaced capital letter.

Submission

Do you feel ready to submit? Or do you think your essay is as good as you can make it, given that the deadline is near? Either way, it's time to add your essay to the application. But where?

Sometimes, the application will have a space for you to upload a separate document. In this case, check the instructions for a list of accepted file types. If your document is not already saved in an acceptable format, you will need to convert it. The most universally compatible format is PDF, so if you are converting your file anyway, try saving it as a PDF. View the newly converted document before submitting to make sure your essay has retained your original formatting. Then go ahead and upload your essay to the online application.

Other applications may provide text boxes so that you can copy and paste your essay directly into the application form. After pasting, scroll through your essay and fix any unexpected formatting issues. Also, check the end of your essay — is it complete? If you accidentally wrote an essay that is longer than the allowed character or word count, you might see an error message, or you might just lose a portion of your essay without any warning!

Although you have now added your essay to the application form, it will not be transmitted to the college until you sign and date your full application and press the Submit button. If you discover a typo at the last minute, you can still edit your essay as long as you have not officially submitted the overall application form.

Supplemental Essays

Many colleges have additional short-answer questions in their applications. Some questions are lighthearted and fun, such as these from USC:

- What is your favorite snack?
- If your life had a theme song, what would it be?
- What TV show will you binge-watch next?

With answer spaces that allow for only fifty characters, responses cannot be too profound. Such questions simply serve to show off your personality. Other questions provide opportunities for thoughtful reflection, asking students to explain the reasons for pursuing a particular major or to describe elements of identity and heritage. Let's explore some of the most common types of supplemental essay questions.

Why Us?

Why do you want to attend this particular institution? Write a love letter to your future university! Do your research first, though. Peruse the website, read the institution's mission and vision statements, take a virtual tour, and check the college's social media accounts. If you are able to visit in person and take a formal tour, that's even better. Then summarize the distinctive qualities of this school that appeal to you personally. Avoid describing basic characteristics that might be considered common knowledge, and de-emphasize superficial elements like weather and location. Instead, look for the less obvious features that make this college a great match for you specifically. If you have anecdotes from a campus tour, or you learned interesting details by making an inquiry by phone or email, consider including those stories. The best "Why us?" essays will be the ones that no one else could write because they address the unique match between you and the university. The best essays also convince the college that you have done your homework and truly want to attend this university for all the right reasons.

Why This Major?

Transfer students are rarely able to apply with an undeclared major. A key factor in the transfer admissions decision process is often the student's readiness to succeed in the specified major. Thus, many colleges ask why a student is interested in the major subject and look for evidence that the student is prepared and eager to take the required classes. Depending on the length of the essay, you may be able to provide a creative retelling of an experience that first sparked your interest, then transition into the classes and experiences that have confirmed this interest as your primary academic and career pathway. If you have limited space, skip the storytelling and focus primarily on your recent preparation for the major. In either case, make sure you go on to personalize the statement to describe how the specific iteration of the major at this college is of particular interest. Read about the major on the department's website and look for any unique programs or concentrations. Check the class schedule for the names of undergraduate classes that appeal to you, and research the professors who teach those classes. As you write about your interests and preparation in the field, drop in details that illustrate your genuine interest in the major as it is configured at this university and explain how attending this university will assist you in achieving your academic and career goals.

Identity/Community

Who are you, and what will you contribute to your next college community? Colleges seek students from diverse backgrounds with interesting lived experiences who will enrich the campus community and foster a vibrant learning environment. Since the 2023 Supreme Court ruling that ended race-based affirmative action in college admissions, schools have gotten creative about diversifying their campuses. Universities can no longer achieve diversity merely by reviewing checked ethnicity boxes on the application form, so they are posing more nuanced questions about students' identities and backgrounds. Diversity isn't just about race, though! Colleges aim to diversify by recruiting students from rural areas, different geographical regions, branches of the military, various age groups, and more. In fact, simply being a transfer student adds a valuable element of diversity! Consider what sets you apart, or how you relate to those who differ from you, and how you plan to contribute to the campus community upon your arrival. Each college wants to understand how you will enrich its student body, making it more interesting and welcoming for everyone.

University of California
Personal Insight Questions (PIQ)

The UC transfer application takes a unique approach to essays. Instead of requesting a main personal statement and a handful of supplemental essays, the UC application asks students to write short answers of up to 350 words responding to four of eight provided prompts.

One prompt, regarding the student's preparation for upper-division coursework in the selected major, is required: "Please describe how you have prepared for your intended major, including your readiness to succeed in your upper-division courses once you enroll at the university." Your approach to this question will be similar to the approach outlined in the personal statement section earlier, combined with the "Why this major?" supplemental essay described above. Because the vast majority of transfer applicants to UC are coming from community colleges, the required question focuses on major rather than reasons for transfer. After all, students transferring from community college have a fairly obvious reason for transfer — to earn a bachelor's degree. However, if you are applying to transfer from a four-year university to UC, you will want to include a few sentences about your reasons for transfer in addition to an explanation of major interest and preparation. Explain not only why you want to pursue the stated major, but also why you will be better off pursuing that major at a UC campus.

The other three topics can be freely selected from the remaining seven options. Choose the questions that allow you to elaborate on areas of strength, and focus primarily on content rather than creativity. The UC application readers are more interested in your answers than in your writing style or ability. Respond to the prompts with language you might use to respond to similar questions in an oral interview — factual and to the point. That said, this is still a piece of writing, so don't forget to proofread before you submit.

Additional Information

Extra detail is always better than not enough. Explain *everything*. Most applications include at least one "additional information" text box where you can explain any special circumstances, such as gaps in your postsecondary education, outlier grades, health challenges, and so on.

186   Application

Although these text boxes may be labeled as optional, most transfer students have relevant information that should be shared with admissions officers.

For example, a student who caught the flu during finals week might wish to explain why that semester's final grades are lower than average. The presence of multiple withdrawals, or W grades, can be a red flag for admissions. However, an explanation of unusual circumstances that necessitated the withdrawals can set admissions officers' minds at ease. Similarly, an unexplained gap, whether it's a single semester or several years, may cause concern, but a description of the student's activities during that time may justify the gap.

Sometimes students wonder if colleges simply won't notice irregularities in their applications, so they hesitate to highlight them by providing explanations. The truth is that admissions officers are trained to read quickly and spot areas of concern. Any explanation the student provides is likely to create a more favorable impression, whereas an unusual but unexplained situation can prompt an application reader to make unfavorable assumptions.

Essay Dos and Don'ts

Here is a summary of the tips presented in this chapter.

Do	Don't
Do explain how you've learned to adapt to various teaching styles.	Don't describe your past professors as "bad teachers" even if you think they were.
Do describe your improved study habits and willingness to seek support.	Don't blame your school for low grades you received in the past.
Do discuss developing self-care routines to improve mental health.	Don't dwell excessively on past mental health crises.
Do research the schools you are applying to and describe unique details that appeal to you.	Don't emphasize superficial qualities like weather and nonacademic amenities as reasons for transfer.

Do write directly about challenges you faced and how they affected your grades.	Don't ignore low grades on your transcript and hope admissions officers won't notice.
Do tell your story and describe how you have benefited from those who have gone before you.	Don't get carried away telling a story about a mentor or role model.
Do utilize spelling and grammar checkers and research confusing grammar rules before accepting automated suggestions.	Don't trust every suggestion provided by spelling and grammar checkers.
Do use your own unique voice to tell your story.	Don't ask ChatGPT to write your essay for you.
Do ask one or two trusted friends, tutors, or family members to provide gentle feedback.	Don't let too many outsiders read and edit your essay.
Do write a narrative of your educational journey.	Don't rewrite your résumé or activities list in your essay.

Common Challenges and Questions

Can I reuse the personal statement I wrote for my first-year applications?

You can, but should you? Does that piece of writing accurately represent the person you are today? The transfer essay gives you the opportunity to reflect on life since high school and show how you have grown and matured. It also needs to explain your educational journey since high school and address your reasons for transferring. Even though that blank piece of paper is intimidating, it's probably best to start fresh with a brand-new essay.

What if I'm really *not* creative?

That's OK. The personal statement for a transfer application can be more straightforward than the essays typically written by first-year applicants. The main goal of your essay is to describe your educational journey and help the reader understand how you became a transfer applicant. If your academic record has unexplained gaps, periods of low grades, or numerous withdrawals, a more direct explanation of your journey might even be a better use of the limited space allotted. Just be sure to proofread carefully so that your essay is a good example of your ability to write in standard academic English.

How personal should I get in the personal statement?

That's entirely up to you. Admissions officers want to understand your academic journey and how that journey has been entwined with your life experiences. Showing a little vulnerability is always welcome. However, you shouldn't feel obligated to divulge more information than you feel comfortable sharing. While you want to explain any unusual variations in your academic record, it's OK to be vague about events in your personal life with phrases like "challenging family circumstances" or "health concerns." Focus on your growth and highlight all the ways that you have prepared for this next chapter of your life.

Can I write about my race, or is that not allowed now?

If your race, heritage, or ethnic background is an important part of your identity, you should feel free to share it! The Supreme Court ruling that banned race-conscious admissions applies to institutions, not individual applicants. Students do not need to worry about breaking the law by sharing demographic information in essays. It is the burden of the receiving institutions to decide how to interpret and utilize the narratives students provide in accordance with the law.

CHAPTER 15

Follow-Up Documentation

You've entered all your data, uploaded your initial documents, written your personal statement, and submitted your applications! Congratulations! Unfortunately, it's not time to rest yet. You still have some work to do.

Most colleges require additional supporting documentation before making an admissions decision or determining transfer credit equivalencies. Official transcripts and test score reports are the most common document requests, but colleges may contact you for others. In some cases, you may need to remind a recommender to submit a letter, or follow up with a school to make sure they sent your transcript to the correct address. Keep a close eye on your applicant portals and submit all requested documents as quickly as possible.

Once you have confirmed that everything has been properly submitted and your prospective colleges have confirmed receipt, you can finally rest. (But keep checking those portals regularly!)

College Applicant Portals

Shortly after submitting an application to a college, you should receive an email inviting you to check the status of your application at the college's online applicant portal. If you don't see such an invitation in your email inbox within a week, first check your spam folder. If you don't find it there either, reach out to the college for assistance. It's extremely important that you have access to the applicant portal for each college you apply to and check them for updates regularly.

If you applied via a school-specific application on a college's website, it's possible that the applicant portal will be the same website you visited to apply in the first place. However, if you applied through one of the central application services, like the Coalition App, Common App, or CBCA, you will certainly need to access a separate portal URL provided by each school to track your application status. Note that once you press Submit on those common application sites, you can no longer edit or add to your submitted information on those sites. All future communications should be directly with the colleges to which you applied. Hence, the importance of the portals.

Portal Setup

The portal invitation email should provide you with a URL, username, and temporary password. In some cases, the message will first provide instructions for selecting a username and/or college-specific email address that will become permanent if you enroll. When you access the portal for the first time, you will need to create a password for future access. It might be wise to create a spreadsheet or keep an offline notebook with each college's portal URL, username, and password, especially if you applied to multiple colleges. A downloadable template is available at TransferSavvy.com/Book.

Counselor or Other Admissions Contact

Now that you are an official applicant, you may be assigned an admissions counselor who will be your contact person throughout the rest of the admissions process. Look for the contact information and biographical details about this person in your portal. This person has been assigned to help you, so don't hesitate to reach out. If you don't see the name of a specific assigned counselor, check the portal for an alternative contact method for updating or inquiring about your submitted application. At this stage, some colleges direct applicants to send inquiries to a general admissions-department email address.

Portal Document Checklist

The core feature of any applicant portal is a checklist of required documents. This list may change frequently as your application is being processed, so check back often. At first, you will probably see a couple of green completion checkmarks confirming receipt of basic elements of the application, such as the application fee and the application form itself. Other items may be red or blank to show that they are still missing. Below is an example of a portal checklist showing all requirements completed.

Application Checklist   Application Submitted: 10/21/2024

This is your checklist. Please ensure all materials are received by the document deadline.

Status		Details	Date
✓	Received	Application fee	10/21/2024
✓	Received	Essay	10/21/2024
✓	Received	Letter of Recommendation	09/30/2024
✓	Received	Mid-Semester Report Form for Transfer Applicants	11/15/2024
✓	Received	College Transcript for Montgomery College	10/31/2024
✓	Received	Resume	10/21/2024
✓	Received	College Transcript for St. Lawrence University	10/30/2024
✓	Received	Test Scores	09/24/2024
✓	Received	Transfer Recommendation Form	11/14/2024
✓	Received	High School Transcript for Walt Whitman High	10/31/2024
✓	Received	Mid-Semester Report Form for Transfer Applicants	11/15/2024

Portal checklists can vary widely by school. Colleges that request significant documentation with the initial application may have very short follow-up checklists. Colleges with deceptively short applications may have long lists of required documents to be submitted later. Every portal will have a unique checklist, so read each one carefully.

Commonly requested portal documents may include the following, which are explained in detail in the next sections.

- Official transcripts
- Official test score reports
- College transfer report(s)
- Midterm grade report
- Financial aid applications: FAFSA, CSS Profile, and/or State Financial Aid Forms
- Letters of recommendation
- Course descriptions or syllabi

192   Application

For documents that you are permitted to upload yourself, there will be an option to do so in the portal. For others, you may need to wait for external recommenders, administrators, and transcript services to submit documents on your behalf. Don't worry if items on your checklist are not immediately marked as complete. It can sometimes take one to two weeks for colleges to process application documents. If you still don't see a green check two or more weeks after submitting a requested document, contact your assigned counselor or use the designated email or phone number in the portal to politely inquire about the missing items. Sometimes the admissions department is simply delayed in processing documents. Other times you may have to resend lost documents or remind your recommenders to submit their letters.

Official Transcripts

Even if you uploaded unofficial transcripts with your application, you may need to send official transcripts before your application can be processed. These transcripts must be sent directly from the high school or college you attended to the university to which you are applying. Alternatively, official transcripts can sometimes be sent to a central service like the Common App for transfer to be distributed to all colleges on your application list. Read the application or portal directions carefully to ensure your transcripts arrive safely at the intended destination.

What makes a transcript official, anyway? Most colleges use a service like Parchment or the National Student Clearinghouse to send official transcripts electronically for a small fee. These transcripts are encrypted, and delivery can be securely tracked and confirmed. If a school does not use a high-tech online service like this, it may have other methods for securing the data and ensuring that the transcripts have not been altered. This could be as simple as a school officer signing across an envelope's flap or securing the envelope with an official school sticker or seal. Avoid having any official transcripts pass through your hands on the way to the receiving institution. In many cases, this will automatically make the transcripts unofficial, simply because the delivery cannot be formally traced.

Remember to send *all* transcripts, even if they only list withdrawals or classes you took as a dual-enrolled high school student. This is no joke! Even if you took just one class and it was already transferred to another college transcript, still send that original transcript. Colleges want official copies of every transcript. Declining to send a transcript can delay the processing of your application, or worse, could be interpreted as a lie of omission.

Official Test Score Reports

If you are using test scores to support your application for transfer admission, colleges may wish to see official score reports. This is especially true when the test scores in question can potentially provide college credits, such as AP, IB, or CLEP tests. Check your portal for instructions, but when in doubt, send official reports. Not only do you want to ensure that your application file is complete, but you also want to claim any credits you earned via testing programs!

College and Grade Reports

Although most of the transfer application process is digitized and available online, there are a few instances where you may need to print a downloaded PDF and take it to your most recent college for signatures from instructors and college administrators. If you are currently enrolled in a brick-and-mortar college, you will probably find it easiest to complete these documents by physically taking them to the appropriate offices on campus. If you are not currently enrolled, or you participate only in distance learning courses, you may have to do some research to find the appropriate email addresses for college officials who can complete these forms on your behalf.

Occasionally, a transfer application will specify that these reports must be completed for every college previously attended, but this is rare. Unless otherwise stated, assume that only documentation from your current or most recent college is needed. If a college is seeking additional information, document requests will be added to your portal.

College Transfer Report(s)

This document has several possible names: It might be called simply a College Report, as it is when downloaded from the Common App for transfer, or it may be referred to as a Letter of Good Standing, Transfer Student Status Report, Dean's Report, Dean's Certification, or similar. Regardless of the name, this document is intended to verify your enrollment status as well as your academic and disciplinary standing at the school.

This form usually includes a section to be completed by the student, with identifying details and possibly a FERPA waiver. Ensure you complete all required student sections before handing the document to your school's registrar or dean's office. Any skipped questions or unsigned waivers can delay the processing of your document. If the deadline and submission instructions are not included on the form, you should provide these details to your registrar or dean. Once completed, the form should be sent directly to the requesting college, where it will be filed with the rest of your application documents.

Midterm Grade Report

Some colleges may request evidence of passing grades in your currently enrolled classes, especially if you are a low-unit transfer. Typically, this request includes a form for you to complete with details about each of your current classes and your estimated in-progress grades. The form may require a signature from each of your instructors to verify the grade estimates, or it may simply include space for each instructor's contact information so that the college can verify the predicted grades, if needed. Students who are primarily enrolled in online classes may have difficulty obtaining instructor signatures. Don't hesitate to ask the requesting college for advice in this case. Options for e-signatures or other alternatives may be available.

Financial Aid Applications

Applying to college is only half the battle. You also need a plan to pay for tuition, housing, and other related costs. The total cost of attendance at some private institutions is nearly six figures per year now! Most families will need to acquire some form of financial assistance to cover these expenses. Even if you believe that you or your family won't qualify for need-based aid, it's wise to file the Free Application for Federal Student Aid (FAFSA) anyway. If your financial circumstances change suddenly, having the FAFSA on file allows you to appeal for financial assistance. Without a submitted FAFSA, your options for requesting emergency aid are extremely limited. Some colleges also have a policy that if you did not file the FAFSA for your first year of attendance at their institution, you will not be eligible to file and request financial assistance in later years. It's better to be safe than sorry, so *file the FAFSA no matter what.*

FAFSA

The Free Application for Federal Student Aid (FAFSA) is managed by the US government and is free to file. It usually becomes available on October 1 of each year, although availability can occasionally be delayed, as it was in 2023 and 2024. Although the form appears daunting at first, the embedded FUTURE Act Direct Data Exchange (FA-DDX) allows most applicants (and their parents, if applicable) to use their previously filed tax returns to auto-complete several sections of the FAFSA form, making the process simpler and more accurate. The FAFSA form also asks students to select up to twenty colleges to receive the results of the financial aid form, but this college list can be edited in the future if plans change.

Submit the FAFSA form as early as possible! It can take several weeks for your FAFSA to be processed, first by the federal government, then by individual college financial aid offices. Filing early increases your chances of receiving a financial aid award letter with your offer of admission or soon after. Also, some funding sources are limited, so late applications might result in reduced aid. After submission, watch your email for a FAFSA Submission Summary message from the US government. This summary of your application should arrive within a couple of weeks and will provide you with an opportunity to review your submission and correct any errors.

CSS Profile

The College Board (yes, the same College Board that administers the SAT, AP, and CLEP tests) manages the CSS Profile. About two hundred universities in North America require submission of the CSS Profile to determine students' eligibility for institutional aid. While the FAFSA relies primarily on tax returns to determine financial need, the CSS Profile goes into much greater detail, requiring families to share the specifics of retirement funds and primary home values, for example. Colleges can also add supplementary questions to the CSS Profile and may require the electronic submission of financial documents such as bank statements and W-2 forms to complete the filing process. If you are required to upload such documents through the Institutional Documentation Service (IDOC) you will receive an email from the College Board after you submit the CSS Profile. Otherwise, follow the instructions provided by the college to submit these documents via their preferred method.

Although the CSS Profile requires much more data, it does not replace the FAFSA! Filing the FAFSA is the only way to access federal funds for college. Most schools that request the CSS Profile will also require the FAFSA to obtain a complete picture of each family's financial situation.

Like the FAFSA, the CSS Profile typically becomes available on October 1 each year. Unlike the FAFSA, filing the CSS Profile is not free. There is one charge to submit the initial application and send the report to one school, and a lesser charge for each additional school selected to receive a report. However, fee waivers are readily available, and nearly half of all applicants file the CSS Profile for free. If you are eligible for a fee waiver, you will be notified as you enter financial data to complete the form.

State Financial Aid Forms

Some states have separate financial aid forms to administer state-based student aid. The rules of each state are unique, so read the directions carefully. Some states provide aid based solely on FAFSA submission. Others require state forms in addition to the FAFSA. Most often, the state-based applications are intended only as an alternative for students who cannot file the FAFSA, such as undocumented students. Only US citizens, permanent residents, and immigrants with certain formal designations from US Citizenship and Immigration Services (USCIS) can file the FAFSA and potentially receive federal money for college. Individual states may have fewer restrictions and can sometimes assist students in circumstances that don't allow them to complete the

FAFSA. If you are ineligible to file the FAFSA, it is definitely worth researching the options in your state.

File on Time Every Year

Regardless of the form(s) you file, a new submission is required every year while you are attending college. Financial aid awards do not automatically renew, so you must file again year after year with your updated financial information. Also check the deadlines (or priority deadlines, if available) for your state and college each year and submit well in advance of the earliest deadline.

Letters of Recommendation

If you requested letters of recommendation but your portal shows that none were received, don't panic! First, confirm that your recommenders sent their letters or submitted their forms to the correct colleges. Services like the Common App for transfer track the electronic submission of letters, so it's easy to see if the letters were submitted on time. Otherwise, you may need to check in with your recommenders and gently remind them to submit their letters if they haven't already done so.

However, sometimes the portal shows missing letters because the college is processing documents by hand and will update your portal once they have verified that the correct recommendations are on file. Look for a note on the portal that describes how long it might take for the college to update your checklist after documents have been received. If you don't see any indication of a specific processing time in the portal, go ahead and email the admissions office and politely ask if you should request that your recommenders resend their letters.

Course Descriptions or Syllabi

As soon as you are admitted to a university, you will want to see how your previously earned credits will transfer to the new institution. To expedite this process and ensure that you receive a transfer credit evaluation report along with your acceptance, some universities ask you to upload syllabi and/or course catalog descriptions either with your application or in your applicant portal. Although the gathering of these materials may seem tedious, this proactive request for course documentation allows the university to provide you with a more accurate credit evaluation in a timely manner.

Scholarship Applications

Merit-based scholarships and grants may be available to you as a transfer student. Students are automatically considered for institutional merit scholarships at many colleges; simply by applying to the college, you have applied for the college's scholarships. This is common practice for schools listed as "buyers" on education journalist Jeffrey Selingo's "Buyers and Sellers List."[1] In his 2020 book, *Who Gets In and Why: A Year Inside College Admissions*, Selingo defines "buyers" as schools that receive fewer applications and therefore must actively recruit students and offer discounted tuition through merit scholarships, and "sellers" as those that are more competitive and therefore do not need to offer discounts. Although Selingo's list is based on data for first-year admissions, its classifications are generally applicable to transfer admissions, too. However, some colleges may offer competitive merit scholarships that require an additional application. Browse each college's website for more information on scholarship requirements.

Some outside organizations also sponsor scholarships for transfer students. The most generous and well-known transfer scholarships are offered by Phi Theta Kappa, an international college honor society, and the Jack Kent Cooke Foundation. Both of these programs are intended to assist community college students as they transition to a four-year university.

Several reputable scholarship search engines list additional opportunities for transfer students. You may even find that you are eligible for some scholarships intended for continuing students. After all, transfer students are continuing in college, just at a different institution! Be mindful of the number of hours you dedicate to scholarship searches and applications, though. Applying for scholarships can be time-consuming, and the payoff is not always worth it. Students often find that working at a part-time job is a more efficient way of earning money for college.

Interviews and Auditions

Universities rarely require transfer applicants to participate in an interview, but some institutions allow students to request an optional interview opportunity. If you believe you could present yourself in a particularly positive light through a live or virtual interview format, contact colleges to see if they offer interviews for transfer students. Since interviews are less common these days, time slots may be limited, so reach out early to inquire about the possibility. Some colleges may not offer real-time interviews but will allow applicants to submit recorded video statements directly or through services like InitialView or Vericant, so be on the lookout for that option, too.

Performing arts majors may be required to participate in live auditions, either in lieu of or alongside recordings submitted in a portfolio. The timeline for application and admission can shift earlier for students in performance majors to allow time for auditions. Check for major-specific application requirements early in your college search process so that you can plan to travel to auditions if necessary.

Common Challenges and Questions

Who signs the college transfer report (or dean's report)?

It can be difficult to find the appropriate college official to sign this form at your school. It often makes sense to begin at the registrar's office or the admissions and records department. The administrators in these offices process transcripts and enrollment records and should have access to all the necessary data to complete and sign this form. Since the form is also sometimes referred to as the Dean's Certification, you might try inquiring with the dean's office as well. But which dean? Larger schools can have many deans of various departments. Check your college's website for a list of administrators, and look for a title such as "Dean of Students" or "Dean of Student Affairs." In most cases, it's not actually the dean who processes these forms, but rather a designated assistant in the dean's office.

200   Application

How do I deal with the transfer report if I'm not currently in school?

Colleges usually specify that they want your transfer report to be completed by someone at your current or most recent college. Sometimes they want to receive reports from all colleges attended. For any school that you are not currently enrolled in, you will need to contact the registrar, dean, or other college administrator for assistance. You may need to email or fax documents if you cannot visit the appropriate offices in person.

What if I miss an important message in the portal?

As soon as you see the message, reach out to your assigned counselor at the college, or contact the admissions office. Politely explain that you overlooked the message and need guidance on how to proceed. It may be too late to rectify the situation — some deadlines are firm. However, most colleges will want to work with you to find a solution. Ask nicely, be respectful, and thank each person who tries to assist you.

How do I file the FAFSA if I'm financially independent?

Students aged twenty-four and older are automatically considered independent. However, if you are under the age of twenty-four, you will generally not be classified as financially independent for the purposes of calculating financial need for college. Even if you work full-time to support yourself, file taxes, and cannot be claimed as a dependent on a parent's tax return, you could still be classified as a dependent student for financial aid. The FAFSA only classifies students under age twenty-four as financially independent under very specific circumstances. For example, students who are married, have children, are veterans, or were legally emancipated as minors may be able to file as independent students. (Note that individual colleges that determine financial need through the CSS Profile may define independence even more narrowly.)

Students under age twenty-four who are unable to contact their parents to obtain their financial information may qualify for "provisional independent" status.[2] This new option allows students to complete the FAFSA without parental information by answering "yes" to the question, "Do unusual circumstances prevent the student from contacting their parents or would contacting their parents pose a risk to the student?" The student can then receive a Student Aid Index (SAI) that reflects their independent status. No additional documentation is required at the time of FAFSA submission, but the student will need to follow up with a financial aid administrator at the college where they ultimately enroll. This administrator will make the final official determination of the student's dependency status. If independent status is confirmed, the student will automatically remain classified as independent in future years as long as they remain at the same institution and their circumstances do not change.

PART VI

DECISIONS

Many colleges have agreed on an admissions season calendar for fall-entry first-time applicants. Aside from special application plans like Early Action and Early Decision, most schools release first-year admissions decisions in March or April and expect students to commit in May. First-year students who apply on a regular decision plan will usually be able to collect and compare all offers of admission before making any decisions.

Not so for transfer admissions! Universities may have fall application deadlines as early as October the year before transfer or as late as August, right before the semester begins. Decisions may be released on a rolling basis or all at once. Commitment and deposit deadlines can be set for any date between May and August. Some schools set deposit deadlines for two weeks after the release of the decision letter, whenever that may be. It is entirely possible that you will be evaluating offers of transfer admission as they come in over a period of several weeks. You may even be asked to commit to one college before you have received a reply from another.

In this section, we will walk through the steps of tracking application results, evaluating admission offers, and deciding to commit to a new university.

CHAPTER 16

Admissions Results

While you might receive fun packages containing your admission offers via snail mail, you will most likely learn which colleges have admitted you via email or the schools' portals first. You may experience various emotions as you receive decisions: elation, surprise, disappointment, confusion. Try not to take any decisions too personally. College admissions decisions are influenced by a number of factors, many of which are entirely out of your control.

Your application documents play a critical role in the admissions decision, but so do factors like the number of available dorm rooms, the popularity of your major, the number of students who deferred entry last year, and the "institutional priorities" of the colleges that year. These priorities might include admitting students from specific regions, students studying in certain fields, students with extracurricular interests in areas the college hopes to promote, and more. Unfortunately, there's no way to know exactly what a college is seeking. So don't let rejections get you down — it's not you; it's them.

Let's focus on the acceptances and decide which college you should attend next!

Tracking Decisions and Deadlines

As you hear back from colleges, keep track of decisions and essential deadlines in a notebook or document. If you created a spreadsheet to keep track of applicant portals, you might want to simply add a few more columns to accommodate this extra information.

Types of Decisions

There are four main decisions you could receive in response to your transfer application:

- Admit
- Need more information
- Waitlist
- Deny

If you are admitted, look for a deposit deadline and instructions for taking the next steps to enrollment. The deposit deadline might be a specific calendar date, like June 1, or it might be relative to the decision date, such as "within two weeks." Carefully make a note of this deposit deadline, and perhaps set a calendar reminder on your smartphone. Each college may provide a different date by which you must commit, and it's easy to mix up dates and miss a deadline.

Sometimes a college will request more information from you before making a final decision. For example, a college might want to review your grades from the most recent term, especially if you are a low-unit transfer. In this case, you may have to wait for the term to end and send a new transcript once your grades have been posted. After providing the requested information, check the portal regularly for updates — a new decision should arrive soon.

Being waitlisted could be due to space limitations on the campus or in your major. Read the details carefully to see if you need to take action to join the waitlist. If the college provides you with an opportunity to send updates on your most recent achievements, take it! On the other hand, if your waitlist decision requests that students *not* send letters of continued interest or updated transcripts and activity lists, it's best to follow those instructions.

If you are denied admission, try not to be discouraged. This decision is from just one university, and it is not an indicator of your value as a student or as a human being. Universities generally receive far more applications from well-qualified candidates than they can possibly accommodate on their campuses.

Case Study: Amelia, University of Miami

Amelia held her breath as she checked her University of Miami portal, but the message it revealed was not very exciting. Miami had requested to see her spring semester grades before making a decision.

As a low-unit transfer, Amelia had been asked to submit both high school and college transcripts. Although her high school grades were mostly strong, she'd had a little case of senioritis during the second semester of her senior year, which caused her GPA to fall. Her first semester of college was a great success, but Miami wanted a little more evidence of Amelia's ability to succeed in challenging classes.

Amelia wrapped up the spring semester with a 3.8 GPA and sent her updated official transcript to the University of Miami. Just a couple of weeks after receiving the transcript, Amelia saw a new message in her portal: Admitted!

Statement of Intent to Register and Deposit Deadlines

To accept an offer of admission, you will need to submit an online form, usually called a Statement of Intent to Register (SIR), and pay the enrollment deposit fee before the stated deadline. Most universities charge deposit fees between $100 and $400, but some may charge up to $1,000 or more! These fees are usually nonrefundable but will be applied to your first tuition bill.

As you track your decisions and the corresponding deposit deadlines, you may find that some deadlines are much earlier than others. In fact, you may be asked to commit to one college before you even receive a decision from another! First-year applicants have "Decision Day," usually on May 1 each year, when colleges nationwide expect students to make their final decisions on where to enroll. Transfer applicants have no such consistency.

In an ideal world, you would be able to collect admission offers, financial aid award letters, and transfer credit evaluation reports from every college on your list before making a decision. Unfortunately, transfer students often have to make decisions with incomplete information. You may be missing financial aid information from one school, a transfer credit report from another, and have no decision at all from a third. If one of your acceptances has an early deposit deadline, you can try contacting the admissions office to request an extension. Some colleges will allow an extra week or two, but in many cases, those deadlines are firm. You may have to pass up one offer while hoping for another, or submit your Statement of Intent to Register (SIR) and put down an enrollment deposit, knowing you might lose that money if you decide to attend a school that admits you later.

Case Study: Jessica, Boston University

Jessica was delighted to receive her acceptance from Boston University (BU). However, she wanted to compare all admission offers before making a final decision. Unfortunately, BU's deposit deadline was before two other universities of interest were scheduled to release their decisions. Jessica wasn't certain that she would like one of those other universities better than BU. She just liked being informed and methodical when making decisions.

Ultimately, Jessica and her parents decided to submit the nonrefundable $800 enrollment deposit for BU. After visiting the school, Jessica felt certain that she would be happy there. If she gained admission to either of her other top choices, she would reevaluate. Although her parents were not thrilled about the idea of losing the $800 deposit, they were willing to risk that money to ensure that Jessica would be able to attend the college she liked most that fall.

A few weeks later, decisions came from the other colleges. Jessica was not accepted to either of them, so she was very glad she'd committed to BU when she did. BU also

> came through with a generous transfer credit evaluation that applied the vast majority of Jessica's credits to her new major program there. All's well that ends well.

Common Challenges and Questions

What if I didn't get in anywhere?

You have a few options:

- **Look for colleges that are still accepting transfer applications.** Some schools continue to evaluate potential transfer students right up to the start of the semester. The National Association for College Admission Counseling (NACAC) compiles a list of colleges accepting late first-year and transfer applications on its website each year.
- **Remain at your current college for another term.** If you still have useful classes to take at your current school, consider staying a little longer. Be careful, though — many universities have maximum unit limits, meaning that they will not accept high-unit transfers or will limit the number of units you can transfer in. Don't earn so many units that you make yourself ineligible for transfer!
- **Take a gap term and apply again.** If you are worried about accumulating too many credits, or if you just need some time off to focus on another round of transfer applications, consider taking a gap term. This will extend your time to degree attainment, but it might be worth the sacrifice to find a college that truly meets your needs.

What if I missed a deposit deadline?

If you realize that you missed a deposit deadline, or you let one pass while you waited for decisions from other schools, reach out to the admissions office immediately. If you were assigned a specific admissions counselor, contact that person directly and politely ask if it might still be possible to enroll. If you cannot enroll for the coming term, ask if you can defer enrollment to the next term or have your application reevaluated for the next admissions season. Universities are not obligated to extend deadlines or readmit you, but it's better to ask than to quietly give up.

I can't decide which college to attend!

If you received multiple acceptances and have the opportunity to compare offers, set aside some time to consider your college priorities. Which aspects of college life are most important to you? List these on the left side of a piece of paper or in the left column of a spreadsheet. Then, write your college options along the top. Go through the features one at a time, assigning a color to each college signifying its rank for that feature. Perhaps green represents the best option, yellow is mediocre, and red is poor. As you color in the page, look for a pattern to emerge. Is one college greener than the others? You can find a downloadable template for this exercise at TransferSavvy.com/Book.

Below is an example in which dark gray represents the best option, light gray is mediocre, and white is poor.

	College A	College B	College C
Feature 1	[best]	[mediocre]	[poor]
Feature 2	[best]	[best]	[mediocre]
Feature 3	[mediocre]	[mediocre]	[poor]

In this example, College A looks like the winner. If there is no clear favorite, think about some additional secondary features, or decide if some features should be weighted more heavily.

If you need more information, take another tour, attend an admitted students day, call your admissions counselor, or seek out current students online to ask them about their experiences. As you gather more information, keep coloring in your chart, and hopefully your top college will emerge.

CHAPTER 17

Transfer Credit Evaluation Report

Ideally, any college that admits you as a transfer student will provide a transfer credit evaluation report either with your decision letter or shortly thereafter. This report outlines how the accepting university has interpreted your previous college credits. At a minimum, this report should indicate which of your prior classes will be accepted for credit. It will likely also include information about which classes are still under review — you may need to provide additional documentation for these classes.

Think of this initial report as a first draft. Some of your classes may be missing or incorrectly categorized. You can appeal these credit decisions if you believe more credits should be transferred or applied to your degree as direct course equivalents. As the student who took the courses, you are the one best qualified to communicate what you learned from them! However, remember that you will need to provide appropriate documentation to support your requests for additional transfer credits.

Note that some universities may not provide transfer credit evaluations immediately after acceptance. These evaluations are typically managed outside of the admissions department and may require additional time and research. Unfortunately, certain schools are reluctant to begin this evaluation process before the student has accepted the admission offer and paid a deposit. In such cases, contact the university and inquire if there is a way to estimate transferable credits or look up equivalencies on your own. It's essential to evaluate your admission offers, including the transfer credit reports, before committing to a school.

Interpreting a Transfer Credit Report

Unfortunately, there is no common format for a college transfer credit evaluation report. Each one you receive will probably look a little different, some more detailed than others. If the report has many codes and abbreviations, look for a key defining them. It may also be helpful to have a copy of the university's course catalog (usually available on the website) handy as you identify course equivalencies, general education requirements, and major prerequisites.

Number of Credits Accepted

Begin by looking at the big picture. How many transfer courses will this new university accept? Compare the transfer credit report with your transcript(s). Every class on your transcript should be listed somewhere on the report and designated as "accepted for credit," "not accepted," or "needs review." If any classes are completely missing, alert the contact shown on the report or reach out to the admissions office.

Then, count the number of credits granted for each accepted class. If this new university follows the same academic calendar and credit system as your previous college(s), the number of credits on the transfer report should closely match the credits on the transcripts you submitted with your application. However, if you are transitioning to a different calendar system, the number of credits granted will differ significantly. (Refer to chapter 4 for additional details on translating credits between different systems.)

Here is an excerpt from a transfer credit evaluation by Colorado College (CC). This student was transferring from a semester-based community college where classes were typically worth 3 to 5 units each. Colorado College operates on a unique block schedule where students take one class at a time, and each class is worth exactly one credit. Calculating equivalencies between courses and credits from such disparate systems is challenging!

	Credit	General Education Requirements	CC Unit Equivalent
	Semester		
Elem Statistics/Probability	4		1
Intro to Social Problems	3		0.75
First Term Spanish	5	LANG	1.25
		Term Total	3 CC Units

This student took three classes at the community college: Statistics, Sociology, and Spanish, worth 4, 3, and 5 units, respectively. The 4-unit semester class was deemed equivalent to a 1-unit block schedule class at Colorado College. The other class credits were calculated proportionately so that the 3-unit class was worth 0.75 and the 5-unit class was worth 1.25 units. Although it may look unusual, this evaluation is a fair assessment of equivalent course credits.

Credits Applied to General Education Requirements

If you have been working on general education (GE), or breadth, requirements at your previous school, you have probably fulfilled some of the GE requirements at your new school. (See chapter 10 for more details on GE requirements.) Most universities require courses in writing, math, a second language, and a variety of fields outside the student's major. For example, English Composition 101 looks pretty similar at most colleges, so you should expect to see that your English 101 class not only transferred for credit but was used to fulfill the introductory writing requirement at the new college.

In the example above, Colorado College accepted the student's Spanish class for credit and noted "LANG" in the column labeled "General Education Requirements." This indicates that the course fulfills CC's second language requirement.

Credits Applied to the Major

Students who declare an intended major during the application process will be curious about how their earned credits might apply to the major at the new university. A thorough transfer credit report will include sections for both general education requirements and major courses. In the example below, Hollie, the "swirling" transfer student from the chapter 1 case study, has applied to Southern New Hampshire University (SNHU) as a general liberal arts major and is hoping to get transfer credit for classes she took over the past thirty years.

The first class listed has been fulfilled by a transfer class from another college. The second class is still unfulfilled, and marked with "1 course needed." The student did not have any transferable credits

214   Decisions

that SNHU deemed equivalent to this required major class, so this course will need to be taken at SNHU.

A: Major Courses (In progress)

Complete the following

Course	Title	Needed	Term	Grade	Credits
1. COM-212	Public Speaking		05/31/01	T	2.01
2. FAS-202	Introduction to Humanities II	1 course needed			

Elective Credits

Some transferable courses simply do not have equivalent classes at the accepting university. The credits are valid and will still be placed on the student's new transcript, but these credits can only be used as electives. Most students need several units of electives to complete a full bachelor's degree, but if too many courses are classified as electives, students may have a difficult time earning a degree in a timely manner. The example below (also from Hollie's SNHU transfer credit report) shows that this student took three transferable classes with no direct equivalent at SNHU.

Other Courses:

Course	Title	Term	Grade	Registered Credits	Earned Credits	Notes
1. MAT-ELE	Mathematics Elective	03/31/20	T	2.68	2.68	*TE
2. ATH-ELE	Anthropology Elective	12/31/20	T	2.68	2.68	*TE
3. SCS-ELE	Social Science Elective	08/31/21	T	2.68	2.68	*TE

Note that the electives are categorized by academic department. Some colleges require a specific number of electives in various subject areas to earn a degree, so these classifications are important. Also, note the unusual credit count of 2.68 per class. This student was transferring from a community college on the quarter system to SNHU, which is on the semester system. These classes were four units each on the quarter system. When multiplied by 0.67 to get semester units, the result is 2.68.

Under Review

Many universities request copies of the syllabi for your classes to evaluate your potential transfer credits. Some colleges, such as the University of Miami, are proactive and organized in this process. Miami has an entire transfer credit portal where a newly admitted transfer student can upload the syllabus for each class under review. Other colleges may wait for students to reach out with questions or an appeal and then provide revised transfer credit evaluations via email.

Some universities, like Pace, will annotate the transfer credit report when a syllabus is needed:

---------- TRANSFER COURSES ------------					---------- PACE EQUIVALENT --------			
SUBJ	CRSE	TITLE	CR.HRS	GRD	SUBJ	CRSE	TITLE	CR.HRS
ANTH	1028-F	First Year Studies: Conne	4.0	B			Submit syllabus	
Full Title: First Year Studies: Connection								
WRIT	3318-R	Place and Fiction	5.0	B			Submit syllabus	
		Acceptable Hours:	9.0				Earned Hours:	0.0

In this example, you can see that the student has nine credits available for potential transfer. Pace University titled this document "Preliminary Transfer Credit Evaluation" and has requested that this student submit the syllabi for further review. The transfer credit evaluation will be updated when the registrar and faculty have reviewed the student's documentation for these classes.

Credits Required for Degree

The most thorough transfer credit evaluations will include a degree audit report, a document that shows not only which classes and credits transferred but also how many additional classes and credits are required for your degree. Universities generally have a transfer policy that limits the number of external credits that can be applied to a degree, often 60 or 90 semester units. The remaining credits, usually 60 or 30 semester units for a 120-unit undergraduate degree, must be taken at the new university that will award your diploma. If your transferable course credits don't match up to exact classes at the new university, you may have to earn even more credits to graduate in your intended major. Before you accept an admission offer, find out how many credits you need to earn for your degree. If that information isn't stated in your transfer evaluation report, ask for it.

Transfer Credit Appeal

You do not have to accept the first offer of transferable credit you receive!

Universities commonly maintain a database of prior transfer credits. Once faculty review a class from a particular school and approve transferable credit, that class is added to the database for automatic credit transfer in the future. The first draft of your credit transfer report may be composed of mostly automated credits like these. To obtain additional credits for classes that are new and unfamiliar to the accepting university, you may need to submit extra documentation.

First Choice Documentation: Syllabi

In the previous section, you saw that Pace University requested syllabi for the courses that had not previously been evaluated for transfer credit. If you are not given appropriate credit for a class and believe the university may have made an error, write an email to the registrar or department that processed your credit report and attach your syllabus. Explain why you believe the class is creditworthy, and reference the university's transfer credit policies, if possible.

For example, here is an excerpt from the University of Chicago's transfer credit policy:

> Generally, the College grants transfer credit for liberal arts courses that carry at least three semester hours or four quarter hours of credit and were passed with a grade of C or better (in some cases, a grade of B or better is required) from an accredited institution that grants bachelor's degrees, subject to review by the Dean of Students office.[1]

In your credit request, describe how the course in question meets the requirements outlined in the policy with a statement such as, "This course from the accredited University of the Pacific was worth three semester credits, and I earned a B+ in the class." Note that you have attached the syllabus, and ask if there is any other documentation you could provide to help the university evaluate your transfer coursework.

Additional Documentation: Course Catalog Descriptions

If a syllabus is not sufficient information, or if you are attempting to prove that a course you took is substantially similar to a course offered by the accepting university, you may need to share course catalog descriptions as well. This step requires some extra effort because you will need to locate the course you took in your previous college's catalog and identify an equivalent course in the accepting university's course catalog. Provide course numbers, names, and descriptions, and ask if the two classes can be compared for possible equivalent credit.

Remember the Colorado College transfer credit evaluation? The Spanish class was clearly noted as fulfilling the second language requirement. But what about that Statistics class? Shouldn't that fulfill a math-related GE requirement?

	Credit	General Education Requirements	CC Unit Equivalent
	Semester		
Elem Statistics/Probability	4		1
Intro to Social Problems	3		0.75
First Term Spanish	5	LANG	1.25
	Term Total		3 CC Units

This student first researched the GE requirements at Colorado College and identified the relevant requirement: Formal Reasoning and Logic (FRL).[2] Colorado offers a class called Elementary Probability and Statistics that fulfills this requirement. So the student compared the course catalog description of the Colorado class with that of the previously completed class and found that they were described in very similar terms. The student submitted these two course descriptions to the registrar and requested a second review. The registrar quickly updated the credit report to add the FRL annotation in the General Education Requirements column. Success!

Additional Documentation: Textbook Details

Textbook details can also provide valuable evidence to support your transfer credit request. Gather the following information for each textbook used in your class:

- Title
- Author(s)
- Edition
- ISBN

You can usually find these details on the course syllabus, campus bookstore website, your textbook purchase/rental receipts, or the title page of the textbook itself. If possible, obtain a copy of the table of contents, either by scanning the relevant pages of the book or downloading a PDF from the publisher's website.

This information can help faculty at your new college understand the content and rigor of your previous course. Compare the textbooks used in the class you took with those required for the equivalent course at your new college. If the textbooks are similar or identical, it strengthens your case for course equivalency.

Request Additional Review

Don't be afraid to ask for an additional review of your credits. The key to efficient transfer and timely graduation is maximizing your previously earned credits. If some classes aren't transferring to the new school, ask why. If courses are classified as electives when they look equivalent to required classes, ask for a reevaluation. Remember that the university administrators have limited time to research every class offered at the four thousand universities in the US. Do a little research for them and ask for credit equivalencies that make sense. Provide the appropriate documentation so that reviewing faculty can easily see the class similarities and grant your request. Not every credit will be applied to your degree exactly as you hope, but it is always worth asking for a second evaluation. Every credit counts!

Case Study: Kate

Kate had always wanted to join the military. In fact, on her high school intake form, she listed the Marine Corps as her post-graduation goal. However, Kate's high school had a strong college-going culture, and military service was not seriously discussed as a post–high school option. So she set aside her military aspirations for three years until a Marine Corps recruiter visited her twelfth-grade band class. He had seen Kate's old intake form and arrived to follow up on her interest now that she was a senior. After speaking with the recruiter, Kate realized that she didn't have to choose between college and the military. If she joined the Marine Corps first, college would still be there when she got out. After serving, she would also be able to use GI Bill funds to afford college independently, without having to take on debt.

As a Marine, Kate specialized in electronics and took college classes in her spare time. When she separated from the military in late 2019, she planned to start college the following year, but unfortunately, Covid-19 derailed her plans. Since Kate did not want her first-year college experience to be entirely online, she went to work and began taking a few classes at the local community college. At first, she lacked confidence and had only modest plans to transfer to the nearest university, but her classmates and advisers inspired her to dream bigger.

Ultimately, Kate was admitted into mechanical engineering at several selective universities, and her final decision came down to Cornell University or the Massachusetts Institute of Technology (MIT). As flattering as the acceptance felt, MIT just wasn't practical for a first-generation veteran transfer student like Kate. MIT's fragmented transfer credit evaluation process was especially concerning for Kate. At MIT, credit review is disaggregated by department and cannot even begin until after the enrollment deadline has passed. Kate was informed that her classes would be evaluated by faculty over the summer and into the fall semester, meaning that she would not only have to commit to enrolling at MIT but also register for first-term classes before learning how her community college credits might (or might not) transfer. That was a leap of faith Kate wasn't willing to take.

Cornell required no such leap. After submitting her Cornell transfer application, Kate received an invitation to view the courses required for her degree and match those to courses she had previously completed. She then uploaded syllabi to the applicant portal so Cornell officials could assess course documentation and make transfer credit decisions during the application review period. As a result of this process, Kate received a preliminary transfer credit evaluation report one day after learning of her acceptance. This efficiency, combined with the prospect of support from Cornell's strong veteran community and robust advising services, convinced Kate that Cornell possessed the necessary infrastructure to fully support her undergraduate journey. Knowing that her community college credits had been accepted and a clear degree path lay ahead, Kate confidently committed to attending Cornell.

Common Challenges and Questions

What if I didn't receive a credit evaluation?

First, check your applicant portal and reread your decision letter. Sometimes the transfer credit report is uploaded to the portal without an announcement and can be overlooked. The decision letter may also mention how and when the transfer credit report will be delivered to you. If you find no mention of a transfer credit evaluation or report, you should contact your admissions counselor or general admissions department at the accepting university and ask when you can expect to receive an evaluation of your transferable credits.

Hopefully, the report will be on its way to you soon. But if you learn that the university's policy is to provide the transfer credit report at a later date, after the enrollment deposit deadline, keep asking questions. Understanding exactly how your credits will transfer before you enroll is essential. You may wish to remind the university of the ethical guidelines put forth by the National Association for College Admission Counseling (NACAC):

> Before requiring an enrollment confirmation, colleges should:
> i) Provide an evaluation of their prior college-level credits that is a good faith estimate of how those credits will be applied toward their degree requirements.[3]

Although these are guidelines, and not rules or laws, universities are strongly urged to abide by NACAC's code of ethics. You should feel empowered to remind universities of their ethical obligations.

What if I don't have a syllabus?

Most universities will request a syllabus in order to review a class for possible transfer credit. If you didn't save a copy of the syllabus yourself, do you have any friends who took the class and might have a copy? Have you tried contacting the professor? If the professor is no longer at the university, or doesn't respond to your request, try contacting the academic department that housed the class (e.g., the history department). Sometimes the administrative assistant or the department head will save copies of past syllabi. If all else fails, try an internet search. Perhaps a classmate or even the professor uploaded the syllabus to an online repository of class documents.

If you have searched everywhere and still cannot locate a copy of the syllabus, then pull together as much information as you can. For example, locate the description of the course in the school's course catalog. Find the name of the textbook you used. Share a final paper or project, if you saved it. Provide any information you can find, and hope for the best. A syllabus is almost always the preferred document, but don't give up on trying to get credits until you have exhausted all your possible options.

CHAPTER 18

Housing Options

You have been admitted, but where are you going to live?
Campus housing for transfer students can be scarce, so begin exploring your options as soon as possible. Keep an eye out for separate housing applications, often linked in your admissions letter or applicant portal. Given the competitive nature of transfer housing, it's wise to submit your application promptly, as spots are typically allocated on a first come, first served basis.

Even if you plan to live off campus, it's important to secure housing right away. In high-demand areas, continuing upper-division students may begin their apartment hunt as early as November of the preceding year. As a transfer student, you'll be entering this race late, so there's no time to lose.

Regardless of your housing preference, securing a place to live should be a top priority. Ideally, you want to have your living arrangements in place before committing to a college. If that's not feasible, at least try to get a sense of the likelihood of acquiring suitable housing nearby before you place a nonrefundable deposit.

Being proactive early on can save you from stress and disappointment down the line.

Campus Housing Application

As soon as you receive your acceptance to a school, start looking for housing application instructions. Even if you are required to live in campus housing, you generally need to complete an application form of some kind to express your housing preferences and prompt the creation of a housing contract. Most universities will require you to submit an enrollment deposit before you can officially apply for housing, but it's still wise to examine the process early and note any important deadlines.

Housing Locations

If you're lucky, the college you choose will have multiple housing options available for transfer students. Some schools may have transfer-specific housing, but others might categorize transfers and continuing students together for housing purposes. If you have the chance to live in a building (or on a dedicated floor) with other transfer students, that's often a great first choice. Many colleges also offer theme houses related to students' identities and interests. Living with peers who share similar backgrounds or interests can ease the transition to a new campus.

After evaluating special-interest housing, investigate the physical locations of available housing options. Get out a campus map and find out what's near each residence. If you have a confirmed major area of interest, check the class schedule to see where classes in your major are often held. Find your likely path to class and see if you pass by any important amenities like libraries, dining halls, or exercise facilities. Also research the types of rooms that are available in each facility. If you have a strong predilection for suite-style apartments, for example, that preference might take priority over map location. Last, if you hope to have a car with you on campus, find out which, if any, residences allow overnight parking for students.

In most cases, the housing application will ask you to rank your favorite housing facilities in order of preference, so be sure to research multiple possibilities. There is no guarantee that you will get your first choice, so be thoughtful about the additional options you rank. Also, consider the cost of each option and how it might affect your estimated cost of attendance calculations. (See chapter 19 for more on estimated costs.)

Room Options

The housing application will also probably ask about your room preferences. In other words, how many roommates do you want to have, and which facilities would you like to share with those roommates?

224   Decisions

Most American universities have a limited number of single rooms, and many of these may be reserved for students with specific disabilities. (If that applies to you, reach out to the disability services office for more information before you submit your housing application.) It's much more common for students to be choosing between double and triple rooms, or between shared and private bathrooms. You may also be asked to select from traditional residence hall arrangements or apartment-style suites, if the university offers both. As you rank your preferences, consider not only social factors but also cleaning responsibilities. Massive bathrooms shared by residents of an entire floor usually include regular professional cleanings, while small bathrooms and kitchens in apartment-style suites are typically the residents' responsibility.

If you already know a student at this school, or if you meet a fellow transfer student who is also planning to enroll, you may be able to request a specific roommate. It's OK if you don't know anyone, though — the college will assign you a roommate if necessary. In fact, some colleges have roommate questionnaires to help place compatible students together. If you have the opportunity to complete one of these surveys, be honest, not aspirational. For example, if you are a night owl, don't say that you are a morning person because you hope to establish new morning routines when you arrive on campus. The more honest your answers, the more compatible your roommate is likely to be.

Dining Plans

Students living in campus residences are often required to purchase meal or dining plans. These plans usually cover several meals at college dining halls and may include additional dollar amounts for snacks, coffee, and so on at school-operated convenience stores. Sometimes funds can also be used at select restaurants and stores in the surrounding neighborhood. Before committing to a plan, research the options and evaluate your likelihood of using the meals and funds provided at each plan level. When in doubt, consult the dining services website to learn about the options for changing your dining plan in the middle of the term. You may need to make an educated guess at first and adjust your plan later.

Exemptions for Campus Housing Requirements

Although it is somewhat rare, some universities require all students, including transfers, to live on campus for a specified number of terms. However, you can usually request an exemption if you have a valid reason for living off campus. Some common reasons for requesting a residential exemption include the following:

- You are above a certain age, or have been out of school for several years.
- You are a veteran.
- You can live with nearby family for free.
- You have a documented medical condition or disability.
- Your religious or moral beliefs cannot be accommodated in student housing.
- You are married or have dependent(s). (Some college campuses have family housing options. If this would be useful for you, inquire with the housing office as early as possible, as space is often limited.)

If you want to request an exemption to housing requirements, search for a form on the college's housing website. The exemption request may be included in the housing application portal for enrolled students and have a deadline similar to the deadline for housing application submission. Please note that you may need to reapply for the exemption each year at a campus with a multi-year campus living requirement.

Off-Campus Housing

If your selected campus does not offer housing for transfer students, or if you simply prefer to live off campus, you will need to search for rentals in the community. Even if you choose to enroll at a college that offers, but does not guarantee, campus housing for transfers, you should start looking for backup options. You may end up on a waitlist for campus housing, which can leave you in limbo until the start of the term. Eventually, you may decide to sign a lease for a nearby apartment rather than remain in waitlist limbo.

Alternatively, if a college can't promise campus housing for you, and off-campus rentals seem too expensive or difficult to secure, that particular college might not be the right choice for you. If so, it's best to discover that early in your decision-making process.

Off-Campus Housing Resources

Many universities create web pages with resources for locating off-campus housing. These university-sponsored pages typically include reliable community options for student housing and serve as a good starting point for your search. By the time you receive your acceptance, many of these student-focused apartments may be full for the upcoming term, though. If that is the case, you will have to get creative.

Check Facebook for a university-sponsored student group, an unofficial housing group, or possibly a group for parents and family members. Users in these groups often post about housing opportunities as they try to cancel leases, sublet apartments, or find roommates. Perhaps you can take over the lease for an outgoing student or someone taking a leave of absence. Or maybe a study-abroad student needs a temporary subletter for a year.

You may also find college forums, Reddit threads, and Craigslist posts about housing opportunities. Be careful to avoid scams, though! Try to visit the apartment in person if at all possible. At the very least, ask the landlord or potential roommate to do a live video walk-through with you from the street to the unit so you know it is legitimate. If you will be subletting, read the original lease or talk to the property manager or owner to make sure that subletting is allowed. Never pay by cash or wire transfer — a credit card with buyer protection is much safer in case of a dispute. Finally, research the average rental rates in the surrounding neighborhood — if it sounds too cheap to be real, it probably is.

Transportation

If your off-campus housing options are not within walking distance to campus, you also need to think about how you will commute to class and account for this mode of travel in both your time management and budget. If you need to buy a bicycle or a parking pass, factor in that expense; see the next chapter for guidelines on doing a financial aid comparison. If you plan to take a bus or other form of public transportation, research the daily timetable to learn how your class schedule might be affected. For example, if you are an astronomy major and need to take lab classes at night, a bus system that stops running at 8 p.m. will present a significant challenge.

Case Study: Caleb

Caleb was delighted to be accepted into George Washington University's engineering program as a sophomore transfer. Of all the schools he applied to, George Washington (GW) was by far his favorite. So, when he received his acceptance letter, he was eager to commit first and ask questions later. Since GW requires all first- and second-year students to live on campus, Caleb wasn't worried about housing. As a sophomore transfer, he would have needed an exemption to live off campus. Surely, GW had a housing space reserved for him.

When orientation was only three weeks away and there was still no confirmed housing assignment from GW, Caleb and his parents began to worry. But finally, GW came through with a room assignment. Caleb was all set to move into the Asian American theme house for continuing GW students. There was just one problem — Caleb is not Asian American. The housing office at GW assured him that this placement was not an accident. Housing spaces were limited, and the Asian American house had a vacancy that no returning Asian American student had requested to fill, so it was up for grabs.

Caleb and his parents flew to Washington, DC, for orientation week and helped him settle in. To their surprise, the house was completely empty. All the other house residents were returning students who had no need to be on campus until the following week. The first night was lonely, but Caleb quickly made friends at the transfer orientation the next day. The rest of orientation week passed smoothly, and Caleb finally met his housemates, who had a good laugh about their honorary Asian American resident.

Case Study: Amelia

Remember Amelia, the lateral transfer who enrolled at the University of Miami? She knew from the start that she would not be able to live on campus, since Miami clearly states on its website that transfer students are ineligible to apply for campus housing. So, as soon as her acceptance arrived, Amelia began searching online for apartments near campus.

It was June by then, and most apartments were already leased to other students for the fall. Miami rental prices were also higher than Amelia had expected. Luckily, she connected with another incoming transfer student online, and together they located an available apartment ten minutes from campus. It was a little farther away than they wanted, but they both had cars and realized that a campus parking permit would be much cheaper than the increased rent to live closer to campus.

Case Studies: Robin and Kate, Military Exemption

Robin and Kate, both veterans and transfer students, had already spent four years living in military barracks during their active-duty contracts and wanted to avoid living in traditional college dormitories. Robin enrolled at Yale, and Kate enrolled at Cornell, both of which require all students to live on campus for at least two years.

Since Robin joined Yale's Eli Whitney program for nontraditional students, she was automatically exempt from the campus housing requirement. She used her GI Bill funds to rent a lovely apartment with a view of campus and relished the independence it provided. Even before classes began, Robin was welcomed into the close-knit Eli Whitney and Yale veteran communities. She appreciated being able to choose between companionship and solitude as she desired. Although Robin lives alone, she does not feel lonely.

As both a veteran and a student over twenty-one years of age, Kate was doubly eligible for an exemption from Cornell's campus housing requirement. Since Kate had been living in her own apartment as a community college student, she recognized the need for her own space at Cornell to remain happy and productive; therefore, she applied for an exemption. Although Kate understood that living in residence halls with other students was a primary way to make new friends at college, as a more mature student, she also knew how to put herself out there to build connections and find the camaraderie and support she needed.

Common Challenges and Questions

Can I live in a sorority/fraternity house?

It would probably be difficult to arrange for Greek housing during your first term as a transfer student. If you are new to Greek life, you probably need to participate in a recruitment process before you can join the chapter, let alone live in the house. If you were a member of a sorority or fraternity at your prior college, you should be able to reaffiliate with the chapter at your new school. However, that process can take time and may require a formal vote by current chapter members while school is in session. It's also important to remember that each chapter of any given sorority or fraternity is unique. You should meet the members of the new chapter before you decide if you want to live in their house. With all that in mind, if you still want to move into a Greek house as soon as possible, you should contact the chapter leadership to inquire about options.

230   Decisions

My campus housing contract starts right *after* my transfer orientation, and I can't afford to go home in between. What should I do?

Since both your housing contract and the orientation schedule are furnished by the college, it's reasonable to ask them for assistance to smooth your transition. Sometimes the housing department can offer a temporary placement for students who need to be on campus for orientations or other activities prior to the start of the main housing contract. Some universities also offer multiple orientation options, with the last option before the start of classes being reserved for international students and others who live too far away to travel back and forth easily.

If you end up moving into campus housing early to accommodate attendance at a new-student orientation, be aware that the first couple of nights might be lonely, depending on your housing placement. Most continuing upper-division students will not be on campus during orientation. So if you aren't living in transfer-specific housing, you might return to an empty suite or floor when the day's orientation activities have ended. To combat loneliness, try to connect with other transfer students during the orientation activities. Find out where they are living and make a plan to eat dinner or watch a show together in the evenings until your roommates or suitemates move in for the upcoming term. Both you and your newfound friends will benefit from the early camaraderie.

CHAPTER 19

Financial Aid Awards and Cost Comparisons

Although the federal government oversees the FAFSA application, your financial aid award letters will not come from the government. Instead, each college that admits you will provide a unique document describing the financial aid that is available to you if you attend that particular college. This document should also show your net cost to attend the college — the total cost that you (or your family) will be responsible for paying each year.

If you submitted the FAFSA (and the CSS Profile, if required) in a timely manner, a financial aid award letter should accompany each admissions decision you receive, or arrive within a few weeks of acceptance. If your FAFSA submission was delayed, colleges may need more time to calculate your financial aid offers. Watch for email notifications that your award letters are ready, and remember to check your applicant portals periodically for updates. You may still be able to apply for financial aid if you have not yet done so. The FAFSA is usually available until June 30 of each year, although some states and universities may have earlier deadlines.

Once you have some financial aid offers in hand, you can begin to compare your options. Try not to be flattered by fancy-sounding scholarship offers and prestigious college names. This is a time to read carefully, think critically, and crunch some numbers.

How to Read a Financial Aid Award Letter

Unfortunately, financial aid award letters are not standardized, so comparing apples to apples can be tricky. Each university can use a

232   Decisions

different format and explain costs with unique terminology. However, if you know which pieces of information to look for, you can find the vital details you need to evaluate each offer. Sample award letters and other financial aid resources are available at TransferSavvy.com/Book.

Total Cost of Attendance

The total cost of attendance (COA) is like the "sticker price" of the college. It is the total dollar amount required to attend the college each year, as stated publicly on its website, before any discounts are applied. Although the exact fees included may vary by college, this number usually consists of full-time tuition plus student fees, housing, food, books, transportation, and other personal expenses. Some universities divide these costs into direct and indirect costs. Direct costs, such as tuition and housing, are billed by the university. Indirect costs are those that you incur as a result of attendance — books, transportation, technology, and so on.

When media outlets report on the rising cost of college, they usually cite the total cost of attendance, even though the average price most students pay is generally much lower. If your financial aid award letter does not include a number that represents the total cost of attendance, you should be able to locate this figure on the university's website.

Note that if the university is a public school funded by the state, the tuition may be marked as either "resident" or "nonresident" tuition. Make sure you are classified correctly, and reach out to the financial aid office immediately if you received an estimate with the wrong residency classification. Private universities generally use the same tuition price for all students, regardless of state residency.

Student Aid Index

Filing the FAFSA triggers an immediate calculation of an important number: the Student Aid Index (SAI). This is the number colleges use to calculate your demonstrated financial need. In the simplest terms, the total cost of attendance minus your SAI equals the dollar amount of financial aid that you need to receive to be able to afford the college. You may see your SAI, and possibly the equation used to determine

Financial Aid Awards and Cost Comparisons   233

your financial need, printed on the financial aid letter. It's OK if you don't, though — your SAI is also stated in the email confirmation you received from the FAFSA when you initially submitted your form.

If you were also required to complete the CSS Profile, there may be an additional note near your SAI or the calculation of your financial need. Since the CSS Profile can be customized with questions specific to each university, schools can develop unique formulas for calculating financial need. These formulas are then known as the school's institutional methodology. So you may see an explanation of how the college calculates your financial need using the FAFSA-determined SAI in combination with the school's institutional methodology.

Grants

Grants are a form of "gift" aid, that is, funds for college that do not need to be repaid. Most often, grants are awarded through federal, state, or institutional programs and are based on the student's level of financial need. The Federal Pell Grant is the primary form of gift aid offered by the US government, and it is awarded to students who demonstrate significant financial need as determined by the FAFSA form. Note that the Pell Grant has a lifetime limit, which is sometimes relevant for transfer students on an extended timeline.[1] As long as you continue to file the FAFSA and qualify, you can use Pell Grant funds for approximately six years of full-time undergraduate study, excluding summer terms. If you make use of the year-round Pell and use funds for summer classes, you will move through your eligibility at a faster rate. Check with a financial aid administrator at your current or future school to learn more.

Most states also offer grants to state residents planning to attend in-state schools.[2] Eligibility requirements vary widely by state. For example, several states allow students to use funds at both public and private in-state universities. A rare few even allow students to enroll at any college in the country and pay with state grant money. Most states base eligibility on demonstrated financial need, but some award grants based on GPA. More than fifteen states also permit undocumented students to apply for state financial aid. On the other hand, some states have more stringent requirements, only allowing grant recipients to use funds at a limited number of public universities, or only in specific degree programs that lead to public service careers like teaching. Visit the website of your state's higher education agency to determine your eligibility for college grants.

Certain individual colleges also offer grants to students whose government-funded grants do not cover the entire cost of attendance. Well-endowed private universities may be able to provide grants that cover 100 percent of a student's demonstrated financial need, but it is more common for colleges to contribute partial grants alongside other forms of financial aid, such as loans or work-study programs.

Institutional Scholarships

Scholarships are another form of "gift" aid, but unlike most grants, scholarships are usually awarded based on academic achievement, athletic talent, or other student qualities rather than financial need. Colleges often use these merit scholarships to attract students with unique talents or high GPAs to their campuses. Some universities have clearly established formulas for offering scholarships to students with certain GPAs. More frequently, though, the requirements for these scholarships and the dollar amounts provided remain mysterious, and criteria may change from year to year. So, when you receive your financial aid letter, you may be pleasantly surprised or deeply disappointed by an unexpected scholarship amount.

Like grants, institutional merit scholarships should be renewable as long as the eligibility requirements are met each year. However, these scholarships will likely expire sooner than the six-year Pell Grant. Most renewable transfer scholarships are valid for only two or three years — the expected timeframe for a transfer student to earn a bachelor's degree.

If you have earned any scholarships from outside organizations like Phi Theta Kappa or Jack Kent Cooke, they will probably not appear on your financial aid award letter yet. You must notify your chosen college and have the outside scholarship funds sent to the school's financial aid office once you enroll. Watch out — while some colleges allow stacking of scholarships, others practice "scholarship displacement," meaning they will reduce the amount of financial aid the college provides and replace it with your outside scholarship on a revised financial aid letter. If you have earned a sizable scholarship from an independent organization, you must carefully research each university's policies to see how your financial aid might be affected.

Loans

Student loans, like car loans and home mortgages, must be repaid with interest. Loans, sometimes listed as "self-help" awards, are likely to be included as part of your overall financial aid package, but you do not have to accept the loans just because they are on your award letter. You have the right to refuse loans, which you should do if you have other options to pay for college. Don't go into debt if you don't have to!

If loans are the only way to make college affordable, begin with Federal Direct Loans. Almost every student who files the FAFSA is eligible for a Federal Direct Unsubsidized Loan. These low-interest loans directly from the US government begin accruing interest immediately, although you do not need to make payments until after you leave college. If you are eligible for a Federal Direct Subsidized Loan (for families with demonstrated financial need), you will save some money because the government pays the interest on your behalf as long as you are enrolled in school. Parents of dependent students may also be able to take out Direct PLUS loans, aka parent PLUS loans, although this option may or may not be listed on your student financial aid award letter. Private loans for students or parents are also possible, but you should not consider these unless you have exhausted all the Federal Direct Loan options available to you.

Work-Study

Another option you might see on your award letter is Federal Work-Study. This is sometimes also listed under "self-help" financial aid because you are not just given money for college — you must work at an on-campus job to earn that money. So how is work-study different from simply getting a part-time job at your school? From the student perspective, it's not actually that different. The main benefit is that certain campus jobs are reserved for work-study students only. You still

236   Decisions

have to apply for the job and show that you have the appropriate experience to succeed, but there may be less competition, since applications are restricted to students who are deemed eligible for work-study via their FAFSA application.

Unmet Need

Subtract grants, scholarships, and any selected self-help aid from the total cost of attendance. The result is the price you will be responsible for paying if you enroll in this college. If this amount exceeds your SAI, it might be categorized on your financial aid award letter as unmet need or outstanding cost. It also could be hidden under a category for private loans. It is crucial that you locate or calculate this number, whatever it may be called, because the college has not offered you a plan for paying this price — it is up to you to find a way to pay if you choose to enroll at this college.

Compare Financial Aid Offers and Expenses

In an ideal scenario, you would receive all your admission offers, credit evaluations, and financial aid award letters before needing to place an enrollment deposit. In reality, with varying transfer application deadlines and decision release dates, you may see offers trickle in over several weeks. However, you want to be able to compare your options with as much detail as possible, especially when it comes to predicting your college costs. So, before the first enrollment deposit deadline, gather all the financial aid award letters you have received and compare them line by line.

Set up a spreadsheet or simply draw a chart on a piece of paper. Put each college under consideration along the top. Down the left side, you'll enter each category of expenses followed by your grants and scholarships, as explained below. See pages 241–42 for an example of a complete comparison chart and download a blank worksheet to complete yourself at TransferSavvy.com/Book.

Total COA

Begin with the total cost of attendance (COA) broken down by category. Remember that the COA includes tuition, housing, food, books, transportation, and any other fees directly related to attending that college. Make sure that the COA of each college lists the same items. If one college includes transportation expenses and another college does not, you won't be comparing apples to apples!

If you think you can make a better estimate of certain expenses than what's given in an award letter, this is a good time to adjust the numbers to match your expected spending. For example, if a school estimates that students spend $3,000 per year on transportation but you live just ten miles from campus, you can safely estimate a lower expense. On the other hand, if your family lives far from campus and you plan to go home for every holiday, birthday, and academic break, you will need to add up the expected costs of multiple flights throughout the year, which would likely increase your travel expenses. Make any practical adjustments necessary and jot down your total COA for each school.

Example COA Calculations

Here is the start of a sample chart comparing three potential colleges: a public in-state college, a public college in another state, and a private college. It shows tallies of the tuition and fees, room and board, and other expenses categories to get an estimated total cost of attendance.

Category	College A: Public in-state	College B: Public out-of-state	College C: Private in-state
Tuition and fees			
Tuition	$15,934.00	$36,516.00[*]	$59,580.00[†]
Fees	$766.00	$1,232.00	$404.00
Subtotal	$16,700.00	$37,748.00	$59,984.00
Room and board			
Housing	$11,960.88	$10,800.00	$11,938.00
Meal plan	$6,614.28	$6,642.00	$5,876.00
Subtotal	$18,575.16	$17,442.00	$17,814.00

Category (continued)	College A: Public in-state	College B: Public out-of-state	College C: Private in-state
Other expenses			
Books and supplies	$1,680.00	$1,300.00	$650.00
Personal expenses	$2,361.00	$3,104.00	$2,006.00
Transportation	$300.00‡	$2,500.00	$876.00
Subtotal	$4,341.00	$6,904.00	$3,532.00
Sum: Total cost of attendance	$39,616.16	$62,094.00	$81,330.00

* You might qualify for in-state tuition next year.
† Has a tuition guarantee so your tuition rate is locked in.
‡ This fee is adjusted because you live nearby.

Grants and Scholarships

Next, list any gift aid awarded. Include federal and state grants, merit scholarships, and any other funds that do not need to be repaid. Colleges may list loans on your financial aid letter, but those are not gifts. Loans will have to be repaid with interest, so that is still *your* money. When you are comparing price tags on colleges, don't include any loans — you want to compare the real cost of each college, whether you are paying the total up-front or spreading payments over the next several years.

Check the conditions for each award. Can the scholarship be renewed each year? Is there a minimum GPA required for the scholarship to be renewed? If so, enter that GPA in your spreadsheet. Is there a limit to the number of renewals of a grant or scholarship? What are the requirements to maintain eligibility for each award? If the time limits or eligibility conditions of any award make it seem unlikely that you would be able to depend on those funds for your full expected time in college, make a note of this — perhaps make a big asterisk with a highlighter so you don't forget this detail.

Remember that outside scholarships are probably not listed on your financial aid letter. If you earned any scholarships from outside organizations, note those amounts in every college's column because those funds can be applied to any school. Consider each college's policy on "scholarship displacement," too. If any of your colleges will decrease your gift aid because you have outside scholarships, find out the exact terms of their policies and adjust the amount of your outside scholarships accordingly.

Your Net Price

Add up all your grants and scholarships for each college and include outside scholarships adjusted to reflect scholarship displacement policies. Then subtract those numbers from the total cost of attendance figure for each college. The price that is left is your responsibility to pay for your first year at that college.

Example Gift Aid Calculations

Continuing the chart from earlier, we've listed the total grants and scholarships received and then subtracted those from the total cost of attendance. The result is your net price.

Sum: Total cost of attendance	$39,616.16	$62,094.00	$81,330.00
Grants and scholarships			
Federal grants	$3,500.00	$3,500.00	$3,500.00
State grants	$8,000.00	$0.00	$0.00
Merit scholarships	$1,500.00	$20,000.00	$35,000.00
Scholarship renewal GPA requirement	3	3.2	3.5
Maximum renewal terms	6 semesters	6 semesters	4 semesters
Subtotal	$13,000.00	$23,500.00	$38,500.00
Your Net Price (after aid)	$26,616.16	$38,594.00	$42,830.00

Future Year Calculations

To keep the math simple, you might just want to multiply the price you've calculated by two or three years (or whatever you estimate your time to graduation will be) to get the overall cost for your degree. However, that won't be entirely accurate. Inflation may drive costs up, and scholarships and grants can expire.

Check each school to see if it offers a guaranteed tuition program or the opportunity to lock in your first-year tuition rate. If it does, the simple math plan will provide a good estimate. At most colleges, though, you can expect tuition rates to rise slightly each year. Actual cost increases and overall inflation rates vary by institution and can be affected by the broader financial markets, but recently, tuition rates have risen at a rate between 2 percent and 5 percent each year.[3] If you don't have guaranteed tuition locked in, multiply this year's tuition by 1.035 to get an estimate of tuition costs for your second year.

Your tuition rates could also change if your state residency status changes. At many public universities, students who enroll as nonresidents continue to pay nonresident tuition every year — residency for tuition purposes cannot be obtained by attending school in the state. Some state universities have more flexible rules for residency, though. If you are considering an out-of-state public university, read about their rules for residency reclassification. You may be able to achieve resident status during your first year so that you can pay in-state tuition from the second year forward. That could be a huge savings, so note that on your chart.

Complete Example Walk-Through

Let's do a full walk-through of this sample financial aid comparison with all the details included. Say you live in the same state as College A, a public university, so you would pay in-state tuition there. College B is a public university in a neighboring state, but the state has lax residency rules, so you may be able to pay nonresident tuition this year and switch to in-state tuition next year. College C is also in the state where you live, but everyone pays the same tuition rate, regardless of residency, because it is a private university. The only college that offers guaranteed tuition is College C. As a private school, it may start with a higher tuition rate, but it's guaranteed not to increase while you are enrolled.

The estimated amounts listed for housing, books, and so on seem reasonable, so the only fee you adjust is transportation. You live a short drive or bus ride away from College A, so you won't spend too much on transportation. Add up the expenses to arrive at your total cost of attendance for each university: $39,616.16, $62,094.00, and $81,330.00. That's quite a difference in cost between the schools!

Next, consider your grants and scholarships. You filed the FAFSA and qualified for a federal grant, so that award ($3,500) is the same at every school. Your state also offers grants, but they can only be used at in-state public universities. (Each state's rules are different, so read the fine print!) Thus, your state grant money ($8,000) can only be used at College A. Each college also awarded you a merit scholarship. College C gave you the largest scholarship at $35,000 per year! It's flattering to win such a prize, but try not to let that flattery persuade you. Crunch those numbers and see which college is going to be the most affordable.

Category	College A: Public in-state	College B: Public out-of-state	College C: Private in-state
Tuition and fees			
Tuition	$15,934.00	$36,516.00*	$59,580.00†
Fees	$766.00	$1,232.00	$404.00
Subtotal	$16,700.00	$37,748.00	$59,984.00
Room and board			
Housing	$11,960.88	$10,800.00	$11,938.00
Meal plan	$6,614.28	$6,642.00	$5,876.00
Subtotal	$18,575.16	$17,442.00	$17,814.00
Other expenses			
Books and supplies	$1,680.00	$1,300.00	$650.00
Personal expenses	$2,361.00	$3,104.00	$2,006.00
Transportation	$300.00‡	$2,500.00	$876.00
Subtotal	$4,341.00	$6,904.00	$3,532.00
Sum: Total cost of attendance	$39,616.16	$62,094.00	$81,330.00

242 Decisions

Category (continued)	College A: Public in-state	College B: Public out-of-state	College C: Private in-state
Grants and scholarships			
Federal grants	$3,500.00	$3,500.00	$3,500.00
State grants	$8,000.00	$0.00	$0.00
Merit scholarships	$1,500.00	$20,000.00	$35,000.00
Scholarship renewal GPA requirement	3	3.2	3.5
Maximum renewal terms	6 semesters	6 semesters	4 semesters
Subtotal	$13,000.00	$23,500.00	$38,500.00
Your Net Price (after aid)	$26,616.16	$38,594.00	$42,830.00

* You might qualify for in-state tuition next year.
† Has a tuition guarantee so your tuition rate is locked in.
‡ This fee is adjusted because you live nearby.

Deduct your grants and scholarships from the total cost of attendance to find your net price for each college. It looks like College A will be the cheapest and College C will be the most expensive. However, College C's price is not much more than College B's, and only College C offers a tuition guarantee. So if you plan to spend two or three years at either of these colleges, you might end up paying a similar overall price. Then again, College C has the highest GPA requirement for scholarship renewal. If you cannot maintain a 3.5 GPA, you could lose your $35,000 merit scholarship. Ponder not only the financial strain that would cause but also the stress you might feel if you are constantly worried about maintaining high grades.

There is one more factor for you to consider, and it's not listed on your financial aid award letter: How many credits do you need to earn for your degree at each school? Look at your transfer credit evaluations. If one of these colleges rejected several of your classes or only accepted some classes for elective credit, you may need to spend an extra

Financial Aid Awards and Cost Comparisons   243

term or two earning the credits needed for a degree. Although College A has the lowest net price in our chart, it won't be the cheapest college overall if you have to spend an extra year earning your degree there.

The chart below shows the total cost for a degree at each school, if College A required an extra year. (To keep it simple, no inflation or changes in residency were included in these calculations.) College A doesn't look like such a good deal anymore, does it?

College A, 3 years	College B, 2 years	College C, 2 years
3 x $26,616.16	2 x $38,594.00	2 x $42,830.00
$79,848.48	**$77,188.00**	**$85,660.00**

Financial Aid Appeal

Family finances can be complicated and nuanced. Even though the FAFSA and CSS Profile forms are extremely detailed, it is still difficult to fully capture complex financial data in standardized forms. As you compare financial aid offers, you may also find inconsistencies in the ways different institutions interpret your financial data and academic background to determine eligibility for scholarships. If the college you most want to attend did not offer the best financial aid awards, or if your financial circumstances have recently changed, it might be worthwhile to file an appeal.

Need-Based Appeal

Remember that the FAFSA and CSS Profile require data from your prior-prior-year tax forms. A lot can change in two years, though. If you feel that the data contained in the FAFSA (and CSS Profile, if applicable) is no longer completely accurate, you may want to file a financial aid appeal based on concrete changes in your financial circumstances. Some examples of concrete changes include divorce, job loss, death of a parent, and extraordinary medical expenses. There may be other situations that necessitate a need-based appeal, too — just be aware that you will be asked to provide documentation of the changes in your financial circumstances. It is difficult to appeal if you don't have verifiable proof of your change in finances.

Merit/Comparison Appeal

If other universities offered more generous grants and scholarships to defray the cost of your college education, you may have the power to request a reconsideration of your financial aid award at a school with a less generous offer. You don't want to call this a negotiation — you aren't haggling over the price of a used car! But if you sincerely want to attend a school that didn't provide a strong offer of gift aid, it may be worth requesting additional funding so that you can choose a college based more on your preferences than the price tag.

How to Appeal

Every school has its own method for processing financial aid appeals. Begin by checking the financial aid pages on the website of the school you hope to attend. Some colleges post clear, step-by-step instructions on how to submit an appeal. They may have a simple form to get the process started. You will likely need to submit some kind of letter or narrative statement describing the reasons for your request. At some point, you may also need to meet with a financial aid administrator on campus or by phone or videoconference to discuss your specific situation.

The federal government empowers college financial aid administrators to use their "professional judgment" to adjust the official data on your FAFSA form.[4] Thus, any requests for additional need-based aid must be directed to the financial aid office. However, at many colleges, the admissions office is the department responsible for determining the value of merit scholarships, so you may need to address a letter to admissions if you hope to receive more merit aid.

Your written statement should be polite and concise and contain the most relevant details. Be sure to include any of the following elements that are applicable to your situation in your letter:

1. Introduction. Who are you?
2. Summary of your reasons for wanting to attend this particular college. Be enthusiastic!
3. Brief summary of the problem.

4. Change(s) in circumstances since FAFSA submission, such as a decrease in salary, or the death of a parent who was to provide financial support.
5. Expenses not included in FAFSA.
6. A statement indicating that the current offer of merit aid makes the college unaffordable for you.
7. Details including dollar amounts.
8. More generous financial aid awards from other colleges (attach copies of the best offer letters).
9. Personal details (especially new facts) that make you worthy of increased scholarship funds.
10. Reiteration of your desire to attend this school and a sincere message of thanks.

You can find sample appeal letters at TransferSavvy.com/Book.

Financial aid appeals can take several weeks, so begin the process as early as possible. Also, be prepared for questions and requests for proof. Responding quickly to messages can expedite the appeal process and help the college arrive at a decision sooner.

Case Study: Nicole

Nicole's family lived comfortably, thanks to her dad's lucrative job as a lawyer. They hadn't saved specifically for college, planning to pay tuition from her dad's high salary and the family's general savings. Additionally, they lived near an excellent public university that had a streamlined community college to university transfer plan. Nicole's planned pathway was affordable and low-stress. Sadly, the year before she planned to transfer, Nicole's father unexpectedly died of a heart attack. Not only did the family's primary source of income suddenly disappear, but the family savings account was now earmarked for necessary survival expenses until Nicole's mom could find a job. While completing the FAFSA,

Nicole and her mom realized that their prior-prior-year tax returns showed wealth they no longer possessed. After allowing herself some time to grieve, Nicole submitted her transfer application to the nearby public university she had always planned to attend. She was admitted, but without need-based financial aid, the net price was just too high. Nicole and her mother wrote a letter to the financial aid office, explaining the change in circumstances. The college asked for a copy of her father's death certificate and an estimate of her mother's earnings, then adjusted Nicole's FAFSA data to reflect the family's current finances. With that, Nicole became eligible for need-based grants and was able to move forward with her education as planned.

Case Study: Morgan

Morgan, a nonbinary student, was an academic star. They earned straight A's in challenging classes at their community college and submitted nearly perfect SAT scores. It's no surprise that several universities offered them transfer admission. Morgan's middle-class family did not qualify for much need-based aid, so Morgan focused their college search on transfer-friendly colleges with generous merit scholarships. Their favorite college offered the largest scholarship, but unfortunately, it also had the highest total cost of attendance among all the colleges on their list. Their second-favorite college offered a smaller scholarship, but due to its lower cost of attendance, it was the most economical option overall. Morgan wrote a financial aid appeal letter and sent it to the admissions office at their favorite college. They described how much they truly wanted to attend this college but explained that they would have to attend their second-choice school for financial reasons and attached the financial aid award letter as proof. In response, Morgan's first-choice college amended their merit award to match the net price of the second-choice college, allowing Morgan to enroll.

Common Challenges and Questions

What if I don't get the award letter in time?

If you submitted the FAFSA (and CSS Profile, if needed) before the college's stated financial aid deadline, you should receive an award letter soon after admittance and well before any deposit deadlines. If you are being asked to make enrollment decisions before receiving your financial aid offer, contact the admissions office, inquire about the delay, and ask for an extension to the enrollment deposit deadline. You may also want to contact the financial aid office to see if they can provide an estimated date for the release of your financial aid letter.

Similar to the ethical guidelines regarding transfer credit evaluations, NACAC also provides a statement regarding the timing of financial aid offers for transfer students:

Before requiring an enrollment confirmation, colleges should:...
ii) Provide a financial aid offer when applicable.[5]

Again, these are just guidelines, but you should feel empowered to remind universities of the NACAC guiding ethics when you ask for financial aid information or an extension to the deposit deadline.

Where do I qualify for in-state tuition?

Gaining state residency for the purpose of paying in-state tuition is a complex topic. If you are under a certain age and your parents still live in your home state, many colleges will continue to consider you a resident of your home state, even if you have been studying elsewhere for years. A relocation to enroll at a particular school is usually classified as a temporary move, not a change in permanent residency. However, some states and universities have different rules and may allow students to claim residency if they can prove the permanence of their relocation through actions such as obtaining a state driver's license, registering a car in the state, or filing state income taxes independently of their parents. To complicate matters even further, residency policies can be different for students who are older, married, military personnel or veterans or their dependents, or whose parents have moved away from the student's original home state while the student was away at college. Every student must carefully research the residency rules for their specific situation and reach out to college financial aid offices with any questions.

These financial aid calculations are confusing! Where can I get help?

Financial aid is a complicated topic! Many students find it confusing. As you begin the process of applying for financial aid, you may find the resources available through the federal government FAFSA Help Center website useful. The Federal Student Aid YouTube channel also has a number of helpful video tutorials.[6] If you really get stuck, you can contact the FAFSA folks for personalized assistance.[7] They even have an online chat option.

Once you have your award letters in hand, you can also use a free online tool such as TuitionFit.org or the FinAide mobile app to evaluate your financial aid offers. TuitionFit.org offers a free service to all students who share their financial aid award letters with the program. When you upload images of your letters, TuitionFit redacts your personal information, allowing you to see how your grants and scholarships compare with those received by other students with similar backgrounds. The FinAide app asks a short series of questions about your Student Aid Index (SAI), each college's total cost of attendance, and the entries on each financial aid award letter. Once you enter the details for a few of your prospective colleges, you will be able to see the financial breakdown for each one and compare the offers directly.

PART VII

POST-ACCEPTANCE

Congratulations on reaching the final stages of your college transfer journey! As you approach the finish line, it's important to understand that the work doesn't end with your acceptance letter. The time period between receiving your offer and stepping onto your new campus is filled with important tasks and exciting opportunities that will set the stage for your success at your new institution. This section will guide you through the essential steps between accepting your offer and thriving in your new environment.

We will start by covering the administrative tasks necessary to finalize your enrollment. Then we'll move on to the more exciting aspects of preparing for your transfer and eventual graduation.

CHAPTER 20

The Fine Print

Once you have decided which school to attend and submitted your enrollment deposit, you can begin planning for a smooth transition to your new college home. The university will likely provide you with checklists and reminder emails, but you should keep your own to-do list as well. At this stage, attention to detail is critical — you've worked hard to reach this point, so it's important not to let anything jeopardize your college dreams.

This chapter will guide you through the essential tasks that must be completed between the deposit deadline and the start of the term. Some of these tasks may seem bureaucratic and tedious. Others provide exciting opportunities to engage with your new campus and fellow students as you prepare for the next phase of your college journey.

Remember, each step you take now is an investment in your future!

Conditional Admission

The phrase "conditional admission" refers to a university acceptance that is planned for the future, provided that the student successfully completes certain tasks on the timeline laid out by the college. For example, an international student might be required to spend a year in an intensive English program to improve language skills. If that student performs well in the English language program, the tentative university acceptance will be confirmed. Cases such as this are unique, and the conditions will be explicitly described in the admissions decision letter.

Many students are unaware that most regular college admission offers are also technically conditional. These offers are tentative, based on the student meeting certain criteria, such as maintaining a minimum GPA or passing in-progress courses. The conditions are usually straightforward and achievable, but they are also important; failure to satisfy these conditions could result in your admission offer being rescinded.

Common Conditions

Review your admission letter carefully — it should outline the specific requirements you need to meet in order to finalize your enrollment. You might also find these details listed on the university website or in your applicant portal.

Here are some of the most common conditions attached to standard offers of transfer admission:

- Maintaining a minimum GPA
- Successfully completing in-progress or planned courses
- Achieving minimum grades in each in-progress or planned course
- Earning an associate degree (if required for your admission pathway)
- Completing a minimum number of credits
- Submitting official final transcripts and test score reports

If you have any doubts or concerns about the requirements you must meet to formally confirm your acceptance, contact the admissions office for clarification. Also, keep a close watch on your email, including your spam folders. When issues arise after acceptance, college administrators often communicate via email and offer opportunities to rectify the situation if possible.

Communicating Changes

Plans change. Sometimes schedule changes are beyond your control — classes fill up before you can register or get canceled when an instructor falls ill. Other times, you may need to adjust your class schedule to accommodate work plans or childcare. Don't panic, but do communicate with the admissions office immediately. Review the minimum requirements for admission and identify potential replacement courses. Then contact your new university and explain the situation. Ask if your updated course schedule is acceptable and find out if there are any other actions you should take to ensure that your enrollment will not be adversely affected by your schedule changes.

Significant GPA changes and unexpected grade dips are also cause for concern. You might hope that a new D on your transcript will go unnoticed, but that is unlikely. It's best to be proactive and contact the admissions office as soon as you realize you are on track to earn an uncharacteristically low grade. University administrators are usually much more willing to work with students who are up-front and honest about the challenges they face. By taking initiative and communicating transparently, you demonstrate maturity and responsibility — traits that universities value in their students.

Submitting Official Documents

It might feel like you have already submitted a million documents with your applications, but you probably aren't done yet! The college you decide to attend will likely ask you to submit more official paperwork before you arrive on campus. Look for a checklist in your portal to know exactly which documents your new school requires, and follow the directions provided to complete and submit them in a timely manner.

Final Official College Transcripts

If you applied for transfer while attending another college, your final official transcript is the most important document you can submit. The new college initially made an admissions decision without knowing your final grades. Now they want to make sure you passed those classes and maintained your GPA. Wait for your final grades to be added to your transcript, then order an official copy to be sent directly to your new college. You may also have the option to order your official transcript in advance and select an option to "hold for final grades." That way, the transcript will be sent as soon as it is ready.

Even if you were not enrolled in college as you went through the transfer application process, you might still need to send new official copies of your transcripts. Many colleges accept unofficial copies of transcripts uploaded to the application site or ask students to

254 Post-Acceptance

self-report courses and grades on the transfer application. Colleges can make initial decisions based on these unofficial reports and then review the official transcripts later. Although your courses and grades may not have changed since you applied, you still need to send official copies now that you are admitted.

Last, remember to send *all* of your official transcripts directly from the schools where you earned credit. You created a transcript at every college you ever attended, and your new university really does want official copies of them all. This may seem unnecessary if all your courses are represented on your most recent college transcript, but many colleges do not accept "pass-along" credits. (See pages 53–54 for more information.)

Note that the details you entered on your application will be checked against your final transcripts, and any discrepancies will need to be investigated. If you realize you made an error and something on the application will not match your official documents, contact the admissions office immediately to explain the situation and ask for guidance.

Proof of Associate Degree Completion

Not all community college students complete an associate degree before they transfer, but if you earn one, be sure to provide your new university with proof of completion. This is especially important if an associate degree is a required part of your transfer agreement or waives certain general education requirements. Remember that the awarding of an associate degree is not automatic in most cases. Students usually have to petition for the degree they wish to earn during their final term, often several weeks before graduation. Get in touch with your academic adviser early if an associate degree is an essential part of your transfer plan.

Proof of High School Graduation

You may need to submit an official copy of your high school transcript. In most cases, colleges that request this document simply want proof of high school graduation. If you completed high school by earning a GED or similar, sending an official score report or confirmation of high school equivalency should achieve the same goal. Completion of an associate degree sometimes waives this requirement entirely.

Official Test Score Reports

Test scores may not have been required for your transfer application, but if they were, be sure to send official score reports. You should also send official score reports for any exams that might provide you with college credit, such as AP or CLEP tests. You may need to follow up on credit for test scores — some colleges require extra paperwork to process credit earned by exam.

Housing Contract

Wherever you decide to live, you will need to sign a housing contract or lease and pay a deposit. If you opted for campus housing, look for a university housing contract on your admitted student dashboard or in your email.

Health Forms

Many universities require students to have a minimum number of vaccinations before arriving on campus. If you are living in university housing, the vaccination requirement may be more comprehensive. You may be able to call your doctor and request proof of immunization, but allow extra time to get new vaccinations if needed. It can take several weeks to get an appointment with a doctor, so look for a list of required immunizations early. Alternatively, you can request an exemption from the immunization requirements if you have a medical or philosophical incompatibility. This usually requires a letter from a doctor as well.

Health Insurance

Most universities require students to have some form of health insurance. Even if your school doesn't require it, you should still investigate options for obtaining health insurance. Medical care is extraordinarily expensive in the US, and an unexpected medical bill could derail your education.

You may already have health insurance through your employer, a family member, or the government health insurance marketplace. Read your policy carefully to understand how medical care may or may not be covered while you attend school. For example, health insurance can be restricted to specific geographic regions; if your school is in a location not typically covered by your existing insurance, you may have difficulty obtaining care. Some employer-sponsored health insurance plans require employees to work a minimum number of hours. If your employer is providing your health insurance, learn the requirements for continuing on your current health plan. You might need to reduce your work hours to focus on school, but you can't risk losing health coverage midyear.

Assuming that your current health insurance plan will provide adequate coverage while you are in college, you can submit evidence of your existing health plan to the university. Check your student dashboard for a section where you can upload a copy of your health insurance card. In many cases, if you fail to provide proof of existing health insurance, you will automatically be enrolled in the student health plan and billed for university-sponsored insurance. Student health plans can offer a good value for some, so explore the options before making a decision. Then, if you choose to decline the college-sponsored health plan, look for a form on your student dashboard where you can opt out of coverage and avoid the unnecessary expense.

Financial Aid

Formally accept any scholarships and grants you were awarded and apply for loans if needed. You can also reject loan offers — just because the college included loans in your financial aid package does not mean you need to accept them. These tasks can usually be completed online through the student dashboard.

Notify All Colleges

First things first — make sure you have confirmed your enrollment and paid the deposit at your selected university. Double-check that the credit card transaction went through, the check was cashed, and/or the payment was acknowledged and accepted by the university. If you have any doubts about your enrollment status, contact the university before taking any other actions.

The next step is to let other universities know that you have decided not to transfer to their institutions. You may also need to withdraw pending transfer applications that you have submitted but from which you have not received decisions. These tasks can often be completed with the click of a button in the applicant portal, but in some cases, you may need to email the admissions office. If you previously accepted another admission offer and made a deposit at a different school, you need to withdraw your Statement of Intent to Register (SIR) and should call or email to inquire about a possible refund.

Once all the details of your enrollment at your new university have been confirmed, you should also notify your current college that you are withdrawing. This step is less important at a community college, where students enroll in classes one at a time. At a four-year university with full-time enrollment, it's important to notify the registrar of your transfer plans so that you don't get billed for classes you won't be attending. You may also want to inform your adviser(s), the housing office, and the financial aid department separately, just to make sure you have a clean break between your prior and future colleges.

Orientation

Don't underestimate the value of attending orientation at your new university. Since you have attended college before, you might feel like you already know everything, but each school offers its own unique features, resources, and culture. Plus, attending orientation is an excellent way to immerse yourself in your new environment and make new friends.

During orientation, you will participate in various activities designed to help you acclimate to campus life. These may include guided campus tours, workshops on academic success strategies, information sessions about class registration, and more. You will also have the chance to meet fellow incoming students, including other transfer students, who may share similar experiences and challenges. Building connections early on can help you establish a support network that will be invaluable as you navigate your new academic journey.

Many universities offer parallel programs during orientation for families and parents to help them understand the transitions their students are experiencing. These sessions typically cover topics such as navigating financial aid resources, understanding student support services, and fostering independence in students. There may also be opportunities to hear from faculty members and administrators to learn more about the university's culture and expectations.

New student orientations can last just a few hours or span multiple days. Transfer students might be invited to the same orientation sessions as first-year students or have an entirely separate orientation program. Some large universities run multiple orientation sessions and offer students a choice of dates, while smaller colleges may only be able to offer a single session. Watch for announcements and follow the instructions to RSVP for your session.

Common Challenges and Questions

What if the official document deadline is before my current college semester ends?

Don't worry — this is a common issue, especially when your current college and future college operate on different academic calendars. Just reach out to your future college and explain the situation. They will likely note in your file that your official transcripts are not late but rather in progress. Do your part by ordering your final official transcript as soon as it becomes available. Even better, preorder your transcript if your college offers an option to "hold for final grades" on the transcript ordering website.

What can I do if my admission is revoked?

In the rare event that your chosen university revokes your admission offer, contact the admissions office or your assigned counselor immediately. Find out what led to the revocation and inquire if it's possible for you to resolve the issue. Sometimes a simple solution exists, like providing a missing document. If your grades dropped or you withdrew from a required class for transfer, you might need to complete additional courses before you can officially enroll. In the worst-case scenario, you may have to spend another term at a community college or your previous university before reapplying for transfer.

CHAPTER 21

Academic Planning

You should begin working with an academic adviser at your new university as soon as you are able. This individual is knowledgeable about the institution, its degree programs, and pathways to graduation. Remember that the adviser is not an expert on your background and needs, though. Think of your relationship with your academic adviser as a partnership — they contribute expertise about the college, while you bring your previous experiences. Together, you and your adviser can develop a degree plan that aligns with your needs.

A detailed course plan will help you earn your degree in a timely manner, but it is not set in stone. As you take courses, you will get to know your professors, develop specific interests, and discover new opportunities in your field. Plan to check in with your adviser at least once or twice each term to discuss your degree plan and make any necessary adjustments.

Your degree is more than a piece of paper to be obtained; it is an experience to be savored. Don't be afraid to ask questions and make changes along the way to create the college experience you desire.

Adviser Sessions and Initial Course Registration

Universities commonly schedule academic advising sessions for incoming transfer students during their new-student orientations. If you are not attending an orientation or don't see an advising session listed in your itinerary, inquire about scheduling a separate appointment. You may even be able to meet via videoconference or by phone before you arrive on campus.

While you might feel ready to schedule your own classes without

260   Post-Acceptance

assistance from an adviser, it's generally beneficial to utilize college-specific expertise whenever it is available. Some universities also restrict new students from registering for classes before having a planning session with an adviser. Since popular courses can fill up quickly, it's important to complete this advising step early and register for your desired classes right away.

Bring Documentation

When meeting with your adviser, bring the following documents with you:

- Past transcripts from all institutions attended
- Transfer credit evaluation report
- AP, IB, or CLEP score reports

Yes, the adviser should have copies of these documents, but sometimes paperwork gets misplaced or delayed, so it's wise to bring your own copies. If the adviser cannot access your educational records during your initial meeting, the assistance you receive may be limited or inaccurate. Incoming students are often encouraged to take a few standard classes in their majors, but if you have already completed equivalent courses, you should inform your adviser and inquire about alternatives.

Prerequisites

Many degree programs have required course sequences that must be taken in a specific order. For example, you might need to complete Calculus before taking Physics, or to finish a writing prerequisite before taking advanced courses in your major. To stay on track:

- review the complete list of required courses in your major.
- find out if any required courses are unavailable during certain terms or seasons.
- start prerequisite course sequences in your first semester, if possible.
- identify multi-term course progressions that must be completed in sequence (e.g., Chemistry 1, 2, and 3).

Academic Planning 261

- meet with your adviser to map out multiple terms of courses.
- check whether some prerequisites can be taken concurrently with other courses (e.g., Calculus and Physics during the same term).

Availability and Waitlists

As an incoming transfer student, you will probably select classes after continuing students have registered for the upcoming term. Consequently, some classes may be full when you attempt to enroll. If a waitlist is available for a full course, join immediately. Waitlisted students are generally offered seats in the class based on the order in which they joined the list. Students often change their schedules just before the semester begins, while others drop classes after the first or second meeting, so keep an eye on the waitlist and be prepared to enroll if a spot opens up. You may have as little as twenty-four hours to confirm your spot once notified. If you are still waitlisted on the first day of class, attend anyway. Your professor may offer class seats to persistent students who attend the first few classes despite not being formally enrolled.

While you wait for updates on the waitlist, discuss a backup plan with your adviser. Identify other courses that can fulfill additional requirements for your degree and enroll in those classes, at least temporarily. Just be sure to officially drop any classes you don't intend to continue! Simply not attending class does not necessarily result in a withdrawal from the course. If you do not take action, you might receive a failing grade for a class you never attended. Check the academic calendar for the add/drop deadline and confirm your withdrawal by that date.

Be Realistic

When creating your class schedule, take an honest look at your daily rhythms and commitments. While that 8 a.m. biology class might be the only section available, it could lead to challenges if you work late nights or have family responsibilities in the morning. Try to find balance between prioritizing essential courses during your first term and developing realistic new routines that will set you up for long-term success. Also, remember to be kind to yourself during this first term at your new school. It is a time of transition, both academically and socially. Allow yourself space to adapt, and try not to overcommit right away.

Long-Term Planning

After your initial registration, scheduling classes should get easier. As a continuing student, your registration priority ranking will likely be based on the number of units you've completed. Once you know your registration day and time, add it to your calendar and set up automated reminders. Then set up a meeting with your adviser to map out your schedule, including backup options. Although you may still encounter full classes and need to join waitlists, entering your registration period with a clear plan will make the process less stressful and increase your chances of success.

Graduation Timeline

When will you graduate with your degree? Taking the time to outline a graduation timeline can help you stay focused on your goals and navigate potential pitfalls along the way. Remember to plan for graduation by identifying the number of required courses you need to complete. While your degree likely requires a minimum number of credits, that number doesn't reflect the specific classes that must be completed to earn a degree in your field. Your total earned credits will likely exceed the minimum required for graduation.

Let's consider an example. Joe just transferred to a new university that accepted 90 credits from the colleges he previously attended. His BA degree requires 120 semester units, so it seems he only has to complete 30 units to earn his degree. If he takes a standard course load of 15 units each semester, he could finish within a year, right? Unfortunately, it's not that straightforward. Joe is pursuing a specialized degree that requires unique courses that were not available at his previous schools. To earn this degree, he must take ten specific classes worth 4 units each. While he could attempt to take 20 units each semester, that would be a very challenging course load. He might want to consider taking summer classes or extending his degree plan by another semester.

Number of Classes and Credits per Term

College students following a four-year graduation plan typically enroll in approximately 15 credits each term. Students who take fewer credits will have a longer graduation timeline, while those taking more can accelerate their time to a degree. Most universities define the minimum number of credits required to qualify as a full-time student. Dropping below this threshold may require special permission from an adviser or dean and can impact financial aid eligibility. Similarly, universities often set a maximum credit limit to prevent students from overenrolling in courses. Students wishing to earn additional credits that would exceed the maximum for that term must first obtain permission from a dean.

To determine how many courses to take each term, reflect on your past college experiences. When did you perform at your best? Some students manage their time more effectively when their days are packed with academic activities, while others require ample downtime and rest between classes. Also, consider your nonacademic responsibilities. If you have a job, care for a family member, or have a long commute to school, you may not be able to handle a demanding full-time course load each term. Aim for the sweet spot where you can continue making tangible progress toward your degree while maintaining your health and managing your outside responsibilities.

Don't forget to factor in extra time to complete any special projects that might be required (or desired) for your degree. You may need to allocate dedicated time to work on a thesis or capstone project as you near the end of your degree.

Summer and Intersession Classes

If you have mapped out a realistic course plan but feel that graduation seems too far away, consider taking extra classes during intersession and/or summer terms. Keep in mind that classes offered during these terms cover the same material in a much shorter timeframe, so the pace will be brisk. While you may be able to succeed in four classes during a regular term, you might only be able to manage one or two classes at an accelerated pace. Avoid overcommitting, and keep track of withdrawal deadlines in case you need to drop a class.

Degree Audit

Make sure you are staying on track by completing an electronic degree audit periodically. This task enables you to compare your current course progress with the degree requirements for your college and major, helping you identify any overlooked requirements. Many colleges provide self-service software, such as DegreeWorks or uAchieve, for this purpose. Look for a degree audit option on your student dashboard and ask your adviser if you don't find anything. Some colleges prefer to have academic advisers conduct degree audits with students in real time, so they restrict direct access for students. Other colleges simply assign unique names for their degree audit software.

Graduation Verification

As you near your planned graduation date, meet with your adviser to learn about the graduation verification and application process. Most degrees are not awarded automatically. Students typically need to apply for graduation several weeks or months before the intended graduation date.

Common Challenges and Questions

My initial advising appointment is just before classes begin. Will I be able to get the classes I need?

Transfer students often encounter challenges when registering for classes after continuing students have already enrolled. Some universities with significant transfer populations reserve seats in popular courses specifically for them, but many others do not. Be prepared to search for backup class options and join waitlists strategically, and don't be afraid to ask your adviser for special consideration. Sometimes an extra student can be squeezed into a full class when it's necessary to keep the student on track for timely graduation.

I have to register for classes, but my transfer credit evaluation hasn't been finalized.

Some universities evaluate transfer credits more quickly than others. If you're still waiting for confirmation of your transfer credits, work with your adviser to make the best course selections based on the information available. Avoid enrolling in classes that sound similar to ones you have already taken — focus on unique courses that advance your learning. Once your transfer credit evaluation is finalized, consult your adviser again to determine if any adjustments should be made to your current schedule and future degree plan in light of this new information.

I see a class that meets two distinct requirements. Can I "double-dip" and take one class to satisfy both requirements?

Perhaps. Policies differ from college to college and also by requirement. For example, many schools permit students to fulfill both a general education requirement and a major requirement with a single class, which can be an efficient way to make progress toward your degree. Conversely, few institutions allow students to apply a single class to multiple general education requirements. You may encounter more variability and nuanced policies for minor or double-major requirements. Colleges often specify the maximum number of classes that can count toward two degree plans, or toward both a major and a minor. Consult your college academic adviser about your specific situation to learn which policies apply.

CHAPTER 22

Tips for Success

Transferring to a new college can be both exciting and intimidating. You have already successfully navigated the admissions process, but now you need to refine some additional skills to thrive in this new environment. Anticipating and preparing for potential challenges improve your ability to overcome them.

This chapter is designed to help you avoid common pitfalls and overcome obstacles on your way to a degree. We will explore practical strategies for managing financial aid, accessing support services, finding community, and maintaining mental health. By focusing on these areas, you'll be better prepared to make the most of your transfer experience and achieve your academic goals.

Financial Aid

Just as you need to revisit your degree plan and course schedule each term, you must also review your financial aid status regularly.

Be sure to file the FAFSA (Free Application for Federal Student Aid) every year to maintain your eligibility for financial aid. It generally becomes available on October 1 each year. If changes to your financial situation are not accurately reflected in the FAFSA, you may need to visit your school's financial aid office for assistance. The financial aid officers at your institution are there to help you navigate the complexities of paying for college, so don't be afraid to ask them questions.

Remember that Pell Grants have lifetime limits — typically equivalent to six years of full-time enrollment. If you have received a Pell Grant, keep track of how much you've used so far to ensure you have enough remaining aid to complete your degree. Similarly, if you are a veteran using GI Bill benefits, make sure you plan your courses to align with your GI Bill eligibility.

If you're taking out loans, carefully evaluate your budget each year to ensure that you are borrowing only what you truly need. Review the repayment terms of your loans, too. Most student loans don't require repayment initiation until six months after graduation, but repayment can begin earlier under certain circumstances (such as dropping below half-time enrollment).

Additionally, look into scholarships and grants for continuing students offered by your college or major department. Once you are established at your new university, you may find that you qualify for special funding programs within your field of study. These can offer valuable financial support to help reduce the burden of tuition and fees.

Support Services

One of the most important steps you can take as a transfer student is to familiarize yourself with the support services available at your new institution. These resources are designed to help you navigate academic challenges and thrive in your new environment. Whether you need accommodations for a disability, academic support, or simply guidance in adjusting to a new campus, knowing where to turn can make all the difference in your success.

If you have a documented disability — whether physical, learning related, or psychological — connect with your university's disability or accessibility resources office as early as possible, ideally before you even arrive on campus. This office can help you obtain accommodations such as extended testing time, note-taking assistance, or alternative formats for course materials. To get started, you'll typically need to provide recent documentation from your healthcare provider. It can also be helpful to share accommodations you've successfully used in the past. Once accommodations are approved, you will need to work with each of your instructors individually to understand how those accommodations can be implemented in their classes. If you need help advocating for yourself with professors, return to the disability/accessibility office for support. Last, find out how often you need to renew your accommodations with the disability/accessibility office, as you may need to check in regularly to keep your accommodations current.

Beyond disability services, universities usually offer a wide variety of academic resources to support your learning. Many schools provide free tutoring in subjects like math, science, and coding through peer tutors or professional staff. Writing centers can help you strengthen your writing skills, format research papers, and refine essays. These services are not just for students who are struggling with coursework — everyone can benefit from expert feedback and outside perspectives.

Visit the career center early and often for assistance with résumé writing, interview coaching, and building a LinkedIn profile. Look for opportunities to attend internship and career fairs to network with potential employers. Simply obtaining a degree is often not enough to secure employment upon graduation — utilize the services of the career center to gain the additional skills you will need to translate your academic knowledge into evidence of career readiness.

Make an effort to attend your professors' office hours as well. Many students believe that office hours are only for students who need additional help with assignments, but in reality, these hours can also be used for exchanging academic ideas and building relationships with professors. Whether you have questions about course material or want to chat about the latest research, visiting your instructors during office hours is always a good idea. Plus, developing relationships with your professors can sometimes lead to mentorship opportunities, research and internship positions, and letters of recommendation for potential graduate school applications in the future.

Community

Adjusting to a new social environment can be daunting for transfer students, especially when entering a well-established campus community where friendships may already have been formed. Nevertheless, building relationships is essential. Gaining a sense of belonging can help you remain motivated and engaged in your new school. Make the most of networking opportunities during orientation, through student-run organizations, or within campus residential communities. Many universities also have transfer student associations or peer mentoring programs designed to help you connect with others who share similar interests and experiences.

Be brave! Step outside your comfort zone by joining clubs or attending campus events that match your interests. Participating in these activities will help you meet new people and connect with the general campus community. As you become more involved, your dedication to your school and motivation to complete your degree will grow. But remember, building relationships takes time — be patient with yourself as you adjust socially while balancing academics.

Mental Health

Don't forget about self-care! Do you remember Maslow's Hierarchy from part 3? You cannot thrive academically until your basic needs, including mental wellness, are met. Locate your college's mental health and wellness services soon after transferring. Moving to a new university can be stressful as you learn to navigate a different academic system and find your community. Since you know the stress is coming, learn how to access support services before you need them.

Most universities offer free or low-cost counseling services and peer mental health support groups through their student health centers. Take advantage of these resources if you're feeling overwhelmed, anxious, or depressed. There is no need to face these challenges alone — seek support so that you can focus on enjoying your academic journey and achieving your goals.

Many schools offer workshops on stress management, mindfulness techniques, and coping strategies that can help you prevent burnout and stay resilient throughout the term. Look for special events around midterms and finals when colleges often organize activities like therapy dog visits, meditation sessions, and late-night comfort food buffets. Participating in activities like these will not only help keep your spirits high but also introduce you to like-minded peers in your community.

Mental and physical health go hand in hand, so make sure that you maintain healthy habits such as exercising regularly, getting enough sleep, eating well, and enjoying fresh air. Most colleges also offer support services in these areas. Check if your new school has resources

270 Post-Acceptance

like a healthy food pantry or napping pods, in addition to the usual exercise center.

If you're balancing work or family responsibilities with school, establish realistic boundaries and communicate them gently to your friends, family, and colleagues. Enlist their support to ensure you have time to recharge mentally and emotionally as you progress through each term.

For a more detailed look at wellness strategies for college students, check out *The College Student's Guide to Mental Health* by Mia Nosanow.[1]

Common Challenges and Questions

I can do telehealth sessions with my current therapist, so I'm not going to research mental health services at my new college.

Not so fast! Have you checked with your therapist about this plan? Therapists and other health practitioners must follow the regulations of the states where they are licensed.[2] Rules regarding telehealth vary from state to state and are rapidly changing as new technologies emerge. If you will be attending college in a different state, the situation becomes even more complex. Don't assume that you will be able to continue with your current therapist via telehealth. Ask your therapist about the feasibility of this option.

I'm nervous about moving to a new school where I don't know anyone. How can I connect to classmates in advance?

You are not alone. Many new transfer students feel worried about transitioning to a new campus where they don't know anyone yet. Look for online student groups you can join. Many colleges host official online groups for incoming students on social media, email lists, and other virtual discussion platforms. If the college doesn't sponsor any official online groups, look for something unofficial or start a group yourself! Begin following student organizations on social media, comment on their posts, and reach out to student leaders to learn about the first events you can attend on campus. You might also reach out to your major department or an affinity group on campus and ask if they have any student ambassadors who might be willing to chat with you and answer your questions before you arrive. Don't worry if you can't connect with many students in advance, though — there will be plenty of opportunities to socialize and network when the term begins.

Final Thoughts

The college transfer journey may seem daunting, but remember that thousands of students successfully navigate this path each year. You have all the tools you need to succeed and are ready to take control of your educational destiny.

As you move forward, keep these final thoughts in mind:

- **Embrace the challenge.** The transfer process (and college in general) may have its ups and downs, but each obstacle is an opportunity for growth. Don't give up!
- **Stay open-minded.** Your new college experience might be different from what you are used to or what you expect. Keep an open mind and explore with optimism.
- **Ask for help.** Remember that you're not alone in this journey. Reach out to advisers, instructors, peer mentors, and support services at your new school. They want to see you succeed.
- **Be bold.** Ask questions, meet interesting people, and try new things. Your college experience is what you make of it.

You've got this!

Acknowledgments

I would like to acknowledge the many individuals who contributed to the creation of this book and supported my journey into authorship:

First and foremost, I thank my family. To my daughter, Kaytlin, the first transfer student I advised — you inspired this adventure! Your experience opened my eyes to the challenges and triumphs of transfer students. You are also my favorite proofreader and em dash enthusiast. To my daughter-in-law, Jordan, thank you for your openness and willingness to share both your story and your emotional support dog. To my husband, Ben, your unwavering support, encouragement, and patience kept me writing even when I wanted to watch TV instead.

This book wouldn't have been possible without Tara Johnson, my closest ally throughout every stage, from research and planning to editing and proofreading. Your pep talks are unrivaled. Thanks also to Kim Golding for being my biggest cheerleader and the first customer to preorder my book despite having no practical need for it.

I am deeply grateful to my agent, Rita Rosenkranz, and editor, Jason Gardner, for their invaluable guidance and expertise. The New World Library team, including managing editor Kristen Cashman, has been an exceptional partner in the publication of this work. A special thanks to Stephanie Chandler of the Nonfiction Authors Association for creating the Nonfiction Writers Conference that led me to Rita and Jason. Thank you all for taking a chance on me.

My mentor, Priscilla Vivio, deserves recognition for providing thoughtful feedback that helped shape this book. You are always willing to be my partner in crime and advocate for transfers and community college students. I'm also grateful to Sheila Akbar for being an excellent accountability partner and sounding board. I'm so glad we connected at "bootcamp."

The heart of this book lies in the stories and wisdom generously shared by transfer students and my fellow professionals. Sydney Matthes from Service to School opened my eyes to the unique challenges veterans face, leading me to Robin and Kate, whose experiences shed light on the veteran transfer experience. Dave Morris provided crucial insights into athletic transfers, while Mark Salisbury and Jason Hamilton clarified the complexities of financial aid. Vipul Patel and Gage Mersereau, thank you for sharing my passion for transfer students and for developing technology tools to support them. Nick Gossett and Avant Assessment, I appreciate your input on world language competencies and credits. Hanna Stotland offered brilliant advice for transfers in crisis. Scot Marken, thank you for sharing stories of neurodiverse transfer student success. Nicole Freeling, your personal and professional experiences with transfer added depth to this work. Hollie Butler, your decades of perseverance reminded me of the crucial need for this book.

Kathy Cordeiro, Melissa Hart, Andrea Brenner, and Jill Shulman, you've been incredible writing role models. Thank you for sharing your wisdom and resources. Beth Gilfillan and Christopher Tremblay, I'm grateful for the opportunity to contribute to the sixth edition of NACAC's *Fundamentals of College Admission Counseling* and for your editorial guidance.

I wish to extend my heartfelt appreciation to Dr. Janet Marling for enthusiastically supporting my continuing education. Your dedication to transfer advocacy is truly inspiring.

Finally, to all the transfer students who have entrusted me with their academic futures over the years, this book is for you. Your resilience, determination, and success stories have been the driving force behind this project.

Notes

Introduction

1. "Jim Rohn — If You Don't Like How Things Are Change It You Are Not a Tree!," talk by Jim Rohn, posted September 1, 2017, by Shaun Muscat, YouTube, https://www.youtube.com/watch?v=L7MuAX-6Yzg&ab_channel=ShaunMuscat.

Chapter 1: All Kinds of Transfers

1. "Table 326.10. Graduation Rate from First Institution Attended for First-Time, Full-Time Bachelor's Degree-Seeking Students at 4-Year Postsecondary Institutions, by Race/Ethnicity, Time to Completion, Sex, Control of Institution, and Percentage of Applications Accepted: Selected Cohort Entry Years, 1996 Through 2016," National Center for Education Statistics Digest of Education Statistics, 2023, https://nces.ed.gov/programs/digest/d23/tables/dt23_326.10.asp.
2. "Signature Report 9," National Student Clearinghouse Research Center, accessed December 15, 2024, https://nscresearchcenter.org/signaturereport9/.
3. Richard L. Drury, "Community Colleges in America: A Historical Perspective," *Inquiry* 8, no. 1 (spring 2003), https://files.eric.ed.gov/fulltext/EJ876835.pdf.
4. Steve Robinson, "From the President's Desk: #EndCCStigma: Social Media as a Tool to Change Public Perception of 2-Year Colleges," *New Directions for Community Colleges*, no. 197 (spring 2022): 141–55, https://eric.ed.gov/?id=EJ1319742.

Chapter 2: Why Transfer?

1. Jennifer Glynn, PhD, "Persistence: The Success of Students Who Transfer from Community Colleges to Selective Four-Year Institutions," Jack Kent Cooke Foundation, January 2019, https://www.jkcf.org/wp-content/uploads/2019/01/Persistance-Jack-Kent-Cooke-Foundation.pdf.
2. "National Program Inventory: Baccalaureate Degrees by State," Community College Baccalaureate Association, last updated March 25, 2025, https://www.accbd.org/state-inventory/.
3. Rachel Burns, Lynneah Brown, Kelsey Heckert, et al., "A Dream Derailed?: Investigating the Impacts of College Closures on Student Outcomes," State Higher Education Executive Officers Association and National Student Clearinghouse

Research Center, November 2022, https://sheeo.org/wp-content/uploads/2022/11/SHEEO_NSCRC_CollegeClosures_Report1.pdf.

4. Tammy English, Jordan Davis, Melissa Wei, and James J. Gross, "Homesickness and Adjustment Across the First Year of College: A Longitudinal Study," *Emotion* 17, no. 1 (October 2016): 1–5, https://pmc.ncbi.nlm.nih.gov/articles/PMC5280212/.

5. Hanna Stotland, "College and Graduate School Applicants in Special Circumstances," accessed December 15, 2024, https://hannastotland.com/crisis-management/.

Chapter 3: Collecting Transcripts

1. Katherine Knott, "U.S. Bans Most Withholding of Transcripts," *Inside Higher Ed*, October 25, 2023, https://www.insidehighered.com/news/government/student-aid-policy/2023/10/25/new-us-rules-ban-transcript-holds-bolster-oversight.

2. "How and Where Can I Obtain a Copy of My Academic Transcript from My School That Closed?," Federal Student Aid, accessed December 15, 2024, https://studentaid.gov/help-center/answers/article/obtaining-copy-of-academic-transcript-from-closed-school.

Chapter 5: Alternative Credit Sources

1. "AP National and State Data," College Board, AP Central, accessed December 15, 2024, https://apcentral.collegeboard.org/about-ap/ap-data-research/national-state-data.

2. Dana Goldstein, "Why Is the College Board Pushing to Expand Advanced Placement?," *New York Times*, November 18, 2023, https://www.nytimes.com/2023/11/18/us/college-board-ap-exams-courses.html.

3. The College Board hosts a database of college AP credit policies. You can search by AP test subject and sort by score to find colleges that might grant credit for your exams. Always double-check with the college directly just to be safe. See "AP Credit Policy Search," College Board, AP Students, accessed December 15, 2024, https://apstudents.collegeboard.org/getting-credit-placement/search-policies.

4. "Take a CLEP Exam with Remote Proctoring," College Board, CLEP, accessed December 15, 2024, https://clep.collegeboard.org/about-remote-proctoring/take-clep-exam-remote-proctoring.

5. "Requesting Transcripts and Certificates," International Baccalaureate, accessed December 15, 2024, https://www.ibo.org/programmes/diploma-programme/assessment-and-exams/requesting-transcripts/.

6. "Learners: Seeking Credit with the National Guide," ACE National Guide, accessed December 15, 2024, https://www.acenet.edu/National-Guide/Pages/Seeking-Credit.aspx.

7. Jim Absher, "GI Bill Top Questions Answered," March 28, 2024, https://www.military.com/education/gi-bill/20-top-faqs-for-the-new-gi-bill.html.

8. "Start Your Journey to 'Admission Accomplished!'," Service to School, accessed December 15, 2024, https://www.service2school.org/.

Chapter 6: The Five P's for College Research

1. "The Jeanne Clery Act," Clery Center, accessed December 15, 2024, https://www.clerycenter.org/the-clery-act.

2. Sara De Felice, Antonia F. de C. Hamilton, Marta Ponari, and Gabriella Vigliocco, "Learning from Others Is Good, with Others Is Better: The Role of Social Interaction in Human Acquisition of New Knowledge" Philosophical Transactions of the Royal Society B, December 26, 2022, https://royalsocietypublishing.org/doi/10.1098/rstb.2021.0357.

3. The Honors Transfer Council of California maintains a list of transfer partners who are eager to assist community college honors students. If you are not a California student, look for a similar resource in your state. See "Transfer Partners," Honors Transfer Council of California, accessed December 15, 2024, https://www.honorstransfercouncil.org/transfer-partners.

4. Garrett Andrews and Brenna Swanston, "What Is Tuition Reciprocity? How to Pay In-State Tuition at Out-of-State Schools," Forbes Advisor, updated March 18, 2024, https://www.forbes.com/advisor/education/student-resources/what-is-tuition-reciprocity/.

5. "Forever Buckeyes," Ohio Department of Higher Education, accessed December 15, 2024, https://highered.ohio.gov/students/pay-for-college/ohio-grants-scholarships/forever-buckeyes.

6. "Grandparent Waiver Information for Prospective & Current State University System Parents & Students," State University System of Florida Board of Governors, updated September 2023, https://www.flbog.edu/wp-content/uploads/2023/09/Grandparent_Waiver_Guidance_for_Parents_Students_Sept_2023.pdf.

7. Sam Jaquez, "Colleges That Offer Tuition Waivers and Scholarships for Native American Students," *College Confidential*, October 16, 2023, https://www.collegeconfidential.com/articles/tuition-waivers-and-scholarships-for-native-american-students/.

8. "Transfer Applicants," UCLA Undergraduate Admission, accessed December 15, 2024, https://admission.ucla.edu/apply/transfer.

9. "H.R.4137 — Higher Education Opportunity Act, 110th Congress (2007–2008)," Congress.gov, accessed February 9, 2025, https://www.congress.gov/bill/110th-congress/house-bill/4137.

10. Justin C. Ortagus, Rodney Hughes, and Hope Allchin, "The Role and Influence of Exclusively Online Degree Programs in Higher Education," *American Educational Research Journal* 61, no. 2 (January 2024): 404–34, https://doi.org/10.3102/00028312231222264.

11. Tatiana Velasco, John Fink, Mariel Bedoya-Guevara, Davis Jenkins, Tania LaViolet, "Tracking Transfer: Community College and Four-Year Institutional Effectiveness in Broadening Bachelor's Degree Attainment," Community College Research Center, Teachers College, Columbia University, February 2024, https://ccrc.tc.columbia.edu/publications/tracking-transfer-community-college-and-four-year-institutional-effectiveness-in-broadening-bachelors-degree-attainment.html.

12. Peter Shea and Temi Bidjerano, "Online Course Enrollment in Community College and Degree Completion: The Tipping Point," *International Review of Research in Open and Distributed Learning* 19, no. 2 (2018), https://doi.org/10.19173/irrodl.v19i2.3460.

278 The Complete Guide to College Transfer

Chapter 7: Qualities of a Transfer-Friendly College

1. See Stephen J. Handel, "Increasing Higher Education Access and Success Using New Pathways to the Baccalaureate: The Emergence of a Transfer-Affirming Culture," College Board, 2013, https://secure-media.collegeboard.org/digitalServices /pdf/rd/StephenJHandel-IncreasingHigherEducationAccess.pdf.
2. "Scholarships (For Academic Year 2024–2025)," University of Southern California, accessed April 8, 2025, https://web.archive.org/web/20231109062439 /https://admission.usc.edu/wp-content/uploads/scholarships-grid.pdf.
3. "Transfer Scholars," University of Oregon, University Housing, accessed December 15, 2024, https://housing.uoregon.edu/transfer-scholars.
4. "Helen Diller Anchor House," UC Berkeley Housing, accessed February 9, 2025, https://housing.berkeley.edu/explore-housing-options/apartments/helen-diller -anchor-house/.
5. Jennifer Teshera-Levye and Heather D. Vance-Chalcraft, "Peer Mentorship and Academic Supports Build Sense of Community and Improve Outcomes for Transfer Students," *Journal of Microbiology & Biology Education* 25, no. 1 (2024): e00163–23, https://pmc.ncbi.nlm.nih.gov/articles/PMC11044626/.
6. "About IPEDS," National Center for Education Statistics, Integrated Postsecondary Education Data System, accessed December 15, 2024, https://nces.ed.gov /ipeds/about-ipeds.
7. "College Navigator," National Center for Education Statistics, accessed December 15, 2024, https://nces.ed.gov/collegenavigator/.
8. "Get Involved & Connect with Transfer Students," University of Texas at Austin Undergraduate College, accessed December 15, 2024, https://undergradcollege .utexas.edu/first-year-experience/transfer-year-experience-program/transfer -student-resources/get-involved-connect-transfer-students.
9. Eric Brooks and Robert Morse, "A More Detailed Look at the Ranking Factors," *U.S. News & World Report*, September 23, 2024, https://www.usnews.com /education/best-colleges/articles/ranking-criteria-and-weights.
10. Kaitlin Mulhere, "How Money Rated the 2024 Best Colleges," *Money*, accessed April 8, 2025, https://money.com/best-colleges/methodology/.

Chapter 8: Partnerships

1. "50-State Comparison: Transfer and Articulation Policies," Education Commission of the States, July 28, 2022, https://www.ecs.org/50-state-comparison -transfer-and-articulation/.
2. Liam Knox and Sara Weissman, "Toward a Transfer Guarantee," Inside Higher Ed, December 14, 2023, https://www.insidehighered.com/news/admissions/transfer /2023/12/14/guaranteed-admission-can-boost-transfer-enrollment-success.
3. "State & Regional College Tuition Discounts," National Association of Student Financial Aid Administrators, accessed December 15, 2024, https://www.nasfaa .org/State_Regional_Tuition_Exchanges.
4. "Transfer Admission Guarantee (TAG)," University of California Admissions, accessed December 15, 2024, https://admission.universityofcalifornia.edu /admission-requirements/transfer-requirements/uc-transfer-programs/transfer -admission-guarantee-tag.html.

Notes 279

5. "Transfer Admission Planner," University of California Admissions, accessed December 15, 2024, https://uctap.universityofcalifornia.edu/students/.
6. "WUE Savings Finder," Western Interstate Commission for Higher Education, accessed December 15, 2024, https://www.wiche.edu/tuition-savings/wue/wue-savings-finder/.

Chapter 9: Minimum Eligibility Requirements

1. "Transfer Requirements," University of Oregon Admissions, accessed December 15, 2024, https://admissions.uoregon.edu/transfer/requirements.

Chapter 10: General Education

1. "Writing Requirement," Brown University, accessed December 15, 2024, https://college.brown.edu/design-your-education/complete-your-degree/degree-requirements/writing-requirement.
2. "Quantitative Reasoning," Boston University Hub, accessed December 15, 2024, https://www.bu.edu/hub/hub-courses/quantitative-reasoning/.
3. "College Core Curriculum: Quantitative Reasoning 2025–2026," NYU College of Arts & Science, accessed April 8, 2025, https://cas.nyu.edu/core/course-listing/2526Courses/QRAY2526.html; for the complete list of the college's Core Curriculum, see "College Core Curriculum," NYU College of Arts & Science, accessed December 15, 2024, https://cas.nyu.edu/core.html.
4. Ashley Mowreader, "Data-Based Decision: Eliminating Developmental Math," Inside Higher Ed, March 12, 2024, https://www.insidehighered.com/news/student-success/academic-life/2024/03/12/how-one-illinois-university-got-rid-developmental.
5. "The Global Seal of Biliteracy Is Your Language Passport to Opportunity," Global Seal of Biliteracy, accessed December 15, 2024, https://theglobalseal.com/.
6. "AICCU Transfer Commitment," Association of Independent California Colleges and Universities, accessed December 15, 2024, https://aiccu.edu/page/transferstudents.
7. "Out-of-State College and Universities," California Community Colleges, Transfer Counselor Website, accessed December 15, 2024, https://ccctransfer.org/oos/.
8. Home page, Study Hall, accessed December 15, 2024, https://gostudyhall.com/.

Chapter 11: Majors and Prerequisites

1. "Table 322.10. Bachelor's Degrees Conferred by Postsecondary Institutions, by Field of Study: Selected Academic Years, 1970–71 Through 2021–22," National Center for Education Statistics Digest of Education Statistics, 2023, https://nces.ed.gov/programs/digest/d23/tables/dt23_322.10.asp.

Chapter 12: Transfer Timeline

1. "Table 326.10. Graduation Rate from First Institution Attended for First-Time, Full-Time Bachelor's Degree-Seeking Students at 4-Year Postsecondary

280   The Complete Guide to College Transfer

Institutions, by Race/Ethnicity, Time to Completion, Sex, Control of Institution, and Percentage of Applications Accepted: Selected Cohort Entry Years, 1996 Through 2016," National Center for Education Statistics Digest of Education Statistics, 2023, https://nces.ed.gov/programs/digest/d23/tables/dt23_326.10.asp.

2. Tatiana Velasco, John Fink, Mariel Bedoya-Guevara, Davis Jenkins, and Tania LaViolet, "Tracking Transfer: Community College and Four-Year Institutional Effectiveness in Broadening Bachelor's Degree Attainment," Community College Research Center, Teachers College, Columbia University, February 2024, https://ccrc.tc.columbia.edu/publications/Tracking-Transfer-Community-College-and-Four-Year-Institutional-Effectiveness-in-Broadening-Bachelors-Degree-Attainment.html.

3. "Eligibility Requirements for Transfer Applicants," Brown Undergraduate Admission, accessed December 15, 2024, https://admission.brown.edu/transfer/eligibility-requirements.

4. "Transfer Admissions Requirements," Virginia Tech Admissions, accessed December 15, 2024, https://www.vt.edu/admissions/transfer/requirements.html.

Chapter 13: Data Entry

1. "Standardized Testing for Transfer Applicants," Yale University, accessed February 9, 2025, https://admissions.yale.edu/standardized-testing-transfer-applicants.

Chapter 15: Follow-Up Documentation

1. Jeff Selingo, "A New Way to Think About Your College List: The Buyers and Sellers," accessed April 9, 2025, https://jeffselingo.com/which-colleges-are-really-buyers-and-which-are-sellers/.

2. "Dependency Status," Federal Student Aid, accessed December 15, 2024, https://studentaid.gov/apply-for-aid/fafsa/filling-out/dependency?sk=AFF-PSW.

Chapter 17: Transfer Credit Evaluation Report

1. "Transfer Credit," University of Chicago Admissions, accessed December 15, 2024, https://collegeadmissions.uchicago.edu/apply/transfer-applicants/transfer-credit.

2. "General Education Requirements," Colorado College, accessed December 15, 2024, https://www.coloradocollege.edu/other/generaleducation/requirements.html.

3. "Guide to Ethical Practice in College Admission," National Association for College Admission Counseling, August 2024, p. 9, https://www.nacacnet.org/wp-content/uploads/NACAC-Guide-to-Ethical-Practice-in-College-Admission_Aug-2024.pdf.

Chapter 19: Financial Aid Awards and Cost Comparisons

1. "Calculating Pell Grant Lifetime Eligibility Used," Federal Student Aid, accessed April 9, 2025, https://studentaid.gov/understand-aid/types/grants/pell/calculate-eligibility.
2. "State Financial Aid Programs," National Association of Student Financial Aid Administrators, accessed December 15, 2024, https://www.nasfaa.org/state_financial_aid_programs.
3. Melanie Hanson, "College Tuition Inflation Rate," Education Data Initiative, last updated September 9, 2024, https://educationdata.org/college-tuition-inflation-rate.
4. "What Is Professional Judgment?," Federal Student Aid, accessed December 15, 2024, https://studentaid.gov/help-center/answers/article/what-is-professional-judgment.
5. "Guide to Ethical Practice in College Admission," National Association for College Admission Counseling, August 2024, p. 9, https://www.nacacnet.org/wp-content/uploads/NACAC-Guide-to-Ethical-Practice-in-College-Admission_Aug-2024.pdf.
6. Federal Student Aid, YouTube, accessed December 15, 2024, https://www.youtube.com/@FederalStudentAid/videos.
7. "Contact Us," Federal Student Aid, accessed December 15, 2024, https://studentaid.gov/help-center/contact.

Chapter 22: Tips for Success

1. Mia Nosanow, *The College Student's Guide to Mental Health: Essential Wellness Strategies for Flourishing in College* (New World Library, 2024).
2. "Licensing Across State Lines," US Department of Health and Human Services, accessed December 15, 2024, https://telehealth.hhs.gov/licensure/licensing-across-state-lines.

Index

academic advisers, 259–62, 264–65
Academic Common Market (ACM), 60, 103
academic notice/probation/suspension: application questions about, 167; disclosure of, 23; "good standing" and, 117; as reason for transfer, 13–14, 15–16; "swirling" transfer due to, 143–44
academic planning: adviser sessions for, 259–62, 264–65; FAQs, 264–65; long-term, 262–64
academic programs, 66–68
academic recommendations, 164, 170
accessibility services programs, 68–69, 127, 267–68
achievements, notable, 163–64
ACT tests, 78, 160, 161
ACTFL tests, 45
admissions: "conditional," 251–53; counselors for, 190, 200, 209–10, 220, 258; direct, 154–55; enrollment figures vs., 90–92; housing applications and, 222–25; need-blind, x; race-conscious, 188; revocation of, 258; understanding the process of, 1
admissions decisions: case studies, 207, 208–9; early, 203; enrollment deposit deadlines and, 207–8, 209–10; FAQs, 209–10; indecision about, 210; release of, 203–4; timeline for, 236; tracking, 204, 204–8; types of, 206
admissions requirements, 71–72, 77–78
admittances, 206
Advanced Placement (AP) classes: as alternative credit source, 43, 44,

112, 193, 255; documentation from, during academic adviser session, 260; GE requirements and, 125; test scores from, 43, 160–61, 193, 255
advisers, 63, 87–88, 95, 259–62, 264–65
affordability, 72–73, 84, 95
AI tools, 172
AI Transcript Transfer (Tassled tool), 82
American Council on Education (ACE), 45; Credly transcripts, 47; Military Guide, 47; military service credits and, 48–49; National Guide database, 46–47
American Council on the Teaching of Foreign Languages (ACTFL) tests, 45
American Sign Language, 127
American Sign Language Proficiency Interview (ASLPI), 127
anxiety, 18–19
appeals: case studies, 245–47; for financial aid, 243–45; merit/comparison, 244; need-based, 243–44; post-acceptance, 137; sample letters, 245; tips for, 244–45; over transfer credit decisions, 137, 211, 216–18, 221
applications: additional, for transfer admission guarantees, 101; "additional information" box on, 185–86; case studies, 132–33; college online portals for, 189–90 (see also college applicant portals); at community colleges, 4; essays for, 128; excerpts from, ix–x; FAQs, 170–71; for financial aid, 191, 194–97 (see also College Scholarship Service (CSS) Profile; Free Application for Federal

Index 283

Student Aid); for graduation, 264;
housing options and, 85, 222–25;
individual school, 154, 170, 189–90;
letters of recommendation, 164–66,
170; managing, ix; multiple, planning for, 130–32; multiple options
for, 151; number of, per year, to one
institution, 147; pending, withdrawal
of, 256–57; processing of, 192;
reapplications, 209; for scholarships,
198; statewide hubs, 153–54; steps
involved in, 149–50 (*see also* data
entry; essays, personal); third-party,
152–53, 170; third-party mobile,
154; transfer-focused associate degree programs and consideration of,
146; websites for, 151–52
ApplyTexas, 153
Arizona General Education Curriculum
(AGEC), 99
Arizona State University, 51, 125, 157
art programs, 64–65, 66
Assist.org, 99–100
associate degrees: completion of, as transfer requirement, 101, 254; completion
of, before transfer, 146; for transfer
(ADTs), 12, 98, 121; types of, 12
Association of Independent California
Colleges and Universities, 107
athletics, 65, 75
auditions, 199
Avant STAMP, 127

bachelor's degrees: completion time for,
137; GI Bill benefits and, 49–50; types
of, 12; use of term, x; vertical transfers for earning, 3–5, 12, 22
backup class options, 264
behavioral dismissals, 23, 117
Beloit College, 175
Belushi, Jim, 10
Berry College, 167, 168
biology, 128
Black students: HBCUs, 63; common
application for, 152–53, 190
block schedules, 40, 213
Boston University, 79, 122, 208–9
brainstorming activities, 175–78
Brown University, 49, 121, 147, 166, 167
business, 128, 130

Cal State Apply, 153
California, 99, 153–54
California Institute of Technology
(Caltech), 91–92
California State University, 124–25, 153
campus housing, 60, 96, 222–25, 255
campus population, 61
Career and Technical Education (CTE), 41
career connections, 59
CareerExplorer.com, 134
case studies: admissions decisions, 207,
208–9; alternative credit sources, 46;
college research, 66, 70–71; eligibility
requirements, 113–14; GE requirements, 124–25; housing options,
227–29; insights from, ix; lateral
transfers, 5–6; majors, 132–33; partnerships, 104–6; reasons for transfer,
15–16, 21–22; reverse transfers,
6–7; "swirling" transfers, 8; transfer
timelines, 144–45; transfer-friendly
colleges/universities, 94–95; vertical
transfers, 4–5
CCCApply, 153
Central Carolina Community College, 82
ChatGPT, 172
cheating, 23, 167
childcare, 89
Citadel, The, 76
City University of New York (CUNY), 82,
153
class registration: advanced/priority, 68,
88; adviser sessions and, 260; information sessions about, during orientation, 257; transfer credit timelines
and, 219–20, 264–65
class sizes, 61–63, 68
Cleary, Beverly, 10
CLEP tests: as alternative credit source, 44,
45, 47, 112; case studies, 46, 51; GE
requirements and, 125, 137; listing,
during data entry, 161; online portal
requests for, 193; "pass-along" credits
and, 53–54; test scores, 255, 260;
transfer timelines and, 137; veteran
students and, 47
closures of schools, 14, 29
club sports, 65
co-admission programs, 101
Coalition App, 151, 152–53, 166, 167, 190

284 The Complete Guide to College Transfer

Coast Guard Training Center (Petaluma, CA), 48–49

college applicant portals: admissions decisions via, 205; document checklist for, 190–98; FAQs, 199–201; invitation email for, 189, 190; location of, 189–90; missed messages on, 200; paying attention to, 189, 190; setting up, 190; tracking, 204

College Board, 44, 53, 161, 195

College Navigator, 91–94

college research: case studies, 66, 70–71; compromise involved in, 55–56; FAQs, 74–76; importance of, 109; organizing for, 58; pastime considerations, 63–65; people considerations, 61–63; place considerations, 59–61, 85; practicality considerations, 71–74, 137; prioritizing for, 56–57; program considerations, 66–70, 131–32; questions for consideration, 58; transfer-friendliness and, 57

College Scholarship Service (CSS) Profile: FAFSA vs., 195–96; family income changes and, 16–17; filing fee for, 196; financial aid award letter and, 231; online portal requests for, 191, 195–96; shortcomings of, 73, 243; submission of, 231; at transfer-friendly colleges/universities, 83

College Student's Guide to Mental Health, The (Nosanow), 270

college transfer reports, 191, 193–94, 199–200

CollegeAthleticAdvisor.com, 65

College-Level Examination Program (CLEP), 44. *See also* CLEP tests

colleges/universities, prior: credit transfers from, 25, 26; "good standing" with, 23–24, 116–17; listing, 27, 157–59; transcripts from, 28, 253–54; unpleasant memories of, 25–26; websites of, 28

Colorado College, 212–13, 217

Common App, 151, 152, 166, 167, 170, 190

Common Black College Application (CBCA), 152–53, 190

common course numbering (CCN) policies, 82–83

Common Data Set (CDS), 90, 161

community: building, 88–89; essays about, 184; tips for finding, 266

Community College of the Air Force (CCAF), 48, 50

Community College Research Center, 146

community colleges: application process at, 4; credit transfer tools at, 81–82; degrees offered by, 12; GI Bill benefits and, 49–50; history of, 10; home-schoolers and, 70–71; noncredit courses at, 40–41; reverse transfers to, 6–7; state-based free, 50; stigma attached to, 9–10; transfer contracts of, 16, 60, 76, 136, 146; vertical transfers from, 3–5, 22, 66, 136. *See also* associate degrees

computer science, 128, 130

contact information, 155

co-op programs, 67

Cornell University, 219–20, 229

cost of attendance (COA), 232, 236–38

Coursera.com, 47

courses: descriptions/syllabi, 191, 197–98, 215, 216–17, 221; in-progress, 130, 159; listing, during data entry, 158–59; overlapping, 131–32; registering for (*see* class registration); yearlong sequences, 135, 138, 260–61. *See also* prerequisite courses

Covid-19 pandemic: financial impact on schools, 14; online classes during, 15, 74, 113, 116; testing requirements following, 78

Craigslist, 226

Crash Course, 125

credit transfers, 79–83; understanding, ix

credits: calculating, 36–39; converting, 33–36, 40; dual enrollment, 9; earned course, 112–13; elective, 214; eligibility requirements and, 111; expiration of, 29–30; FAQs, 40–42, 118; levels and, 36–37; loss of, 137; nonstandard systems, 33, 36, 40; online courses and, 115–16, 125–26; "pass-along," 53–54; post-acceptance appeals, 137; transfer, 79–83, 137, 146; for transfer admission guarantees, 101

credits, alternative sources: case studies, 46, 51–52; FAQs, 52–54; military service, 47–50; prior learning/work experience, 46–47; test scores, 43–46, 52–53

Credly, 47
crime, 60–61
criminal history, 166, 167–68
CSS Profile. *See* College Scholarship
Service (CSS) Profile
Curry College, 107
CVs, 169, 268

DANTES Subject Standardized Tests
(DSST), 45, 47, 51
data entry: academic history, 156–59;
application forms, 152–55; common,
155–56; disciplinary questions,
166–68; extracurricular activities,
162–64, 171; FAQs, 170–71; test
scores, 160–62; as transfer application
step, 149–50
De Anza Community College, 80
deadlines: add/drop, 261; college applicant
portal messages and, 200; for document
submission, 258; for eligibility
requirements, 111, 112, 118; enrollment deposit, 204, 207, 209–10; for
financial aid filing, 197; for transfer
admission guarantees, 101
"Decision Day" (May 1), 207
Defense Language Institute Foreign
Language Center (DLIFLC;
Monterey, CA), 51
Defense Language Proficiency Test
(DLPT), 45
degree audit, 264; reports, 215
degrees, types of, 12
demographics, 63, 156
depression, 18–19
dining plans, 224
disability resource centers, 68–69, 127,
267–68
disciplinary issues, 23, 117, 166–68
discrimination, 9
Disney College Program, 47
Divemaster certification, 47
diversity, 63, 126, 184, 188
doctoral degrees, 12
documentation, additional: FAQs,
199–201; interviews/auditions, 199;
portal document checklist, 190–98;
requirements for, 189, 206; scholarship applications, 198; as transfer application step, 150; for transfer credit
appeals, 216–17; uploading, 169

dual admission programs, 101
dual enrollment credits, 9, 70, 112, 115,
192–93

education departments, 29
Edvisorly, 154
electives, 214
Eli Whitney Students Program (Yale
University), 52, 228–29
eligibility requirements: case studies,
113–14; common types of, 111; conditional, 111; deadlines for meeting,
111, 112, 118; earned course credits,
112–13; FAQs, 118–19; good standing, 116–17; grades/GPA, 114–15;
for grants, 233–34; high school GPA/
graduation, 116; minimum, 111–12;
practicality considerations and,
71–72; required courses, 115–16; for
scholarships, 234
elitism, 9–10
email, 28, 155, 205, 233
#EndCCStigma campaign, 10
engineering, 128, 130
English as a Second Language (ESL)
classes, 41, 251
English Composition classes: completion
of, before transfer, 121; eligibility
requirements and, 115; transfer credit
for, 214; transfer requirements involving, 101, 121
English fluency tests, 161
enrollment deposits: amount of, 207; deadlines for, 204, 207, 209–10; housing
applications and, 222–23; submission
of, 251; timelines for, 207–8; transfer
credit evaluation reports and, 219–20
essays, personal: "additional information"
box, 185–86; brainstorming activities,
175–78; case studies, 178–79; diversity issues and, 188; editing/revising,
181–82; FAQs, 187–88; importance
of, 173; objectives of, 173, 187–88;
organizing/drafting, 180–81; prompts
and length of, 174–75; reusing,
187; submitting, 182; supplemental,
183–85; writing tips, 172–73, 186–87
Expected Family Contribution (EFC), 73
expulsion, 23–24, 29. *See also* suspension,
academic
extracurricular activities, 162–64, 171

286   The Complete Guide to College Transfer

Facebook, 226
FAFSA. *See* Free Application for Federal Student Aid (FAFSA)
faith-based educational institutions, 63, 126
fall entry, 137–38
fall orientations, 87
family: background, in data entry, 156; boundary establishment with, 270; emergencies, 42; financial support from, 74; housing options for, 89, 96, 225; income of, and financial aid, 16–17; keeping in touch with, 21; transfer choices and, 4, 19
Family Educational Rights and Privacy Act (FERPA) rights, 165–66, 194
Federal Direct Loans, 235
Federal Student Aid Estimator, 72–73
Federal Student Aid YouTube channel, 248
Federal Work-Study, 235–36
FinAide, 248
financial aid: acceptance of, 256; appealing, 243–45; applications for, 191, 194–97 (*see also* College Scholarship Service (CSS) Profile; Free Application for Federal Student Aid); award letters, 207–8, 231–36, 247; calculating, 17–18; case studies, 245–47; FAQs, 247–48; filing deadlines, 197, 247, 266; help for understanding, 248; managing, ix, 266–67; need-based, 16–17, 194; new student orientations and, 257; offers vs. expenses, 232, 236–43; researching, 69–70; "self-help," 235–36; state forms, 196–97; timeline for, 236, 247; at transfer-friendly colleges/universities, 83–85; unmet need and, 236
financial considerations, 4, 16–18. *See also* cost of attendance (COA); financial aid; net price
financial programs, 66, 69–70
first-year students, 49; new student orientations for, 86; scholarships awarded to, 84–85; use of term, x
first-year vs. transfer students: academic background, 11; admissions decisions, 203–4, 207–8; application services, 151, 152–53; college research data and, 77; direct admissions programs, 155; extracurricular activities

and, 162, 171; financial aid policies, 83–85; graduation rates, 92–94; Greek life, 64; housing options, 60, 86, 96; major decision-making and, 67; military veterans and, 49; new student orientations, 86–87, 137–38, 258; personal essay, 173, 187–88; scholarship applications, 198; support services, 87–88; test score requirements, 160–61; tuition reciprocity programs, 103
Florida, 70, 83
food expenses, 236–37
Foothill Community College (CA), 71, 79–80
Forever Buckeyes program, 70
foundational courses, 41
four-year colleges/universities: admitted student profiles at, 161–62; "buyers" vs. "sellers," 198; credit transfer tools at, 81; GI Bill benefits and, 49–50; "good standing" with, 23–24; GPA requirements for transfer, 13; "institutional priorities" of, 205; lateral transfers between, 5–6; public, 70; reverse transfers from, 6–7; social life expectations at, 19, 20–21; transfer contracts of, 16, 60; use of term, 136; vertical transfers to, 3–5, 66; websites of, 18, 77, 78, 83, 90, 170
fraternities, 20, 64, 229
Free Application for Federal Student Aid (FAFSA): advantages of filing, 194–95; calculators available from, 72; case studies, 245–46; CSS vs., 195–96; family income changes and, 16–17; federal oversight of, 231; financial aid award letter and, 231; financial independence and, 200–201; Help Center website, 248; online portal requests for, 191, 195; refiling of, 266; SAI calculated from, 232–33; shortcomings of, 243; student loan eligibility and, 235; submission of, 231, 235; at transfer-friendly colleges/universities, 83; work-study eligibility and, 236
frequency of transfer, 3, 55
FUTURE Act Direct Data Exchange (FA-DDX), 195

Index 287

Gallaudet University, 127
gap terms, 24, 137, 139, 145, 209
General Education Development (GED) certificate, 116, 157, 254
general education (GE) requirements: alternative ways to fulfill, 125–26; case studies, 124–25, 126; college definitions of, 120; completion of, before transfer, 120–21; "double-dipping" to satisfy, 265; English Composition, 121; FAQs, 127, 265; mathematics, 121–22; second language proficiency, 122–23; for transfer admission guarantees, 101; transfer credits applied to, 213, 217; transferable, 98–99; transfer-focused associate degree programs and completion of, 146
George Washington University, 227
Georgia, 99
GI Bill benefits, 49–50, 52, 228–29, 267
Google, 47
grade point average (GPA): calculating, 32, 38–39; eligibility requirements and, 72, 111, 114–15, 131; FAQs, 118; grant awards based on, 233; improvement of, for transfer, 13–14, 23, 114, 118; major GPA, 114, 128, 130; recommendations and, 171; scholarships and, 234, 238; on transcripts, 38; transfer requirements, 13, 42, 101, 105; for tuition reciprocity programs, 103; withdrawals and, 41–42
grades: listing, during data entry, 158–59; midterm, 191, 194; minimum, in specific classes, 101; online portal requests for, 191, 193, 194; poor, retaking classes to replace, 118–19
graduate school, 268
graduation rates, 77, 89, 92–94, 95
graduation timeline, 262
graduation verification/application, 264
Grandparent Waiver, 70
grants: acceptance of, 256; applications for, 198; COA vs., 238, 239, 241–42; expiration of, 240, 266–67; financial aid award letter and, 233–34; researching, 267. See also Pell grants
Greek life, 20, 64, 66, 229
Green, Hank, 125
Green, John, 125

Hanks, Tom, 10
Harvard University, 167–68
health forms, 255
health insurance, 69, 89, 255–56
health problems, 18, 42
healthcare options, 89
Hierarchy of Needs, 56–57
high schools: academic background in, 11; AP courses taken in, 43, 44, 112, 125, 160–61 (see also Advanced Placement (AP) classes; International Baccalaureate (IB) programs); college courses taken in, 9, 27, 45; graduation proof, 116; IEPs in, 7; transcripts from, 27, 37, 111, 116, 157, 254
high-unit transfers, 9, 37, 107, 112
Hispanic-Serving Institution (HSI), 63
Historically Black College or University (HBCU), 63, 152–53
homeschoolers, 70–71
homesickness, 20
honors, 163–64
honors programs, 20, 67–68, 71
"honors-to-honors" programs, 68
housing contracts, 14, 222, 230, 255
housing options: campus housing, 60, 96, 222–25, 255; case studies, 227–29; competition for, 222; cost of, 236–37, 240; dining plans, 224; exemptions, 96, 225, 228–29; FAQs, 229–30; honors programs and, 68; new student orientations and contracts for, 230; off-campus housing, 225–27; researching, 60; residency requirements and, 37, 96, 225, 248; room options, 223–24; theme houses, 223, 227; transfer-specific, 85–86; transportation and, 226–27

Idaho, 155
identity, essays about, 184
IELTS test scores, 161
illness, 18
impostor syndrome, 89
incarcerated students, 14
Individualized Education Plans (IEPs), 7
inflation, 240
InitialView, 199
Institutional Documentation Service (IDOC), 196
instructors, 63

288 The Complete Guide to College Transfer

International Baccalaureate (IB) programs: as alternative credit source, 43, 45, 112, 193; documentation from, during academic adviser session, 260; GE requirements and, 125; test scores from, 45, 160–61, 193
international students, 161, 251
internships: case studies, 71; credit recommendations for, 47; at current college, 24; during gap terms, 137; researching, 59, 67; tips for accessing, 268
Intersegmental General Education Transfer Curriculum (IGETC; CA), 99, 124–25
Interstate Passport program, 98
interviews, 199, 268
intramural sports, 65, 75
ITHAKA, 82

Jack Kent Cooke Foundation, 198, 234
January intersession courses, 114
jobs, part-time, 198, 235–36
Joint Services Transcript (JST), 48–49, 50
joint-admission programs, 101
junior colleges, 10. See also community colleges

Landers University, 82
language proficiency. See English as a Second Language (ESL) classes; English fluency tests; second language proficiency
language tests, 45
lateral transfers, 5–6, 109–10, 136, 142
learning disabilities, 68–69, 127
legacy status, 156
letters of recommendation, 164–66, 170, 191, 197, 268
LinkedIn, 47, 268
loans, 235, 267
local surroundings, 59–60
loneliness. See social isolation
low-income students, 89
low-unit transfers, 37, 128

major pathways, 99–100
majors: case studies, 132–33; choice of, in personal essays, 183–84, 185; curriculum organization for, 129; declaring, 12–13; discontinued, 14; disenchantment with, 22; FAQs, 134–35, 265;

GPA minimums for, 114, 128, 130; indecision about, 134; most selective, 128; popularity of, 205, 206; prerequisites for, 101, 115, 129–30, 132, 135, 265; researching, 67; specialized, 20; STEM, 99; transfer applications for, 128; transfer credits applied to, 213–14; transfer-focused associate degree programs and entry into, 146
married students, 248
Maslow, Abraham, 56
Massachusetts, 99, 107
Massachusetts Institute of Technology (MIT), 219–20
MassTransfer, 99
master's degrees, 12
mathematics courses: completion of, before transfer, 121–22; eligibility requirements and, 115; transfer requirements involving, 101, 121
meal plans, 224
mental health: maintaining, 266, 269; researching support services for, 69, 269–70; telehealth sessions and, 270; transfer choices and, 18–19
merit scholarships, 84–85
Me3.careers, 134
Microsoft, 47
Midwest Student Exchange Program, 103
midyear entry, 87, 138–39
military service: ACE Military Guide, 47; as alternative credit source, 43, 47–50, 79; campus diversity and, 184; case studies, 51–52, 218–20, 228–29; GI Bill benefits from, 49–50; personal essay and, 184; tests designed for, 45 (see also DANTES Subject Standardized Tests); transcripts from, 47, 48–49; transfer choices and, 15; transfer credit evaluation reports and, 218–20; transfer-friendly colleges/universities and, 79; uploading papers from, 169. See also veteran students
military service academies, 75–76
Minnesota, 155
ModernStates.org, 44
Money magazine, 95
Moorpark College, 99–100
multipotentialites, 4
MyMajors.com, 134
MyNextMove.org, 134

Index 289

National Association for College Admission Counseling (NACAC), 221, 247
National Association of Intercollegiate Athletics (NAIA), 65
National Center for Educational Statistics, 89
National Collegiate Athletic Association (NCAA), 65
National Panhellenic Conference, 64
National Student Clearinghouse, 28, 29, 192
Native Americans, 70
needs, hierarchy of, 56–57
net price: calculating/calculators, 18, 69, 73, 84, 239–43; case studies, 246, 247; college rankings and, 95; defined, 73, 236, 239
neurodivergent students, 68–69, 127
New England Regional Student Program, 103
new student orientations, 86–87, 230, 257–58, 259, 268
New York State, 153–54
New York Times, 44
New York University (NYU), 90–91, 122, 166–67, 174
Niche, 155
noncredit courses, 40–41
nontraditional students: case studies, 51–52, 228–29; housing exemptions for, 96, 248; university programs for, 52, 161, 228–29. *See also* veteran students
North American Interfraternity Conference, 64
Nosanow, Mia, 270
nursing, 128, 129–30, 132–33

off-campus housing, 225–27
Ohio, 70
Ohio Transfer 36 (OT36), 99
O*Net Interest Profiler, 134
online colleges, 15, 51, 74–75
online learning, 7, 44, 47, 115–16, 125–26
online student groups, 270–71
Oregon State University, 107
orientation programs, 86–87. *See also* new student orientations
outcome measures, 92–94. *See also* graduation rates

Pace University, 215, 216
Parchment, 28, 192
partnerships: benefits of, 146; case studies, 104–6; FAQs, 106–7; streamlining effect of, 97; transfer admission guarantees, 100–102, 104–7, 130, 146; transfer articulation agreements, 97–100, 107, 129. *See also* tuition reciprocity programs
pass/fail (P/F) grades, 36, 38, 39
Pathways Planner (Tassled tool), 81
peer mentors, 89, 268–69
Pell grants, 50, 83, 93, 233, 266–67
personal statements. *See* essays, personal
Phi Beta Kappa, 163, 198, 234
plagiarism, 23, 167
planning: importance of, 109–10; for multiple options, 130–32. *See also* academic planning; college research
portfolios, 169
post-acceptance timeline: administrative tasks, 251–56; appeals, 137; enrollment finalization, 249, 252; FAQs, 258; new student orientations, 257–58; other college notifications, 256–57
predegree preparatory classes, 41
pre-med programs, 128
prerequisite courses: academic planning for, 260–61; deadlines for completing, 129–30; in-progress, 130; for majors, 101, 115, 129–30, 132, 135, 265; overlapping, 131–32; researching, 131; yearlong sequences for, 135
prior colleges/universities: credit transfers from, 25, 26; "good standing" with, 23–24, 116–17; listing, 27, 157–59; transcripts from, 28, 253–54; unpleasant memories of, 25–26; websites of, 28
prioritization skills, 162
prison partnerships, 14
privacy waivers, 165–66, 194
Professional Association of Diving Instructors (PADI), 47
professional recommendations, 164–65, 170
professors, 63, 268
programs, researching during college search, 66–68

proofreading, 172–73

psychology, 128

quantitative reasoning requirements,
    121–22

quarter system: credit conversion for,
    33–36; schools changing from semes-
    ter system to, 40; semester system vs.,
    32–33; transfer credits and, 212

queer students, 126

race-consciousness, 188

rankings, 95

reasons for transfer: academic, 11–16;
    application essay explaining, 173;
    case studies, 15–16, 21–22; financial,
    16–18; individual, uniqueness of, 11,
    22; personal, 18–19; social, 19–21

recommendation letters, 164–66, 170, 191,
    197, 268

Reddit, 226

rejections, 205, 206, 209

relocation, temporary vs. permanent, 59

requirements: admissions, 71–72, 77–78;
    course, 115–16; for transfer ad-
    mission guarantees, 101. See also
    deadlines; eligibility requirements;
    general education (GE) requirements;
    prerequisite courses

research programs, 67

residency policies, 37, 96, 225, 248

restrictions: for transfer admission guar-
    antees, 102; for tuition reciprocity
    programs, 103

résumés, 169, 268

reverse transfers, 6–7

Rodgers, Aaron, 10

Rohn, Jim, ix

roommate issues, 20

safety, 60–61

SAT college entrance exams, 44, 78, 160,
    161

scholarship displacement, 234–35, 239

scholarships: acceptance of, 256; applica-
    tions for, 198; COA vs., 238–39, 241–
    42; expiration of, 17, 240; financial
    aid award letter and, 234–35, 238–39;
    first-year vs. transfer students, 84–85;
    outside, 239; renewability of, 17, 234,

238; researching, 69, 267; stacking
    of, 234

school closures, 14, 29

second language proficiency, 115, 122–23,
    127, 213

self-actualization, 56

Selingo, Jeff, 198

semester system: credit conversion for, 33–
    36; quarter system vs., 32–33; schools
    changing from quarter system to, 40;
    transfer credits and, 212

Service to School (S2S), 50

Shepard, Dax, 10

Sign Language, American, 127

skills, 162, 163, 266

social isolation: case studies, 105–6; entry
    timing and, 138; new student orien-
    tations and, 230; online vs. in-person
    classes and, 75; tips for avoiding, 270–
    71; transfer choices and, 20, 105–6;
    transfer-specific housing and, 86

social media, 10, 64, 183, 226, 270–71

sororities, 20, 64, 66, 229

Southern New Hampshire University
    (SNHU), 8, 213–14

split-term schedules, 40

sports, 65, 75

STAndards-Based Measurement of Profi-
    ciency (STAMP 4s) test, 45

state education departments, 29

state residency, 240

State University of New York (SUNY), 153

Statement of Intent to Register (SIR),
    207–8, 257

Stotland, Hanna, 23

stress, 69

Student Aid Index (SAI), 73, 201, 232–33,
    248

student clubs, 20, 64, 269

student conduct, 23, 24

student health centers, 69

student health plans, 256

student loans, 235, 267

student profiles, 155

student safety, 60–61

Study Hall, 125–26

study-abroad programs, 21, 24

Study.com, 47

summer entry, 139

support services: new student orientations
    and, 257–58; researching, 66, 68–69;

tips for accessing, 266, 267–68; at transfer-friendly colleges/universities, 87–89; for veterans, 15

suspension. *See* academic notice/probation/suspension

"swirling" transfers, 7–8, 9, 143–44

Tan, Amy, 10

Tassled.com, 81–82, 115

technical certificates, 47

telehealth sessions, 270

test scores: during adviser sessions, 260; as alternative credit source, 43–46; eligibility requirements and, 111; FAQs, 52–53; first-year vs. transfer students, 78; GE requirements and, 125; listing, during data entry, 160–62; old, 52–53; online portal requests for, 191, 193; requests for, 27; researching, 78; submission of, 255; uploading reports, 169

test-free policies, x, 78

Texas, 153–54

Texas Core Curriculum (TCC), 99

Texas Tech University (TTU), 81

text communications, 155

textbooks, 217–18, 221, 236–37, 240

theme houses, 223, 227

time management, 162

timelines: extracurricular, 162–63; for recommendations, 165. *See also* transfer timelines

TOEFL test scores, 161

transcendence, 56

transcript sites, 28, 192

transcripts: accessibility to, during data entry, 156; ACE/Credly, 47; during adviser sessions, 260; declining to send, 193; FAQs, 28–30; fees for, 28; final, submission of, 253–54, 258; GPAs on, 38; high school, 27, 37, 111, 116, 157, 254; military, 47–49; online portal requests for, 191, 192–93; "pre-reads" of, 81; quarter system vs. semester system, 32–33; reading, 31–32; unofficial, 28, 169, 192

transfer admission guarantees, 100–102, 104–7, 130

transfer articulation agreements, 97–100, 107, 129

transfer contracts, 16, 60

transfer credit evaluation reports: during adviser sessions, 260; appealing, 211, 216–18, 221; case studies, 9, 208–9, 218–20; COA and, 242–43; FAQs, 220–21, 264–65; interpreting, 212–15; preliminary, 220; timeline for, 83, 207–8, 211, 220–21, 236, 264–65

transfer credits, 79–83; degree requirements and, 215; elective, 214; finalization of, 264–65; GE requirements and, 213; majors and, 213–14; number accepted, 212–13; rejections, and COA, 242–43; under review, 215

transfer equivalencies, 82–83

transfer guides, 99–100

transfer scholarships, 198

transfer shock, 89

transfer student associations, 268–69

transfer student centers, 88–89

transfer students, 49; admission and enrollment statistics, 90–92; CLEP test scores for, 161; housing options specific to, 85–86; orientation needs of, 86–87, 230; profiles of, 72, 155; scholarships awarded to, 84–85; university definitions of, 112

transfer timelines: bachelor's degree completion time and, 137; case studies, 144–45; entry timing, 137–39; FAQs, 146–47; lateral transfers and, 136; planning for, 136; sample, 140–44; vertical transfers and, 136

TransferExplorer.org, 82

transfer-friendly colleges/universities: admissions requirements at, 77–78; case studies, 94–95; credit transfers at, 79–83; enrollment and outcome data at, 89–94; FAQs, 95–96; financial aid at, 83–85; graduation rates and, 77; housing options at, 85–86; new student orientations at, 86–87; support services at, 87–89

Transferology.com, 79, 81, 82, 83, 115

TransferSavvy.com, ix, 27, 36, 39, 58, 68, 131, 163–64, 190, 210, 236

Transfer-Year Experience Program, 94

Transfer-Year Interest Groups (TrIGs), 94–95

Transition Assistance Program (TAP), 50

transparency, 84

transportation, 226–27, 237, 240–41

292 The Complete Guide to College Transfer

travel expenses, 59
tuition, guaranteed, 240
tuition, in-state, 247–48
Tuition Break, 103
tuition costs, 16, 17–18, 232, 236–37
tuition discount programs, 104
tuition reciprocity programs: defined, 97, 102; eligibility for, 102–3; popular examples, 103–4; researching, 60, 69–70; restrictions for, 103
TuitionFit.org, 248
tutoring, 268
"2+2" degree programs, 76, 136
types of transfer: lateral, 5–6, 109–10, 136, 142; reverse, 6–7; "swirling," 7–8, 9, 143–44; vertical, 3–5, 12, 22, 140–41

universities, public land-grant, 10. *See also* four-year colleges/universities
University of California (UC): Berkeley, 4–5, 86, 99–100; Davis, 71; Los Angeles (UCLA), 72; Santa Barbara, 104–5; Santa Cruz, 80; UC system, 88, 124–25, 153, 185
University of Chicago, 216
University of Miami, 207, 215, 228
University of North Texas (UNT), 93–94
University of Oregon, 62, 86, 115, 117
University of Phoenix, 158–59
University of Southern California (USC), 84, 174
University of Texas at Austin, 94–95
University of Virginia, 115
university policies, excerpts from, ix–x
University System of Georgia, 99
unmet need, 236
U.S. News & World Report, 95

Vericant, 199
vertical transfers, 3–5, 12, 22, 140–41
veteran students: case studies, 51–52, 218–20, 228–29; expert help for, 50; as first-year vs. transfer students, 49; housing exemptions for, 96, 228–29, 248; transcripts of, 47; transfer choices and, 15; transfer credit evaluation reports and, 218–20. *See also* military service
video statements, 199
Virginia Military Institute, 76
Virginia Tech, 147
vocational training, 12, 40–41

waitlisting, 206, 261, 264
Washington 45, 99
Wesleyan University, 49
Western Undergraduate Exchange (WUE), 60, 70, 103, 106
Who Gets In and Why (Selingo), 198
withdrawals, 39, 41–42, 113, 192–93, 258
women's colleges, 63
working students, 4
work-study, 235–36
writing centers, 268
writing classes. *See* English Composition classes
writing proficiency, 121
writing sample, 149–50, 169. *See also* essays, personal

Yale University, 52, 228–29
yearlong sequences, 135, 138
YouTube, 125, 248

About the Author

Jaime Smith is a certified educational planner specializing in college transfer admissions. She earned a Post-Master's Certificate in Transfer Leadership and Practice from the University of North Georgia in collaboration with the National Institute for the Study of Transfer Students in 2023. Jaime also authored the chapter on transfer students for the sixth edition of NACAC's *Fundamentals of College Admission Counseling* textbook for counselors in training.

With over twenty-five years of experience in education across all levels, Jaime embodies the spirit of lifelong learning. Her academic credentials include a BA in linguistics from UC Berkeley, an MA in TESOL, and an MSEd in eLearning. Additionally, she has earned certificates in college counseling, online teaching and learning, and English instruction for nonnative speakers. In 2022, Jaime became a certified educational planner through AICEP, further solidifying her expertise in the field.

As an advocate for alternative K–12 learning options, Jaime founded OnlineG3.com, an independent online education program for gifted and twice-exceptional students. There, she continues to teach English and advise homeschooling families on the college admissions process.

A California native, Jaime now lives in Oregon with her husband and pet bunny. She has one daughter, a former homeschooler turned transfer student who is now in grad school. She blogs about college transfer at TransferSavvy.com.

NEW WORLD LIBRARY is dedicated to publishing books and other media that inspire and challenge us to improve the quality of our lives and the world.

We are a socially and environmentally aware company. We recognize that we have an ethical responsibility to our readers, our authors, our staff members, and our planet.

We serve our readers by creating the finest publications possible on personal growth, creativity, spirituality, wellness, and other areas of emerging importance. We serve our authors by working with them to produce and promote quality books that reach a wide audience. We serve New World Library employees with generous benefits, significant profit sharing, and constant encouragement to pursue their most expansive dreams.

We print our books with soy-based ink on paper from sustainably managed forests. We power our Northern California office with solar energy, and we respectfully acknowledge that it is located on the ancestral lands of the Coast Miwok Indians. We also contribute to nonprofit organizations working to make the world a better place for us all.

Our products are available wherever books are sold.

customerservice@NewWorldLibrary.com
Phone: 415-884-2100 or 800-972-6657
Orders: Ext. 110
Fax: 415-884-2199
NewWorldLibrary.com

Scan below to access our newsletter
and learn more about our books and authors.